"One of The Most Daring of Men"

"One of The Most Daring of Men":

The Life of
Confederate General
William Tatum Wofford

by
Gerald J. Smith

Southern Heritage Press
4035 Emerald Drive
Murfreesboro, TN 37130

Journal of Confederate History Series
VOL. XVI
John McGlone, Series Editor

First printing 1997.

Library of Congress Cataloging-in-Publication Data
96-072-554

Smith, Gerald J., Author
"One of The Most Daring of Men": The Life of Confederate General William Tatum Wofford
Includes bibliographical references; index
ISBN 1-889332-03-8

Southern Heritage Press
4035 Emerald Drive
Murfreesboro, TN 37130

DEDICATION

To my dear friend and mentor, Dr. Carlyle Cross, who, like the subject of this biography, was a humble and gracious gentleman.

Gerald Smith
Martinez, Georgia 1997

TABLE OF CONTENTS

PREFACE   xi

CHAPTER 1   1
Antebellum Days

CHAPTER 2   23
War!

CHAPTER 3   39
First Blood

CHAPTER 4   51
Deadly Autumn

CHAPTER 5   65
High Tide

CHAPTER 6   107
Wilderness to Guard Hill

CHAPTER 7   131
Department of North Georgia

CHAPTER 8   149
Postbellum Days

ADDENDUM   171

FOOTNOTES   173

BIBLIOGRAPHY   213

INDEX   237

Cover photograph, General William T. Wofford.
Courtesy of Dwight Harley, Sr.

ILLUSTRATIONS

Captain Dilmus L. Jarrett, ... 46
Company C, 18th Georgia Regiment

Private William W. Beard, ... 70
Company D, 16th Georgia Regiment

Private Jesse M. Pendley, ... 84
Company C, Phillips' Legion

Private William W. Fitts, ... 117
Company D, 16th Georgia Regiment

Privates William T. Bailey and Henry M. Bailey, ... 121
Company C, 16th Georgia Regiment

Confederate Congressman Herschel V. Johnson 134

MAPS

Hood's Texas Brigade at Second Manassas, ... 44
August 30, 1862

Hood's Texas Brigade at Sharpsburg, ... 54
September 17, 1862

Wofford's Brigade at Chancellorsville, ... 71
May 3, 1863

Wofford's Brigade at Gettysburg, ... 87
July 2, 1863

Wofford's Brigade at the Wilderness, ... 110
May 6, 1864

PREFACE

Brigadier General William Tatum Wofford's life spanned the greater part of the 19th century. He managed to be a part of most of the momentous issues that shaped Georgia history in that era. From the Mexican War in 1847-48 to the famous Georgia Constitutional Convention of 1877, Wofford left an indelible impression among his contemporaries. In the state legislature and in the Confederate military, he knew well the likes of Robert Toombs, A. R. Lawton, the Cobb brothers, Joseph E. Brown, the Stephens brothers, James Longstreet, Robert E. Lee, and Jefferson Davis. Even when they disagreed with him on political or military matters, these men were impressed with his probity, generosity, and high-mindedness.

Yet, perhaps because he was from a milieu which spawned such great persons - the 1800's were a century mirabilis in that respect - he has been virtually forgotten by 20th century historians. His considerable contributions in the debates surrounding the Wilmot Proviso, secession, and the 1877 state constitution have for the most part not even warranted a footnote in modern histories of Georgia. His leadership of Hood's Texas Brigade of the Army of Northern Virginia at Sharpsburg, Maryland in 1862; his own Georgia brigade's performances at Chancellorsville and Gettysburg with pivotal activities in each battle; his leadership in suggesting and implementing Longstreet's famous flank attack of the Federal left at the Wilderness - all of this has been relegated to the scrubby undergrowth of Civil War scholarship with hardly a mention. Most significantly, perhaps, his efforts to feed the impoverished people of North Georgia - certainly appreciated at the time - have been glossed over if not totally forgotten in subsequent histories.

The Wofford papers, in private possession, illuminate much about this great Georgian, but the file is fragmented largely because most of his war letters to his wife, as well as his antebellum personal and legal correspondence, went up in smoke

xii

when his home and office were torched with most of the town of Cassville by enraged Yankees in October 1864. Even the records of his beloved 18th Georgia Regiment were fragmented by the war, including his personal service record.

Diaries, letters, and memoirs of friends and members of his brigade shed light on his war activities, but his propensity for not submitting after-action reports - and they may have been lost - is a sorely distressing matter. Contemporary newspaper reports of the doings of his brigade are revealing and helpful. The Official Records are still the best source for his leadership in North Georgia as the war closed.

I gratefully acknowledge the generous help of the following persons and institutions: Doyle A. Buck; John McGlone; Ann Seith; Keith Bohannon; Richard Coffman; John Stevenson; James Hinton; Ira Pindley; Dwight Harley, Sr.; Dwight Harley, Jr.; Robert Thomas; Thomas Holley; Mark Lemon; Robert Rybolt; Gerald Judson Smith, Jr.; Elizabeth W. Roberson; Etowah Valley Historical Society; Murray County Historical Society; Woodruff Library, Emory University; Perkins Library, Duke University; Southern Historical Collection, University of North Carolina; Gettysburg National Military Park; Kennesaw Mountain NMP; Fredericksburg-Spottsylvania NMP; Museum of the Confederacy; United States Army Military History Institute; South Carolina Historical Society; New York Historical Society; New Hampshire Historical Society; South Carolina Library; National Archives; Library, University of Georgia; Antietam NMP; Manassas NMP; Wofford College; Augusta College; Paine College; Georgia Department of Archives and History; Harold B. Simpson Confederate Research Center; Piedmont College; Augusta State University; Georgia Southern University; Paine College; Confederate Stamp Alliance; Bartow History Center.

By Gerald J. Smith

<u>"I'm Going Whether You Swear Me In Or Not!"</u>:
<u>Diaries, Letters and Reminiscences from the Union and the
Confederacy</u>
1995

<u>"Smite Them Hip and Thigh!"</u>
<u>Georgia Methodist Ministers in the Confederate Military</u>
1993

<u>Oglethorpe County and The Bicentennial</u>
1976

<u>The Agrarian Thought of John Donald Wade</u>
1972

Chapter 1

Antebellum Days

William Tatum Wofford's pedigree was solid. His great grandfather, Colonel William Wofford of Virginia, a Revolutionary War hero, settled in then Franklin County, Georgia, along the line which separated the state from the Cherokee Nation. The settlement bore his name - Wofford's Settlement - and included friends and relatives. When it was discovered by survey that the settlement was indeed on the Cherokee side of the line, the Indians demanded that the whites leave. Colonel Wofford and others sent a petition to Governor James Jackson to do whatever was necessary to rectify the situation. Jackson parleyed with the Cherokees; the result was the "Four Mile Purchase of 1804," in which the Indians ceded "a strip of land four miles wide and twenty miles long. . . ." [1] This treaty brought Wofford's Settlement legally into the state of Georgia. When Habersham County was created in 1818, most of the settlement was included.

One of the sons of the colonel, Benjamin J. Wofford, also a veteran of the American Revolution, settled in the strip and raised a son, William Hollingsworth Wofford, who married Nancy M. Tatum, who had migrated with her family from Virginia. To them were born two daughters, Rachel and Martha, and a son, William Tatum Wofford, born June 28, 1823. [2] When the son was three years old, the father died. The widow and her three children were deeded 25 acres on Broad River in Habersham County. [3]

In the Land Lottery of 1827, Benjamin Wofford drew a lot in western Georgia. He and Nancy sold their land in the Settlement and moved to Cass County, settling near the town of Cassville. [4] This community, the county seat, was a thriving village of "near 100 houses, besides stores, offices, shops. . . ." [5] It was an ideal place for rearing children. Young William Tatum attended the local school for his elementary training.

In 1836, at the age of thirteen, he was sent to the new Gwinnett Manual Labor Institute in Lawrenceville, Georgia. Founded by the Presbyterians in 1835, "the school was located on a farm of 250 or more acres. . . . " [6] The students paid for their schooling by working the farm. Spending at least two hours a day in class, they spent three hours a day in the fields. The curriculum included "logic, rhetoric, moral and mental philosophy, chemistry, mathematics, and anatomy." [7] Agricultural theory and methods were also taught as a part of the student's work experience. William Tatum's interest in agricultural experimentation and diversity was to serve him well in the years to come. "He was to become a passionate lover of rural life and spent his happiest days in the superintendance of his thrifty farming operations." [8]

One of Wofford's schoolmates at Gwinnett was Charles Henry Smith, who later in life wrote the famous "Bill Arp" stories. In a reminiscence entitled "The Old School Days," Smith described a recitation day at the school:

> And General Wofford was there too, and his speech was the speech of an Indian chief to the pale faces, and most every sentence began with "brothers," and he whipped a big sassy Spaniard by the name of Del Gardo for imposing on us little boys, and then went off to fight the Mexicans for imposing on Uncle Sam, and ever since he has been fighting somebody for imposing on somebody, and I think he had rather do it than not. [9]

In 1839, he graduated from Gwinnett Institute and entered Franklin College in Athens, Georgia. There he developed a talent for oratory which was to mark him among the state's finest in declamation. [10] In 1843, he studied law in Athens under Judge Nathan Lewis Hutchins, and on August 10,

1844, he was admitted into Clarke County Superior Court by Judge Junius Hillyer, and "to all the several courts of Law and Equity in this State." [11] He returned to Cassville and opened a law practice in the courthouse on March 14, 1845. [12] The next year he applied for admission to the Supreme Court of Georgia and was granted license. [13]

Wofford lived with his mother and sister Martha - Rachel had married - on his plantation near Cassville. In the years between 1845 and the agricultural census of 1850, he would acquire 110 acres of improved land, 370 unimproved, all valued at $6,000.00. He owned one horse for transportation, 6 mules for farm work, a cow, 5 oxen, and 60 hogs, all valued at $413.00. He raised per year, with fluctuations according to weather, an average of 12 bushels of wheat, 1,250 bushels of corn, 100 bushels of oats, 20 bales of cotton, 6 bushels of peas, 20 bushels of potatoes, and 600 bushels of sweet potatoes. Beehives yielded 90 gallons of honey. [14] As James Bonner wrote, "The average Georgia farmer in 1850 was neither a landless hireling nor the traditional planter. He was a practical farmer who diversified his activities when he thought cotton likely to be unprofitable." [15] Wofford was nothing if not practical.

With a livelihood in his law practice, he did not have to rely solely on his farming. With ten slaves, he worked the plantation, which reached by 1860 a value in real property of $7,500.00, and a personal property value of $16,700.00. [16] He was thus in the mainstream of Georgia's destiny. As E. Merton Coulter stated, "The mass of Georgians during the antebellum times were the yeomanry or middle class. Some of them owned a few slaves, but most of them were the small farmers who did their own labor, the small business men who needed little help. . . . " As late as 1877, Wofford was inviting thrifty farmers to settle in his county. [17]

By the standards of the day, Wofford was comfortably set in life. Early on, and probably as the result of his rearing as an only son who felt responsible for his fatherless family, he acquired a sensitivity for human need and an affinity with the working man that informed his thinking politically and morally. He was to view the elitist aristocracy of the South with suspicion in the years ahead.

When the Mexican War began, Wofford was appointed as a captain on August 8, 1847, by Governor George Towns and ordered to raise a company of mounted volunteers. Eighty-six men signed up from the area. The company marched to Columbus, Georgia, for the general rendezvous. There they became Company E, First Battalion, Georgia Mounted Volunteers, commanded by Lieutenant Colonel J. P. Calhoun, on August 28. In mid-September, they marched to New Orleans where they boarded the transport "Beauford District" bound for Matagorda, Mexico. [18]

The voyage was rough on the battalion's horses; Wofford's company alone lost twenty-five, the carcasses of which were tossed overboard in mid-October. After the battalion disembarked at its destination on November 1, the losses in stock were remedied, and they set out to join General Zachary Scott at Vera Cruz. The weather and terrain were harsh on both men and mounts; several of the latter died of fatigue and some of the men were discharged with disability. In Vera Cruz, a glanders epidemic broke out. This equine disease, fatal to horses, was contracted by some of the men. Wofford's own horse died and had to be replaced. [19]

Wofford's men were engaged in combat only twice. In November of 1847, he led his unit in a cavalry clash with the "Castilian Lancers" near Vera Cruz. In the melee, a lancer killed one of the Georgians. Wofford snatched the weapon from the enemy soldier, killed him and kept the lance as a souvenir. [20] The other confrontation occurred after the treaty between the United States and Mexico was signed, February 2, 1848. As a part of the force of occupation, Company E was ambushed at the village of Matesordera by a large force of Mexican guerrillas on February 19, 1848. Though outnumbered, Wofford skillfully led his men to safety, with five men killed in action. From then until July, the company did picket duty or languished in camp.

The battalion was discharged in Mobile, Alabama, July 12, 1848. Of the original eighty-six, twelve had died in battle or of disease, five had been discharged with disability, two had deserted, and one was missing in action. [21]

Wofford received the gratitude of the State in a resolution of February, 1850, by the Georgia House of Representatives. [22] His tenure as a captain of volunteers with all its responsibilities, heartaches, and military action, confirmed him as a true leader of armed men. Later, when the crisis of the 1860's appeared, his Mexican War days would serve him well as a leader of a much larger group of volunteers.

He returned to his law practice a local hero, with the people of Cassville and the county looking to him for leadership. Whether he wanted this honor is not known, but he was not one to shirk what to him was a matter of duty. For example, in January, 1849, the Cassville newspaper, *The Georgia Pioneer*, printed its last issue before moving to Rome, Georgia. Wofford, feeling that his community needed a public forum, prevailed on a friend of his Athens days to come to Cassville. John W. Burke, who with his brother published the *Athens Southern Banner*, came to Wofford's town and established the *Cassville Standard*, the first issue appearing March 15, 1849. It was a weekly newspaper with a Democratic political bent. [23]

Wofford, with Burke's support, then ran for the position of state representative. In October, 1849, he received the highest vote in Cass County. As a Jackson Union Democrat, he went to Milledgeville to begin his career in politics. In the Lower House of the State Legislature, he soon bolstered his growing reputation as a humane, fair, and sensible man. "He was said to be one of the most attentive and useful members of the two Legislatures of which he was a member." [24] He was appointed by the House to the Committee on the Judiciary and the Committee on Finance. Through the first committee, he introduced a bill to "require the action of justices of the peace in granting peace warrants." This bill passed. [25] On a personal note, he introduced a bill to allow a dam or watershed to be built on his land to aid in irrigation. This, too, passed. [26]

For the future of his county, he asked the House to extend the Western and Atlantic Railroad by spur from Cass Station to Cassville, a distance of six miles. [27] Wofford was clearly visionary in this request, for he saw that the future of Cassville as a trade center was linked with the rail tracks that connected Chattanooga with the heartland of Georgia. When the railroad was being built in the 1840's, however, Cassville was left out:

> The original surveys of the Western and Atlantic Railroad developed the fact that it was impracticable to build the line through Cassville, then one of the most flourishing towns in North Georgia. The citizens of Cassville finally succeeded in getting the Legislature to pass an act providing for an alternate route via the town, leaving the Western and Atlantic above Cartersville and again intersecting it at some point south of Kingston; and also requiring the citizens of Cassville to bear all the expenses connected with surveys and costs of constructing the new route. [28]

At that time, the Cassville people considered the cost too great, and so forwent a grand opportunity. Cass Station became a signal stop, as noted, leaving any trade cargo bound for Cassville to be hauled by freight wagons to Cassville with attendant expenses. In effect, Cassville's thriving trade was visibly at an end. Like other cities in Georgia, which opted also against the rails, Cassville would wither on the vine, as it were. Wofford saw all this and thus asked the House for help in the 1850 session. The bill, however, languished, and unfortunately, so did Cassville's future. When in the next session he chaired the Committee on the Western and Atlantic Railroad, Wofford reintroduced the matter, it was to no avail. [29]

On the national level, stormclouds were gathering, stirred up by the recent victory over Mexico. The immense lands ceded to the United States as part of the treaty with its erstwhile foe lay for Congress's disposition. Even before the end of the war, slavery entered the picture when in 1846, Pennsylvania Congressman David Wilmot proposed a rider to any peace measure "to prohibit slavery in all the territory which might be secured by treaty with Mexico." [30] The Southern gentlemen were horrified at any such suggestion. The "Wilmot Proviso" never passed, but its ghost was to linger. Henry Clay's Omnibus Bill which was passed September 18, 1850, compromised on slavery, one of its codicils being "the enactment of a more rigorous law for the recovery of fugitive slaves." [31]

During this national debate, the Georgia House was also considering the Wilmot issue. On January 24, 1850, a debate centered on the following protest:

> That in the event of the passage of the Wilmot Proviso by Congress, the abolition of slavery in the District of Columbia, the admission of California as a state in its present pretended organization, or the continued refusal of the non-slave holding states to deliver up fugitive slaves as provided in the constitution, it will become the immediate and imperative duty of the people in this state to meet in convention to take into consideration the mode and measure of redress. [32]

Offering a compromise of his own as a Union Democrat, Wofford suggested that the phrase, "the passage of the Wilmot Proviso by Congress," be amended by inserting after the word

"Proviso" the phrase "over territory south of 36 degrees x 30 minutes North latitude, known as the Missouri Compromise Line." [33] Supported by Charles J. Jenkins, J. A. Nesbit, and Lucius Gartrell, the debate on his amendment lasted until January 27. Defeated in the end by the majority, Wofford and his supporters drew up a minority report, signed on January 28, which read: "This line we are willing to take as a compromise and because the South has heretofore, without tarnishing the honor of her free sons, abided by it." Wofford's rhetoric and sensibility in upholding the Missouri Compromise garnered for him wide support, and although his amendment failed, his reputation was enhanced. [34]

When the southern states called conventions to act on Clay's compromise in the United States Congress, Georgia set December 10, 1850, for her forum. Despite much anti-compromise rhetoric, a public referendum was held November 25: "Georgians decided by a heavy majority of 42,000 to 24,000 that the Compromise of 1850 was to be accepted. . . . " [35] Wofford, always the moderate, was pleased. He was among the 264 delegates to the December 10 convention in Milledgeville. The famous Georgia Platform, written by Charles Jenkins, was adopted:

> It declared Georgia attached to the Union; it regretted the agitation on the slavery question, and insisted on the right of the states to settle the matter for themselves; it avowed the willingness of the State of Georgia to abide by the compromise measures of Henry Clay; it declared the State of Georgia ought to and will resist any action of Congress that would disturb the safety and violate the rights and honor of the slave-holding States. [36]

One historian called the Georgia Platform "the State's most significant utterance. . . . " [37] Another was more specific: "The Georgia Platform saved the Union in 1850, as the other Southern states followed Georgia's lead and accepted the Compromise." [38] To Wofford's mind, maintaining the Union was paramount, and he was to maintain this conviction until the State seceded a decade later. He had no qualms about his Unionist stance, and became a leader in moderate political circles.

During the 1851-52 session, he chaired the Committee on the Western and Atlantic Railroad and sat on the Committees on Privileges and Elections and on Journals. [39] During the session he mentored an aspiring young representative from Putnam County, Joseph Addison Turner, a poet and journalist, who had published a political satire entitled "The Hasty Plate of Soup," in which he commented on Georgia politics. Sales were not good, so Wofford bought the remainder and distributed them gratis. [40]

On April 29, 1852, Wofford attended a state convention of a recently formed body of Democrats named the Constitutional Unionists. These men, including Alexander H. Stephens and Robert Toombs, were leery of the secessionist rhetoric and state rights bombast of the Southern Rights Party. The meeting was held in Milledgeville; the 111 delegates agreed to meet again at the Democratic Convention on July 15 to solidify a platform. At this session, Wofford drew up a minority report in which was stated that the national constitution, with subsequent compromises regarding fugitive slaves and such, would be supported; the report also offered to voters who were of the same mind a slate of electors who were trustworthy, among whom was his uncle, General William B. Wofford of Stephens County, a state senator. [41]

In the bizarre political machinations which followed the July convention, Wofford and his uncle, with many of the Constitutional Unionists, pulled out, calling themselves "Tugalo Democrats," taking the name of a river in his uncle's district. Hopkins Holsey, editor of the *Athens Southern Banner*, explained the Tugalo position: "It claims no party allegiance whatever. It appeals to the judgment and the sympathies of all men who hate tyranny in whatever form it may present itself, and who at the same time desire to support (Franklin) Pierce ... " [42]

Ironically, by November the Tugalos were joined by the Southern Rights Democrats who with them supported Franklin Pierce, a moderate on political matters, for president. As Coulter wrote: "The Southern Rights Party, who were in fact mostly Democrats, readily embraced the Democratic national ticket, and the Democrats who had formerly been in the Constitutional Union Party supported the same ticket." [43]

Strange bedfellows, perhaps, but Captain Wofford was dead serious about the change. When in October 1852 he bought the *Cassville Standard* from his friend Burke, he emblazoned on the masthead of the editorial page "FRANKLIN PIERCE FOR PRESIDENT" in his inaugural issue of October 7. [44] Until it was sold two years later, Wofford maintained a strong Democratic commitment, uncompromising in pro-Unionist sentiment. [45] He was a Jackson Union Democrat as it was defined by the editor of the *Atlanta Daily Intelligencer:*

> We are for the Union as Gen. Jackson understood it, a Union of equal rights to every citizen . . . a Union which secured to the slave-holder the same privileges as a non-slaveholder; a Union which afforded protection to slave property throughout the length and breadth of our vast domain; a Union which guarantees the right of property of every kind in the common Territories of the Union. [46]

In September 1852, he attended a meeting of the Cassville Temperance Society. The *Cassville Standard* carried the following report:

According to a previous notice, the
Cassville Temperance Society met in
September 1852. The president being
absent, Major John W. Burke, 1st vice
president, was called to the chair. T. C.
Shropshire, Esq., was then called on and
responded to a very eloquent address,
setting forth the evils of intemperance, and
claiming that moral suasion could not avail
anything as a remedy. His remedy was the
law, when a majority of the people wished.
Col. Warren Akin being present was
invited to speak but declined . . . an
animated discussion arose, in which Col.
Akin, Capt. Wofford, M. A. Higgs, Gen. J.
H. Rice and the chairman participated. . . [47]

Wofford chose not to run for the next term of the
Legislature. When the body convened, however, he was elected
by a 3/4 vote of the Lower House to serve as the Clerk. [48] This
was a great honor for him and attested to his influence around
the state as an astute statesman. He attended to his duties with
customary thoroughness, as he wrote to his mother in
November 1853:

Dear Mother,
Excuse me for not writing to you
sooner, but I have been so busy that I have
not had time. I am well excepting a cold. I
was elected by a very large majority Clerk
of the House of Representatives, nearly two
votes to one, and I am very grateful to my
friends for their influence. Mr. Price and
Mr. Vaughn did me much good, and a
good many told me of the strong letters Mr.
Clayton had written to them for me I

> cannot come home before the Legislature
> adjourns, and I cannot tell when that will
> be, perhaps not before the first of
> January. [49]

The Lower House, during the term Wofford served as Clerk, entertained and passed a proposal to found a college in Cassville for young men within the "lower financial brackets." Reverend John Crawford offered land and money for the building. [50] The Legislature granted permission and appointed Wofford to serve as a trustee of the new college. He also served as a trustee of Cassville Female Institute, a Methodist school, and the Georgia Military Institute in Marietta. [51]

In 1856, Wofford helped form the Cass County Agricultural Society to discuss the future of agriculture and economics in the area. The Society reported in the *Cassville Standard*, January 8, 1857, that cotton culture was the most "important branch of agriculture" and "aids in the extension of civilization." But they realized, too, the need for a careful husbandry of the land. On February 19, 1857, the *Standard* reported: "Our wheatfields begin to look green and prosperous. . . . Almost every farmer is experimenting, to test and determine the kinds (of seed) best adapted to our soil and climate." [52]

A friend of Wofford's, Charles Wallace Howard of Cass County, had a large farm and a small home-boarding school at "Springbank." He edited the *Southern Countryman* and the *Southern Cultivator* and influenced agricultural thinking for years. [53] His ideas were decidedly revolutionary in a cotton-based economy:

> The grass farm, he pointed out, gave leisure
> for reading, study, and the amenities of
> social life. "When we add . . . [the products
> of livestock] to our cotton, rice and sugar,"
> he said, "we shall perhaps live more
> independently than any other people in

Christendom." He maintained that the low
price of land in the South was not caused
by slavery, climate, depressed agricultural
prices, or even by the presence of cheap
land in the West, but rather by the South's
unbalanced and defective system of
agriculture. [54]

Wofford, concerned about better methods of farming
since his days at Gwinnett Institute, agreed with Howard and
by 1860 had 1,100 acres in grass for grazing. The agricultural
census of that same year revealed that Wofford had acquired
1,225 hogs and 38 sheep. His corn production dropped to 500
bushels per year, since the bulk of his land was in pasturage. [55]
His leadership in agriculture led the citizens of Cass County to
send him as a delegate to the Southern Commercial Convention
in Knoxville, Tennessee, August, 1857. [56] These annual
conventions had been held since 1845. "Their purpose was to
examine the economic conditions of the South and to offer plans
for improvement. . . . " [57] Beginning with the 1857 meeting, and
leading up to the Civil War, these conventions became less
agricultural and more of a forum for southern rights rhetoric
and anti-abolitionist ventilation.
        Captain Wofford went to Knoxville to hear at the onset a
charge to the Convention to "prepare the South for commercial
independence as she would soon, in all probability, seek
political independence." The moving spirit behind the
Convention, James DeBow of New Orleans, was even
suggesting that the South was ready now for disunion because
of her acquisition of railroads, colleges, shipping, and
factories. [58] The convention then endorsed "the need for a
Southern Pacific railroad," postponed a vote on tariffs - a sticky
question for southerners, appointed committees to petition
Congress on free trade, supported southern manufacturing and
mining, rolling stock, and machine shops, and entertained
discussion on reopening the slave trade. [59]

Slavery for Wofford had always been more of a convenience than a way of life, so he was alarmed no doubt at the pro-secession rhetoric which closed the convention at Knoxville. [60] "The radical forces . . . had effectively taken over the movement . . . and they had come away from Knoxville firmly in the driver's seat for the 1858 session." [61]

Wofford's friend, Joseph E. Brown, Governor of Georgia, asked him to attend the next commercial convention in Montgomery, May 1858. His reasons are not known, but in view of the radical talk at Knoxville, Brown may have wanted Wofford's moderation to be represented. It may be that he was simply responding to the invitation in *Debow's Review* of 1858 to send "your ablest, best tried, and most trusted sons.   . . ." [62] That invitation also assured the Southern people that disunion would not be discussed. Yet, when the Convention met on May 10, symbolically perhaps in the "new" warehouse of the Montgomery and West Point Railroad Company, Mr. William Yancey of Alabama in his official welcome made reference to an "independent sovereignty." [63]

The Convention was given over to discussion of the African slave trade almost exclusively. Wofford voted to table resolutions which sounded to him as radical or smacked of such. The most significant of these was the following:

> Resolved,
> That we recommend to the Governors of the Southern States, or such of them as think with us, to call on the people of their respective States to elect delegates, equal to their representation in Congress, to meet in convention at _____, on the first Monday in _____, to take into consideration the present critical position of the South, and the dangers that threaten her in the future, and to endeavor to devise, if possible, effectual safeguards for her future security

and equality in the Union, or, failing in
that, to get out of it. [64]

With his interest in agriculture and his abiding stance as
a Unionist, Wofford was disappointed in both commercial
conventions.   Indeed, as Johnson states in her study of the
conventions, "Despite the sizable number of planters . . ., other
than endorsing the need for public education on the subject, the
conventions seldom discussed farming methods." [65]

Yet, education on agriculture was not to be gainsaid for
Wofford, for in 1859, he and a group from Cassville petitioned
the Legislature in December to endow a professorship in natural
science and agriculture at Cherokee Baptist College. [66]   The
Legislature did not accept the proposal. Even a local bond drive
was unsuccessful because the War was to empty the college of
its young men, and eventually, Sherman's army was to burn the
building in 1864. [67]

Wofford's social life was not neglected during the 1850's.
He was an eligible bachelor if ever there was one, with good
reputation, a profession, and an estate. The following poem,
dated February 26, 1852, was kept by him in his personal
papers:

>Come back, oh come! The past shall be
>   A cloud forever removed;
>Come back, and in my welcome see
>   How thou art still beloved.
>I strove in vain to bid my heart
>   Forget its early dream
>For ah! the dream would not depart,
>   And thou wert still its theme.
>
>Come back, and never more shall doubt
>   Or cold distrust be mine;
>My heart hath cast these demons out
>   And now is wholly thine.

Not written in his hand, it is probably from an admirer of the fair sex who will ever remain anonymous.

On September 28, 1858, he wrote the following invitation to Miss Nannie Wofford. This, too, was a keepsake in his personal papers, so one wonders if it or a copy were ever sent:

> Capt. Wofford's Compliments to Miss Nannie Wofford and asks the favor of her company on Saturday next. Mrs. Rich, Mrs. Vaughan, and Mrs. Bagle have kindly consented to fill the place of _____ for the occasion.

He met Miss Julia Adelaide Dwight, daughter of Dr. Samuel B. and M. A. Dwight, Spring Place, Murray County, Georgia, sometime in 1858. Apparently, they had discussed marriage early on, for he received the following Valentine "hint" on February 14, 1859, in Julia's handwriting:

> A Gentle Hint:
> What are all the charms of earth
> All its pride, its treasures worth,
> With no partner at your side,
> Thoughts and feelings to divide!
> Therefore God with gracious plan
> Saw, and said, and showed that man
> Ne'er was made to live alone -
> Therefore marriage first was known,
> - Your Valentine

On July 4, 1859, a Cotillion Party was held in Howard's Hall, Cassville, for which Wofford served as a manager and sponsor. His coming nuptials were announced publicly at this event. On July 11, he wrote to Julia:

> Dear Julia
>
> Without your consent I pen this note. I will be at Hopedale (the Dwight Plantation) on Thursday next; for Monday will be too long. Say to Miss Rosa and to no one else that a friend of mine is very much pleased with her. Give my love to all that are near to you and for yourself feel assured of the fidelity and sincerity of the heart you already have. This is not a letter; only a notice of my coming. I will come by Dalton.

He and Julia were married on August 1, 1859, at her home by Reverend Thomas Rambant. [68] On July 25, 1860, a daughter was born to them and christened Mary Tatum Wofford. [69]

Wofford was a Fifth District delegate to the State Democratic Convention, which met December 8, 1859, in Milledgeville to select delegates to the national convention to be held the next year in Charleston, South Carolina. The Georgia convention adjourned because of dissension over nominee Howell Cobb for the presidency. They met again on March 14, 1860, to decide the matter. Wofford, according to one historian, breached the party by not upholding Cobb. [70] He could not forget the wavering of Cobb (Americans of a later time would call it "waffling") in the years subsequent to the 1850 Compromise. Wofford, however, was not alone in non-support of Cobb, who "generously removed himself as a disturbing influence." [71]

Elected a national delegate, Wofford went to Charleston. Even the setting boded ill for the Democratic Party in America:

> Had the Democrats deliberately set out to pick the worst place in the country for their 1860 convention, they would have chosen Charleston. The city's Old World charm,

> beautiful homes, and shaded walks hardly
> compensated for its glaring deficiencies:
> the most radical citizenry in the South,
> abysmal accommodations for large
> numbers of people, and a convention hall
> barely suitable for half the number of
> people crammed into it each day. [72]

In addition, wrote another, "At the time of holding the Convention there was probably no place in the United States where Stephen Douglas (the national Democratic candidate for president) and the doctrine of popular sovereignty were more detested than they were in Charleston." [73]

Physically uncomfortable, Wofford was no less discomfited politically. He supported Douglas against the secession-minded Southern Rights Democrats who backed John C. Breckinridge and the Constitutional Unionists who backed John Bell. As the motto of the *Cassville Standard*, his former newspaper, said, "The Constitution must be maintained Inviolate in all its parts." [74] But Wofford also knew the strength of the Southern Rights men. Consequently, as Michael Johnson wrote, "Expectation of a Breckinridge victory in Georgia sapped the energy that might otherwise have gone into more effective Bell or Douglas organizations. . . . Even the popular former governor, H. V. Johnson, Douglas' running mate, could not overcome the grass-roots opposition to Douglas." [75] At the November election, to no one's great surprise, Breckinridge garnered 51,893 votes; Bell, 42,855; and Douglas, 11,580. Lincoln, the Republican candidate, of course, won. [76]

Governor Brown immediately called on November 21 a state convention to consider alternatives to the Lincoln election. On January 2, 1861, Wofford was elected, with Turner W. Trippe and Hankins F. Price, to represent Cass County. All three were anti-secession. They listened with alarm and sadness, no doubt, to the pro-secessionist talk. "Little was thought or spoken of but secession . . . " [77] Wofford and all of his Unionist colleagues made, however, a grave omission during the time between the national election and the January 1861 convention. Historian Schott states it best: "The conservatives were despondent, demoralized, unorganized, and confused. They had let eight weeks go by without the first move toward concentration on a common strategy, much less a concerted attack on their enemies. Momentum was the paramount advantage the radicals took into the convention." [78] The secession of South Carolina in December 1860 increased this momentum.

The convention met at Milledgeville, January 16, 1861. The radicals carried the day. Wofford and his colleagues from Cass County voted "yes" on Herschel Johnson's resolution that a convention of the Southern states be called to decide on secession. This was defeated. Eugenius Nesbit offered an ordinance on the secession of Georgia on January 19. Wofford was among those who voted against it; the "yeas" carried the motion 208 to 89. The President of the convention, George W. Crawford, then announced, "it was his privilege and pleasure to declare that the State of Georgia was free, sovereign, and independent." [79]

Wofford's thoughts after this momentous decision can only be divined since no record is available. He must have sympathized with Herschel Johnson, however, who stated years later:

> And so the Rubicon was crossed and the State of Georgia was launched upon a dark, uncertain and dangerous sea. Peals of cannon announced the fact, in token of exultation. The secessionists were jubilant. I never felt so sad before. [80]

On January 21, 1861, Wofford, will all the convention delegates, signed the Ordinance of Secession. Since speeches during the convention were not recorded, Wofford's pleas for moderation are not to be seen, but one reported that "with exceptional prescience he saw the certain fatality of the step and with rare and almost convincing eloquence combated it." [81] After the final vote was rendered, however, he stood with his state.   As Lawton Evans wrote, "Now that the State had seceded, there was no longer any division of sentiment." [82]

Wofford returned to Cassville where all were preparing for the expected Union reaction. Companies were already being raised by January 26. The "Cherokee Cavalry" was mustered that same day at the Cassville Armory. The "Etowah Infantry" had already mustered in nearby Cartersville three days earlier. [83] Wofford was asked to recommend suitable men to Governor Brown; on February 23, for example, he sent to Brown the following:

> Dear Sir:
> I am informed that John O. T. Herrill of Savannah is an applicant for a Lieutenancy in the Regular Army of Georgia and I take the liberty of asking you as a favor to myself to give him the position he desires. Mr. Herrill is thoroughly enlisted in the cause of the south, and would add to our military the experience and taste necessary to success. [84]

On March 7, Wofford rejoined the delegates in Savannah. The next day he had to return home for personal reasons and was granted leave of absence from the Convention. [85]   He returned before March 16 when the Confederate Constitution was ratified, and offered the following resolution which was considered and adopted:

Whereas, under the Government of the United States, prior to the secession of Georgia, there has been annually paid to the pensioners resident in said State a sum of money amounting to about $23,000.00:

1. Resolved, that this Convention urge the Congress of the Confederate States to make immediate provision for the payment of the pensioners resident in this State the amounts heretofore allowed them by the Government of the United States.

2. Resolved, that the secretary communicate the above to the Congress of the Confederate States. [86]

Chapter 2

War !

So the fateful die was cast. The heady wine of patriotism mesmerized the people of Georgia. Sidney Lanier, writing afterward, described the intense emotion:

> The whole South was satisfied it could whip five Norths. The newspapers said we could do it; the preachers pronounced anathemas against the man that didn't believe we could do it; our old men said at the street corners, if they were young they could do it, and by the Eternal, they believed they could do it anyhow . . . the young men said they'd be blanked if they couldn't do it, and the young ladies said they wouldn't marry a man who couldn't do it. [1]

Wofford, now that secession was a fiat accompli, offered his services to Governor Brown. On May 3, 1861, he was elected Colonel of the First Regiment, Fourth Brigade, Georgia State Volunteers, at Camp Brown, Smyrna, Georgia. [2] The infantry companies which comprised the First Regiment consisted of the Acworth Infantry, Newton Rifles, Jackson County Volunteers, Davis Invincibles, Stephens Infantry, Davis Guards, Lewis Volunteers, Rowland Highlanders, Dooly Light Infantry, and the Rowland Infantry. [3]

Governor Brown in the meantime was in a skirmish with the new Confederate government and President Jefferson Davis over the use of Georgia troops which the state had gone to great expense to equip and train. On May 8, Wofford sent the hardpressed governor a note of support:

> Dear Sir
> The dispatch I sent you on yesterday was
> forwarded before Gen. Phillips (William)
> received yours; and your answer to me was
> as we expected after seeing the one to him.
> As I informed you when you were here, I
> am content with the dispositions you may,
> in your wisdom make of our Brigade or of
> my Regiment. In a word, my Regiment is
> ready at <u>your call</u> to serve our state or the
> Confederate States. [4]

On May 30, Wofford wrote Brown about surgeons for the
Regiment: "I have selected as surgeon of the 1st Regt, 4th Brg
Ga Vol Dr. E. I. Roach of Atlanta and Dr. I. B. Brown as assistant
surgeon and ask that they may be commissioned as such." [5]

In June, 1861, Wofford moved his men to a newly
established training center at Big Shanty, about seven miles
north of Marietta. Named for Charles M. McDonald, a former
governor, Camp McDonald became a huge, sprawling tent city
adjacent to the Western and Atlantic Railroad. "The Brigade
was composed of two Regiments and one Battalion of infantry,
one Battalion of artillery and a Battalion of cavalry." [6] Milton
Barrett of the Acworth Infantry wrote, "We have bin hear ever
senc the 11th of June last a drilling. we are well drill and armd
. . . " [7] The drilling of the troops was done by the cadets of the
nearby Georgia Military Institute. [8]

Wofford's leadership was put to the test early on. On
June 13, Governor Brown visited the camp to muster in the
troops for the duration of the war instead of for twelve months
as the men had been promised. In addition to this, he declared
in a very haughty and derogatory manner that martial law
would be imposed forthwith. If this were not bad enough, he
also dismissed the sutlers and "grog shops." [9] In the view of the
men, he had quit preaching and gone to meddling. The
immediate reaction was that "every company in camp packed

up to leave . . . Colonel Wofford called us together and pledged himself for our rations if we would stay tight. . . . " He also promised to catch the next train, go to Atlanta, and speak with Governor Brown. The correspondent to the *Augusta Daily Chronicle and Sentinel* took up the story:

> During the Colonel's absence, Gen. Phillips appeared in front of the headquarters of the 1st Regiment, when the Sergeant Major ordered the 1st Regiment to fall into line - and not a solitary man obeyed the call - One entire company of the 1st Regiment had already left, and two others disorganized. Col. Wofford returned in the evening, when all rushed to his quarters, eager to hear the result of his mission. In a few moments he appeared and delivered an eloquent and patriotic address. He said the arrangements were not as satisfactory as he wished; stated the difficulty in the way of getting into service except to remain in the brigade, as that was the only chance to get arms. His eloquent and patriotic appeals to the men to go with him and stand by him were irresistible. There was probably not a man who heard the speech but what agreed to be mustered into service. [10]

The men returned to their posts, mollified by the sincerity of Wofford. What transpired between the Colonel and the Governor over this incident is not known, but one might surmise that Wofford told his friend to leave military matters to the officers. The Colonel was also concerned that the Governor had not yet commissioned his regimental surgeons who were already busy with the sick:

> June 16, 1861
> Dear Sir
> When I saw you at Camp Brown I informed
> you that I had selected Drs. Roach and
> Brown as Surgeon and Asst Surgeon of the
> 1st Regt 4th Brgd Ga Vol and understood
> that you approved of my selection and
> would use your influence with the
> Secretary of War in their favor. As we are
> in the service of the state and as the
> commissioning of Surgeons is with you in
> our present service I hope you will appoint
> the above gentlemen . . . both gentlemen
> are competent and I know that they are the
> choice of the Regiment. [11]

In all truth, the Governor had all he could handle in his
struggle with President Davis over the disposition of the Fourth
Brigade. Brown offered in July to tender the unit to the
Confederacy if Davis would keep the brigade intact and appoint
Phillips to Brigadier General, PACS. To punctuate his
earnestness, he sent Wofford to Richmond on July 20 to speak
with the Chief Executive on the matter. Davis was not to be
budged, so Brown had to comply: The Fourth Brigade was to be
broken up and its regiments sent to Richmond in August. [12]

In the meantime, the citizens of Marietta and
surrounding towns were enjoying the camp of instruction at Big
Shanty immensely. They visited daily the tent city, watching
the soldiers drilling and marching. On July 31, on the eve of
their departure for Virginia, a grand review was held:

> People from the entire upper part of the
> state crowded into the little town to witness
> it. It was a memorable day in the county.
> The northbound W. and A. train which
> arrived at Big Shanty at twelve o'clock

brought a hundred or more people. Others
came in wagons, carriages, and ox carts. At
two o'clock, the two regiments and the
three battalions formed in line and the more
than two thousand men passed in review
before Governor Brown. [13]

Afterward, Wofford left for Richmond to prepare for the coming
of his troops. He arrived on the third of August. His men left
Camp McDonald that day. R. A. Quinn of the Newton Rifles
described the journey:

> . . . the 1st Regiment left Camp McDonald,
> Georgia, for Virginia on the 3rd of August,
> passing on the State R. R. to Dalton,
> Georgia, from thence to Knoxville,
> Tennessee; from thence to Bristol on the
> line of the Tennessee and Virginia, from
> thence to Lynchburg, Virginia on James
> River, here we lay over one night, and from
> Lynchburg to Petersburg, Virginia and
> from Petersburg to Richmond, Virginia,
> arriving at Richmond on the 8th of
> August. . . . [14]

En route, the men were cheered at every stop. Private Barrett
recounted, "we had a fine time of hit. we was cherd all a long
the way by croud of sitisens. a flag was a waven over most ever
house and every winder crouded with lady. . . . " [15]

On August 9, the Regiment was mustered into the Army
of the Confederate States of America and was numbered the
18th Georgia Regiment. [16] It was then camped about three miles
from Richmond at Camp Scott, which was near the city
reservoir and thus in an unhealthy location. [17] After many fell
ill, Wofford moved the regiment to Oregon Camp on August 31,
where they drilled for a few weeks. In mid-September, he was

directed to take his men to Camp Winder in Richmond to guard prisoners-of-war. They were assigned to Liggon's Factory on Main and 25th Streets where the prisoners were incarcerated in warehouses. [18] "The rooms of the buildings were about 75 by 30 feet; a row of tobacco presses divided the quarters of the officers and occupied about one-half of the room on their floor." [19]

The prisoners were heavily guarded all around the compound. The Georgia soldiers were new to war in general and to guarding prisoners-of-war in particular. On September 21, a prisoner was shot to death for looking out of a window. Of course, there were two sides to the story: The Federals said he was shaking out his blanket; the Georgians maintained he was leaning out shouting imprecations at the guards. [20] Either way, he was just as dead!

On October 25, Wofford was ordered to take the 18th to Goldsboro, North Carolina, to reinforce the garrison against a rumored Yankee amphibious assault up the Neuse River. [21] They arrived by train on the 26th, no doubt excited about the prospects of a fight. They had missed the big showdown at Manassas on July 21; so far the only shot fired at the enemy was directed at a poor wretch looking out of a prison window. They had been in the army five months, so perhaps now they would "see the elephant." It was not to be this time however. A gale disrupted the Union offensive on November 1. That same night, all the tents of the regiment, including Wofford's, were blown down "an every thing rining wet and the earth so soft and the wind bloing we could not get our tents to stand. . . . " [22] Ordered back to Richmond, the 18th boarded a rickety train on the 7th, arriving at their old camp in the capital the next day. [23]

On November 17, 1861, Wofford received the following telegram from the Quartermaster Department: "I am instructed to inform you that arrangements have been made to transport your Regiment to Manassas via Fredericksburg tomorrow morning at 9 A.M. Wagons will be sent to your camp at 6 o'clock to convey baggage to the Depot. Please be punctual." [24] They were taken on the 18th to a station ten miles from

Fredericksburg where they camped for the night. [25] On the 19th, they marched toward the Potomac River. The way was hard with streams and bad roads to negotiate. "Colnel Woffer [sic] put a privet on his horse an he is a take hit a foot." [26] They camped for the night and next day arrived "about three miles from Dumfries at a place known as Camp Fisher on the Potomac between Powell's Run and Neabsco Creek." This was 18 miles below Manassas and half-mile from the river. [27]

Three Texas regiments were also in the vicinity (1st, 4th, and 5th Texas). According to historian Harold Simpson, the "close physical location of the Georgia Regiment to the three Texas units probably accounted for the assignment of the 18th Georgia as the fourth regiment to complete the organization of the Texas Brigade." [28] That may be, but Wofford had written to G.W.C. Lee in the War Department to have the 18th "temporarily attached to the Texas Brigade, having no permanent assignment." [29] Whatever, the 18th was attached to the three Texas units, thus beginning an illustrious career as a part of one of the premiere fighting units in military history. Lieutenant James Lemon of the 18th confided to his journal that the Texans are " a right hard looking set of fellows . . . we all spent a while giving each other the 'look'." [30] They soon warmed up and became close comrades. The 18th was soon nicknamed "the Third Texas." They were commanded by Brigadier General Louis T. Wigfall, a South Carolinian. The brigade was in Major General William Whiting's division with Colonel Evander M. Law's Brigade, in General G. W. Smith's Reserve Corps. [31]

On the 23rd of November, the men were ordered to build houses, for with the close proximity of the Potomac River, the winter months promised much discomfort. The men were also prohibited by Wofford from scavenging the countryside. As Private William Shockley wrote to his wife, "some of the boys went out this morning and hooked some pumpkins Colonel Wofford found it out and made them pay for them. The Texians go out occassionally and kill a hog or anything they come across but our Colonel will not allow us to take them. . . . " [32]

The 18th Georgia, having at last found a home within a brigade, settled down for the winter. The men built their log cabins against the cold and amused themselves with cards, et cetera, for Wofford refused to turn them out into the elements except for picket duty to watch the enemy ships in the Potomac. Shockley made camp chairs and sold them for seventy-five cents each. [33] Two other entrepreneurs opened a ginger cake bakery in their hut. [34]

A. F. Burnett and W. W. White of Company A published "The Spirit of '61," a camp newspaper. [35] Subtitled "A Spark May Lurk Unseen," it was an eight page document, handwritten on ledger sheets: "The Spirit of 61 edited and published by Burnett and White of the Acworth Infantry will be issued weekly Terms of subscription 50 cts per single copy. Office at No. 4 Acworth Street Comp A 18th Regmt. Ga. Vol." This first issue contained letters to the editors, an article on the Adirondacks, and news items from the *Richmond Dispatch*. There was a patriotic message against "blackhearted abolitionists" in which is the following: "This regiment I trust and believe will do honor to the glorious cause for which we are fighting." [36] Another article complimenting the officers, urged the soldiers of the 18th to observe the situation of other units and see "that the 18th is better cared for than any other regt in the field . . . " [37]

The men were entertained at times by the eccentricities of General Wigfall, who, according to J. B. Polley of the 5th Texas, "sees a Yankee in every shadow, hears one approaching in every breeze that rustles and clinks together the ice encrusted boughs of the pine trees . . . " over the headquarters hut. Wigfall would then beat the long roll for the brigade to fall in, regardless of the weather. After two or three of these false alarms, the colonels decided to wait for verbal orders before "arousing their commands." [38] Twice a week the men were issued 5 pounds of meal, 3 pounds of flour, 1 1/4 pounds of beef, and 3/4 pound of bacon, coffee and sugar. [39] Except for some sickness in February, the men weathered the harsh Potomac winter very well.

Wofford developed a bad cold which was to plague him for several months. He was cheered, however, by letters from home. His wife Julia was overseeing the harvest - 50 bushels of wheat, 21 wagonloads of corn, 20 bushels of potatoes, and several bales of cotton. Eight hogs were slaughtered and dressed, hampered however by the cost of salt for preserving - $10.00 a sack in Cassville. Coffee also was almost impossible to find anywhere. [40]

On November 21, 1861, she mentioned the latest development politically in Cassville: "Is it not too bad about our county being changed to Bartow? What confusion it will create, before it is known. I think our men had better be thinking of something of more importance." She referred therewith to the recent action of the Georgia Legislature which had granted in November a name change for their county from Cass to Bartow:

> WHEREAS, The county of Cass, in this state, in its organization, was named in memory of Lewis Cass, of Michigan; and the said Lewis Cass having recently shown himself inimical to the South by voluntary donation of his private property to sustain a wicked war upon her people, and by the utterance of sentiments such as the South must be subjugated, the Union must be preserved; and has therefore become unworthy of the honor conferred by the naming of said county:

> AND WHEREAS, deeming it their duty, it is always the pleasure of a brave and free people to perpetuate the memory of those who have fallen upon the field of battle in

> defence of the honor, rights, and liberties of
> our common country, and by their noble
> deeds and self sacrificing devotion, have
> endeared their names in the hearts of the
> present generation. We should in some
> measure hand down their names to live
> ever green in the hearts of succeeding
> generations. [41]

The name of Cass County was changed to Bartow in memory of
General Francis Bartow who had died at First Manassas.
Attempts were made to change Cassville to Manassas, and
instructions were sent to the Confederate Postal Department to
that effect. Wofford and his wife continued to use "Cassville." [42]

On March 6, 1862, upon the resignation of General
Wigfall, Colonel John Bell Hood of the 4th Texas was promoted
to Brigadier General and given command of the Texas
Brigade. [43] Thus and for posterity, the unit would be called
"Hood's Texas Brigade." As Douglas Southall Freeman wrote,
"These were as good soldiers as the Army of Northern Virginia
had." [44] Bruce Catton was more discerning: Hood's troops
"were generally considered the hardest fighters in Lee's Army,
which is about all the compliment any troops need." [45]

On March 8, the Brigade was ordered to pack up and get
ready for a move toward Fredericksburg. This order was in the
context of General Joseph Johnston's retreat in the face of a
Union buildup of forces in the Potomac area. [46] The Texas
Brigade was the rearguard. The men, according to Val Giles of
the 4th Texas, "took a lingering look at the old camp and moved
off in the direction of the Rappahannock River." [47] The
afternoon of the 8th, the men began their long march. For five
days, they slogged through mud and sleet, reaching on the 12th,
"a beautiful pine orchard near Fredericksburg, . . . called Camp
Wigfall." [48]

The men settled down in the new location. On the 14th,
the 18th Georgia was taken out on picket duty. When they

returned to camp, they discovered they did not have one! The "Texians" had raided the camp and stolen everything, even the tents! [49] Wofford's reaction is unknown, but in view of his care for the men, it is reasonable to believe that he remonstrated with Hood and most of the stolen goods reappeared. Ironically, Hood prided himself on his discipline, as he wrote later:

> Moreover, their conduct in camp should be such as not to require punishment, and, when thrown near or within towns, should one of their comrades be led to commit some breach of military discipline, they should, themselves, take him in charge, and not allow his misconduct to bring discredit upon the regiment; proper deportment was obligatory upon them at home, and, consequently, I should exact the same of them whilst in the Army. [50]

This statement notwithstanding, the Texans still managed their shenanigans. Perhaps it was their freewheeling style, their total lack of fear, and the constant drilling of the brigade; at any rate, they were already making a name for themselves among their compatriots. Brigadier General Dorsey Pender observed to his wife: "I have North Carolina troops and am determined that if any effort of mine can do it, this Brigade shall be second to none but Hood's Texas boys. He has the best material on the continent without a doubt." [51]

On April 4, Hood volunteered to take his brigade back towards Dumfries to intercept Union General Daniel Sickles' Brigade, rumored to have crossed the Potomac. The men thought they would surely test their mettle this time, and "not a man lagged by the wayside." [52] Reaching the place where the Yanks were supposed to be, nothing was found. "The Texas Brigade, therefore, had to return to its camp and await another opportunity. . . . " [53] One of Wofford's men was more sanguine

about the matter. "On the 4th of April we were ordered to
Stafford Court House to drive the enemy from that place; this
we did and returned to camp on the 5th of April." [54]

In all truth, it was not as easy as all that. Underneath the
bluster and braggadocio was a terrible letdown.   In their
eagerness to catch the enemy, the men had quickstepped along
unmindful of the toll it was exacting from them physically and
mentally. Finding no enemy, "without hope of either glory or
plunder, privates and officers alike became footsore and
weary." [55] To exacerbate the situation, the men camped without
shelter in a snowfall and the next day had to struggle back to
Fredericksburg. [56]

On April 10, the troops were ordered to march to
Yorktown, on the Peninsula below Richmond, to reinforce
General John B. Magruder's force against invasion.   Private
Shockley of the 18th described the extreme hardship of the first
leg of the march:

> When we left camp we did not know which
> way we were going we took the road to
> Richmond and marched about 30 miles to
> Milford   Station   on   the   Richmond-
> Fredericksburg Railroad, there we took the
> cars and rode to this place which is 35 miles
> from Milford . . . I got all I bargained for in
> the way of hardship . . . we marched all day
> through the rain and mud lay down on the
> wet ground that night the next morning it
> was still raining we took up the line of
> march very early and marched til about
> three o'clock in the evening . . . it had
> begun to snow . . . we got on the cars about
> 12 o'clock Thursday Aprile the 10 and came
> down here [Ashland] in little over an hour
> . . . they are looking for a fight at Yorktown
> and it is thought we will go there. [57]

Nine of Wofford's men sickened on the march, three of whom died.

After resting until the 14th, the brigade set out for Yorktown, 85 miles away, arriving on the 19th, tired and footsore. The weather was dreadful, and sandy soil made the going rough indeed. Some of the men had blisters on their feet as "large as a quarter dollar." [58] Thirty men of the 18th were left at Ashland and Richmond in the hospitals. [59] For the next two weeks, the men stayed near Yorktown. "I was here," wrote Hood, "placed in reserve with my brigade . . . and continued the system of instruction and training. . . . " [60] The men of the 18th had lost their cooking utensils in the Texas raid on their camp, so they improvised by mixing dough in bark trays and cooking it on boards leaned against the fire. [61]

In the general retreat from Yorktown by the army before McClellan's blue legions, the brigade was again the rear guard element. The men left at daybreak on May 4th, in a cold rain which turned the roads into deep mud. They overtook the main body of Confederates four miles from Williamsburg; passing it, they marched on through the town, turned left and headed for the York River and the village of West Point. As they moved along at route step, the men could hear the battle of Williamsburg start up and rage behind them. They may have longed to stay and fight, but Hood had been ordered to go to the York River to counter a flanking movement by the enemy. [62] After marching well into the night, they halted in wooded country six miles from Eltham's Landing on the York.

Cavalry scouts reported to Hood that a Federal advance across the river was in the making. On the 7th, he led the brigade to Eltham's to thwart the flanking movement. Hood narrowly escaped death and in a brief skirmish with some loss to the Texas regiments, drove the enemy back. [63] The 18th Georgia was held in reserve defending the brigade artillery. In one Georgian's words, the regiment "was placed in rear of the artillery to defend hit . . . the 18th Ga. did not get to fier a gun but took prisoners. . . ." [64] Not all of the Georgians liked being out of the fracas. Lieutenant Lemon wrote in his journal: "The boys are claiming Hood is playing favorites with his own boys but I do not believe this. Our guns are inferior. . . . " [65] The battle, small by comparison to what the future held for the Texas Brigade, was strategically important, for "our bold front had prevented the debarkation of Franklin's Corps and the capture of our immense wagon trains." [66]

Afterwards, the men marched to Baltimore Crossroads five miles from Richmond. While there, the new regimental flag arrived. "It is a beautiful crimson flag with blue bars and 12 stars," wrote Lemon. Wofford called the regiment out on parade, and gave a speech. The men swore to live or die in its defense. [67] Subsequent events were to test the veracity of their oath to the fullest. After a five day rest, the brigade moved to Chickahominy Creek nearer the capital. The men were hungry, and though well camped, had to supplement meager rations the best they could. As one wrote, "what the people would not sell, the soldiers stole." [68] Camp sickness took its toll also. Colonel Wofford fell ill and had to take sick leave the last week in May. [69]

Back in Cassville, Wofford recuperated from the pneumonia. He delighted in his family; Mary Tatum was toddling around, chattering constantly. Wofford's mother was 71 years old and well. Julia was ever busy tending the farm and the family. He recovered slowly under her attention. [70] This enforced inactivity gave him time for serious reflection on the events in the state. In April of 1862, a band of Union soldiers under James Andrews had stolen a locomotive in full view of the sentries at Camp McDonald at Big Shanty and driven it up through Cass (Bartow) County along the W and A Railroad, trying to burn bridges all the way to Chattanooga and generally disrupt communications. Finally caught and foiled, the Yanks had still made an impression on the local folk - Georgia was vulnerable to invasion. [71]

The disaster at Shiloh on the 6th and 7th of April, although hailed a victory for the South, had also adversely affected the morale of the people: "There was developing an apprehension, an uneasiness, which communicated itself to the most optimistic." [72] If nothing else, the Southern people realized that the North was in the war for keeps, and hard times were coming.   Indicative of those difficult times ahead, the Confederate Congress had also that April passed the Conscription Act which among other things compelled twelve-month soldiers to re-enlist or be drafted.   One of Wofford's own men expressed his feelings and those of his comrades when he wrote home the following: "I am comin when my time is out. I volunteered for six months and I am perfectly willing to serve my time out, and come home and stay a while and go again, but I dont want to be forced to go." [73]

Wofford, ever the conservative and always concerned for his soldiers, could see where all of this could lead: The farmer-soldier, or the yeoman of the South, would have to bear the weight of the military of the Confederacy while worrying about his family and farm back home. Wofford and other county leaders began discussing the possibility of some form of public relief for the wives and children of the farmers from the county who were in the armies. [74]

One other matter caused him deep personal concern. Julia had intimated in an earlier letter: "It is reported here that it is probable that you will be elected Brigadier General." There was no such foundation, but he was as concerned about his military career as the next man. General Lafayette McLaws, his division commander later in the war, wrote that Wofford was "very ambitious of military fame and one of the most daring of men." [75] He had not gone to West Point, to be sure, but he had led a company in the Mexican War and was senior officer in the Texas Brigade. When Wigfall had resigned on February 20, to enter the Confederate Congress, Wofford as senior colonel was in line for promotion to brigadier general. When Colonel Hood had been promoted on March 6 and given command of the Texas Brigade, Wofford must have wondered. Hood was at that time of the war undistinguished, so the question remained and no doubt hurt the Georgian. [76] Nonetheless, he returned to the regiment the first week in July and as a good soldier, put personal misgivings aside. His day, after all, was coming.

Chapter 3

First Blood

Wofford had good reason to be proud of his regiment when he returned to them. At the battle of Seven Pines, May 31 - June 1, the men had been held in reserve with the rest of the brigade, moving hither and yon in the Chickahominy swamps in water to their waists while the battle raged. [1] In the week following, however, some of Wofford's men had, commando-style, raided behind the Union lines and captured a New York colonel. Taking him to Hood, they had been presented the prisoner's pistol as a trophy. [2]

General Joseph Johnston had been wounded at Seven Pines, and Robert E. Lee assumed command of the army. In rearranging his units, he added the infantry of Hampton's Legion to the Texas Brigade. He then commenced the offensive to clear the Virginia Peninsula of McClellan's forces and relieve pressure on Richmond. Wofford's Georgians "shed their first blood" finally during the famous Seven Days' Campaign which followed. On June 27, at Gaines Mill, they aided in the first major victory spearheaded by Hood's Texas Brigade. The Texas regiments received full share of the glory of that fight; a writer from the 18th Georgia, pennamed "Chickahominie," sent an article to the *Richmond Whig* detailing the 18th's part in the action:

> The regiment was under fire for about three hours, and lost one hundred and forty-eight in killed and wounded. Two officers killed and six wounded. Carried into action five hundred and seven men. Every officer and man acted with great gallantry and coolness.

> . . . The commander of the cavalry that
> charged our lines and who fell into our
> hands a wounded prisoner, declared he had
> as leave charge a wall of fire. [3]

John Fannin of the 18th wrote a friend after the battle: "I went through the fight unhurt but how I escaped I cannot tell, it looks like Providence smiled on me as well as on several others . . . I never saw the like before in my life, nor I never want to see such a sight again in my life." [4] Another 18th veteran wrote of it as "one of the greatest battles of modern times. . . . " [5] The Georgians had undergone their initiation successfully but at great cost. Old Stonewall himself pronounced them veterans: After riding over the Union lines which the Texas Brigade had broken, he said somberly, "The men who carried this position were soldiers indeed." [6] The brigade served in a supporting role in the rest of the campaign and went into camp near Richmond for a much-needed rest.

Hood was elevated to command of the division on July 26, when Whiting took medical leave. [7] Wofford as senior colonel took command of the Texas Brigade. Again, the question as to why he was not promoted at this time no doubt reared its head. Perhaps the fact that Wofford had missed the big show at Gaines Mill had something to do with the issue - that is, he had yet to prove his leadership on the field of battle. Hood's star as a combat leader had risen perceptibly. Wofford was still essentially an unknown quantity.

As the men rested and refitted, they were allowed to visit the capital where they spent their money in the shops and stews. Sutlers brought their wares out to the camps - tobacco, canned goods, and what-not. One of these sold the men some sausage which they enjoyed immensely until they discovered he had used cat meat! [8] The soldiers also picked wild berries, appropriated milk from nearby cows, or when Wofford was not looking, stole from the sutler's wagons. [9] One soldier, however, asked his wife to send him shoes, clothes, and a Bible. [10]

During this time, the Federal government sent an army under bombastic General John Pope to the Rappahannock River area in northern Virginia to threaten Lee's rear. Lee, still wary of McClellan's army on the Peninsula, decided to send Stonewall Jackson's corps to inderdict Pope. Hood's division was attached to Longstreet's corps and left on the Peninsula for the time being. On August 7, Wofford received orders to have all baggage sent to Richmond and rations cooked for hard marching. [11] Lee had decided to follow Jackson with the rest of the Army of Northern Virginia. One member of the Texas Brigade wrote: "Our fine tents . . . were sent off that evening and we never saw them again. Carey Street where they were stored was burned to the ground, as well as many other places, when Richmond was taken." [12]

When the march began, the Texas Brigade led Longstreet's column, heading for the Rapidan River and Gordonsville where Jackson was waiting, watching Pope. The brigade reached Raccoon Ford on the Rapidan on the 15th of August. Pope, with the approach of Lee's army, pulled back north of the Rappahannock. For several days, the two armies maneuvered for position. On August 21, Hood's men clashed with Federal outposts at Kelly's Ford on the Rappahannock, driving them back. On the 22nd, they were sent to Freeman's Ford to relieve Brigadier General Isaac Trimble's Brigade. The Federals attacked and were worsted by Hood's and Trimble's commands. [13]

Lee at length decided to send Jackson's corps on a wide swing around Pope through Thoroughfare Gap to Manassas Junction where Pope's huge supply base was located. Longstreet with the rest of the army would occupy Pope's attention along the Rappahannock front. [14] Accordingly, Hood's men took over General A. P. Hill's camps on the 24th and watched Pope's rear guard. [15] At two o'clock on the 26th, Longstreet's corps started a forced march toward Thoroughfare Gap to link up with Jackson beyond. "We kept tramping," remembered a veteran in Wofford's command, "all that evening and all that night, and at about 8 p.m. next day the 27th we halted within a few miles of Thoroughfare Gap, and bivouacked . . . tired and footsore. . . . " [16] To break the monotony and fatigue of the long trek, the Georgians of the Texas Brigade sang what was virtually the Georgia state song, "Goober Peas." The Texans responded with a lusty rendition of "The Yellow Rose of Texas." [17] With arms at will, the veterans strode at route step mile after weary mile. They no doubt reflected on a somber incident of the trek: A spy, who had deliberately sought to delay Longstreet's progress with false orders, had been summarily hanged beside the road near Stevensburg. His body hung from the tree as the men marched by. [18]

On the 28th, hearing that the Federals occupied the Gap, Hood and General D. R. Jones were ordered to clear it posthaste since Jackson was at bay before Pope's rapidly concentrating force. [19] Jones's men encountered infantry and artillery in the pass but brushed it aside. In the meantime, Law's Brigade, followed by Wofford's men, was ordered to cross the mountain and flank the enemy. "We could see a long line of troops passing obliquely up the mountain north of the Gap," remembered a veteran; "The Texas Brigade was ordered to follow, which it did until we marched one third of a mile, when the brigade was counter-marched at dark to the mouth of the Gap." [20] Law's Brigade was brought back also, and, reunited, the division passed through and camped. [21]

"At daylight of the 29th, we were awakened by the noise of musketry and artillery firing." [22] The men knew it was Jackson's corps engaging the enemy. Hood's division led off toward the sound of battle. At Gainesville, they turned onto the Warrenton Turnpike and by 10 A.M. were nearing Jackson's position near the old Manassas battlefield. [23] The division was deployed perpendicular to Jackson's right wing. Law's Brigade was on the left of the Turnpike; the Texas Brigade to the right. The First Texas was the left unit, its extreme left in the road; then the Fourth Texas, the 18th Georgia in the center, the Fifth Texas, and Hampton's Legion. They then moved forward to a line pointed out by Jackson under cover of some woods near Groveton. Skirmishers were sent forward, and the men settled down to watch the battle raging against Jackson's troops. [24]

At army headquarters, Lee spoke with Longstreet about attacking up the Warrenton Turnpike to relieve pressure on Jackson. Longstreet suggested that because of the lateness of the day, a general advance would not go far, but a "reconnaissance in force" at dark might show a weakness in the enemy position. Lee agreed and Longstreet gave the job to Hood. [25]

At sunset, the Texas Brigade and Law's men moved out, only to find that the Federals were advancing toward them. The Yankees had been ordered to pursue fleeing Rebels - which existed only in the far reaches of Pope's imagination - and got the surprise of their lives. Theron Haight of the 24th New York remembered: "Suddenly a body of troops was seen moving toward us from among the trees along the lane on our left . . . They shouted 'Don't fire at us, boys, we're coming to help you'; and some of us felt reassured . . . " [26] But not for long. Wofford reported, "My regiment opened a well-directed fire and charged into a ravine, silencing the enemy and completely routing him." [27] Their volley lit the darkness and struck enemy bodies "like hailstones against a window." [28] The Rebels then pitched into their foe. Correspondent "Potomac" of the 18th Georgia wrote to the *Atlanta Southern Confederacy:*

> A hand-to-hand conflict is awful enough in day time, but amid pitch darkness it is absolutely diabolical. Bayonets, butts of muskets, and even fists were used freely. The yells of the victors, the shrieks of the wounded, and the groans of the dying, together with the rattle and flash of musketry in the darkness . . . made up a scene which beggars all description. [29]

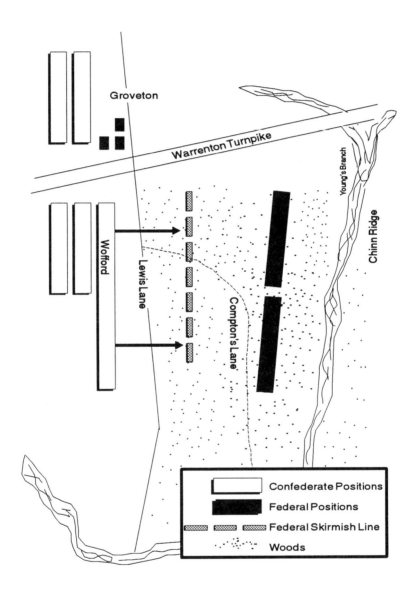

The Texas Brigade at Second Manassas, August 30, 1862.

Courtesy G. Judson Smith, Jr.

Private T. H. Northcutt of the 18th captured the flag of the 24th New York. Fifty-three prisoners were taken; the 18th had only two wounded. [30]

As the 18th continued its charge, someone halted it. Wofford's battle blood was up; he angrily asked Adjutant General W. H. Sellars of Hood's staff, "Who halted us?" Sellars replied he did not know. Wofford then ordered his men to continue the attack. The enemy had fled, however, so he halted them at a stream ahead. The rest of the brigade was soon brought up after chasing the enemy for a mile. Hood, discovering that they were surrounded in the darkness by the unsuspecting enemy, quietly brought the division back to its former position. [31] The reconnaissance had been successful, netting prisoners and a cannon taken by Law's men. It was a hint of things to come and made the Yankees - the enlisted men anyway - very wary about their left flank in the next day's events.

The 30th of August dawned bright and lovely. The men of the Texas Brigade lounged about, eating the last of their green "roastneers," their only ration:

> As we lay there in the shade of the little oaks, no one casting a casual glance around would have dreamed of the real situation. Some were reading novels and newspapers, some playing cards, and betting great rolls of Confederate money on their hands, regardless of the cannon balls which occasionally came tearing through the treetops. [32]

Except for the steady riflefire of the skirmishers in the clover field in their front, the day passed quietly for the men until noon when the Federals launched an assault on Jackson's position. Wofford's men had to watch the show before them until at 3:30 P.M., they were ordered to load and fix bayonets. [33]

Captain Dilmus L. Jarrett, Commander of Company C, Jackson County Volunteers, 18th Georgia Regiment, was wounded at Second Manassas, August 30, 1862, and died September 6, 1862.

Courtesy of Hazel M. Glenn Collection,
United States Army Military History Institute.

On the other side, Alfred Davenport of Duryea's 5th New York Zouaves looked out over the woods in his front, where the 10th New York skirmishers were disputing with the enemy: "It struck me that some mischief was brewing." [34] So it was. He saw the 10th New Yorkers suddenly run from the woods toward him, followed by a crash of massed rifle fire. "It was a continual hiss, snap, whiz, and slug," wrote Davenport. [35] And Hell followed after - the men of Hood's division streamed out of the woods, firing and yelling as they came.

Wofford wrote: "As we passed the field in front of our line, the brigade moved in splendid order, and with a shout advanced through the second strip of woods on the enemy's lines, which we carried so quickly that no halt was perceptible." [36] Some of the 5th New Yorkers volleyed high, for the retreating skirmishers of the 10th New York masked their fire, but some units of the 18th Georgia felt the volley: "At this first fire at least 40 Georgians fell, but the remainder returned the fire with equal effect, and with a wild yell rushed on the foe with the bayonet, literally pushing them back and forcing them to retire down the hill." [37] Lieutenant Lemon wrote, "they fired a volley at us that went high and hurt no one - we halted and fired a volley right into them and their screams were plainly heard above the musketry. . . . " [38] Cowtan, brigade historian of the 10th New York, recorded, "the graycoats were seen through the woods, and the next instant a destructive volley tore through the two devoted regiments. . . . " [39] Andrew Coats of the 5th New York wrote, "Not only were men wounded or killed, but they were riddled. . . . " [40]

The Federals were pursued to Young's Branch ravine in their rear where they were killed or captured "nearly every man. . . . " [41] One Texan remembered a terrible sight: "Many of them were shot in the back of the head, while up in the air, in their jumpings, they would turn complete summersaults [sic] and fall with their feet forward." [42] Sergeant T. C. Albergotti of Hampton's Legion saw Young's Branch glutted with Zouaves: "It was pitiful to hear the poor devils crying from pain and drowning, leg, arm, and some mortally wounded and unable to get out . . . " [43]   The 10th New York flag was captured by the Georgians who then charged a battery, capturing four cannon. [44] Surging on toward Chinn Ridge, they confronted another battery.

At this point, the charge bogged down from lack of proper supports. Wofford wrote,

> I halted my regiment as soon as my left was covered by the woods, and moved in line to the second battery through the woods, and over a slight declivity to within forty yards of the enemy's guns and their lines of support . . . At this point I had no support except a mere fragment of a regiment (supposed to be the Holcombe Legion which fought with much spirit and gallantry) . . . Seeing my men falling rapidly . . . and no reinforcements arriving, I withdrew my regiment . . . [45]

In this last action, "the battleflag of the 18th was shot down three times . . . the color bearer, Sergeant Weems, bore this flag to the front until he fell with two painful wounds, the colors being pierced by 17 balls and the staff by one . . . " [46] Truly, as Private Fletcher recalled, "the bluecoats on the ridge were a tough set to move." [47]

Except for the Fifth Texas, which strayed and went on fighting, the Texas Brigade rested from its exertions in the Young's Branch ravine. In all truth, they needed it. The 18th Georgia had lost 19 killed and 114 wounded. The aggregate loss of the brigade was 77 dead, 496 wounded. The 5th New York had 79 killed, 170 wounded, and 48 missing; the 10th New York lost 23 killed, 65 wounded, and 27 missing. A battery was also captured. [48]   A Rebel veteran summed it up: "It is no exaggeration to say that hillside was strewn thick with the flower of those two (New York) regiments. An observer said that it was possible to walk on corpses from the edge of the wood to the creek, so thickly were they strewn." [49] J. B. Polley's description of the same scene is oft-quoted:

> As we looked up the hill, a ghastly spectacle met our eyes. An acre of ground was literally covered with dead, dying and wounded of the 5th New York Zouaves, the variegated colors of whose peculiar uniforms gave the scene the appearance of a Texas hillside in spring, painted with wild flowers of every hue and color. [50]

The Texas Brigade had done a marvelous work in their charge of the 30th at Chinn Ridge. Objectivity compels one to think, however, that the brigade was seriously hampered by an interior command problem: It was not clear, apparently, who was in charge of the men. The regiments fought separate battles instead of a massive thrust of brigade strength. Topography conceivably could have scattered the regiments over a wide area, but Wofford, for example, could find only a section of the Holcombe Legion of Evans' Brigade at the position fronting Weidrich's battery on the Ridge. The First Texas got lost for a time. [51] The Fifth Texas "slipped the bridle" and joined another unit to fight further. Hampton's Legion recuperated in a separate location. All of this smacks of disorder on a high level.

Tactically, the brigade was exhausted early on and rested while the remainder of Longstreet's corps mopped up. True, the Texas Brigade was considered a shock unit after Gaines Mill, but properly coordinated, the Texans, Georgians, and South Carolinians - to say nothing of Law's Brigade - may have gone much further in disorganizing the foe, thus saving Lee's army much-needed manpower by decreasing the casualty lists. Indicative of the confusion was the fact that the regimental commanders were not sure to whom to address their after-action reports.   Frobel, brigade artillery chief, directed his to Major Sellars, Hood's adjutant; Wofford sent his to Hood; Gary of the Legion sent his to Wofford; Work of the First Texas to Hood; Carter, Fourth Texas, to Sellars; and Robertson, Fifth Texas, to Sellars. [52] Surgeon LaFayette Guild's casualty report of the Army lists Wofford as commander of the Texas Brigade. This confusion no doubt contributed to such problems as Colonel Work mentioned at the close of his report: "I received no notice and did not discover the movements of the other regiments of the brigade in time to have changed my front. . . . " [53]

Much momentum and many lives were affected by this problem. Apparently Wofford had no clear idea of his role as brigade chief, a charge which must be laid at the feet of his superiors.   Hood stated in his memoirs that he had placed Sellars in temporary command of the Texas Brigade, a direct rebuff, unintended or not, of Wofford: Sellars was a major, Wofford a senior colonel. The latter must have discussed this with Hood, for after the subsequent battle at Sharpsburg, all the regiments sent reports to Wofford who forwarded them with a brigade report to the division headquarters. [54]

On the day following the battle, the brigade buried its dead and moved up to the Henry House Hill. [55] The next day they left the battlefield, pursuing the Federals. At Fairfax Court House on September 3, the men rested. Wofford took the opportunity to send the two captured battleflags to Governor Brown with the following letter:

I present to the state of Georgia two stands of colors captured by my regiment in the battles of the 29 & 30 August. The plain one belonging to the 24th N. Y. Regt was taken by T. H. Northcutt of Capt Oneill's Co from Cobb. The other belonging to the 10th NY Zouaves by Wm Key of Capt Ropers Co from Bartow Co. My Regiment took a battery of four splendid brass pieces on the 30th. [56]

Chapter 4

Deadly Autumn

The Texas Brigade, on September 5, 1862, crossed the Potomac River at White's Ford into Maryland. "About noon, . . . it came to the turn of the Texas Brigade to cross over. In we bulged, our bands playing, and the boys yelling, as jolly as any who had gone before or any who came after us." [1] The men were impressed by the natural beauty around them. Barrett, marching with the 18th Georgia, gazed at the setting and wrote to the folks at home: "This is butiful contry with rich valeys and lofty mountains. tha rase large amount of hay and gain . . . " [2] Private Stephen Welch of Hampton's Legion wrote, "The beauty of the scenery charmed me and if I live till after the war I should like to have a farm and settle down there." [3] On September 7, they went into camp on the Monocacy River near Frederick, Maryland. Hood ordered the men to get into the water and wash their clothes. [4] The grime and blood of the Second Manassas campaign was washed off, albeit the men were still in rags. After resting for a few days, they marched on to Hagerstown.

Lee again separated his army, sending Jackson to invest Harper's Ferry. Union General McClellan advanced his host in the hopes of trapping Lee against the Potomac before he could reunite with Jackson. On the 14th of September, Confederate General D. H. Hill fought a delaying action at South Mountain near Boonesboro. Hood's division was sent to reinforce him. Shockley of the 18th Georgia wrote:

> on Sunday the 14th Sept we left Hagerstown and went back to the gap in the mountain near Middletown . . . Longstreet to whose choir (sic!) we belong got there about an hour by the sun did not fight much our Regt was not in the fight

though they doublequicked over the
mountain. [5]

That night, the Texas Brigade moved on to a picturesque little
village in the shadow of South Mountain, a place called
Sharpsburg.

On the morning of September 15, the division marched
up the Hagerstown Pike near Sharpsburg, passed a white-
framed Dunkard Church and filed off to the left into the West
Woods around the church; Federal long-range artillery across
Antietam Creek probed the area, dropping shells among the
Texas Brigade, but doing no physical damage other than
wounding two men. [6] The 15th and 16th were spent in this
position, the men resting and eating what was left of their
rations of green corn and apples. Many were without shoes;
clothes were ragged and patched; dysentery from the raw food
was taking its toll. But to a man, from General to drummer boy,
they were spoiling for a fight. They knew "the old man" had
stopped retreating; they knew also that their backs were against
a river; it was, in their country parlance, time to "root hog or
die," "fish or cut bait."

On the evening of the 16th, Hood received orders to take
his division and meet a Federal advance by Union General
Joseph Hooker, who had brought most of his corps across the
Antietam and was threatening the Confederate left flank.
Wofford and Law led their brigades across the Hagerstown
Pike, spread out in a long line perpendicular to the Pike in a
large field of clover. Wofford deployed his men: Hampton's
Legion, with its left in the Pike, then the 18th Georgia, First
Texas, Fourth Texas, and Fifth Texas. The Fifth's right
connected with Law's Brigade whose right rested on the edge of
a patch of woodland known as East Woods. [7]

Aligned, the division tramped 700 yards north until they
reached a 40-acre cornfield of shoulder-high corn. Pushing into
this natural cover, the men waited for the enemy. Federal
cannon probed the immensity of the corn from the northern end

of the field and Miller's farmyard. The Confederates lay down to remain undetected. Much to their discomfiture and to Wofford's ire, a Confederate battery, referred to by him contemptuously as "a little battery of ours . . . ," unlimbered on the Pike and fired at the Yankees, thus giving away the division's presence in the corn. It then, in Wofford's words, "hastily beat a retreat as soon as their guns opened on us." [8] One of Wofford's officers and several men were thus wounded. Stephen Welch of Hampton's Legion remembered, "we were under a terrific fire of shot and shell. . . . " [9]

Skirmishers were sent out who soon got into a shooting match with the enemy. Except for this action, the rest of the brigade lay quietly among the cornstalks. As Hood recalled, "When the firing had in a great measure ceased, we were so close to the enemy that we could distinctly hear him massing in our immediate front." [10] After dark, Hood requested and received permission to lead the division back to the Dunkard Church area to cook and eat much-needed food: "We had had issued to us no meat for several days, and little or no bread." [11] The brigades moved back quietly and were replaced by Brigadier General A. R. Lawton's division.

Back in the West Woods, behind the church, details were sent to get rations from the division wagons. The men "had not partaken of any food since morning and were now anxiously waiting for it to come." [12] But not that day. John Stevens of the Fifth Texas remembered:

> But daylight came too soon, the smoke of our fires proving a good mark to indicate to the Federals where our lines were. They began to shell us with their canister shot and at the same time to advance their lines. The falling shot raked our bread pans, skillets, and fires right and left, putting a complete check to all preparations for the much needed breakfast. [13]

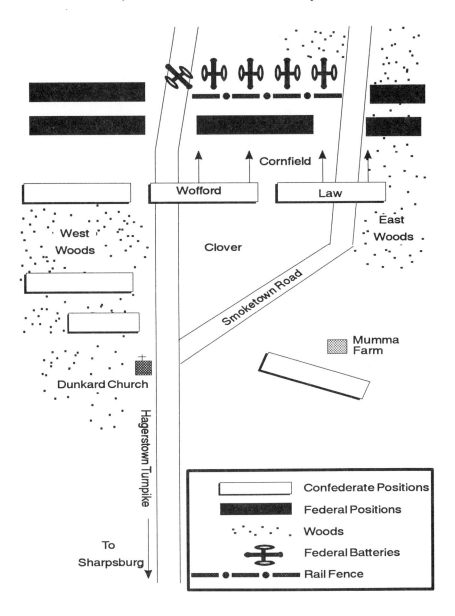

The Texas Brigade at Sharpsburg, September 17, 1862.

Courtesy G. Judson Smith, Jr.

The Yankees attacked Lawton in overwhelming force at dawn, and Hood's men stood to arms, food forgotten and uneaten. Jackson had made Hood promise to come immediately if he were needed. He was. [14]

Two Federal corps, the First and Twelfth, had crossed the Antietam during the night. Joseph Hooker's First Corps had deployed in massive formations stretching from Miller's Farm on the left of the Pike eastward to the Smoketown Road which paralleled the Pike several hundred yards. General Abner Doubleday's division attacked General J. R. Jones' units in the West Woods; General Rickett's division came through the East Woods near the Mumma Farm. General Meade struck due south through Miller's Cornfield, soon to be as famous a plot of ground anywhere in the world. This field was bordered on the north by a rail fence, on the west by a post and rail fence along the Hagerstown Pike, and on the right by the East Woods.

In the early light of September 17, Meade's division struck Lawton's outnumbered units in the tall corn and woods. Union artillery also blasted the Rebels mercilessly, taking down entire ranks. In an hour, Lawton had to call for help from Hood. Wrote the latter: "At 6 o'clock I received notice from him that he would require all the assistance I could give him." [15] Hood led his men forward. The soldiers, mad at having to leave their unfinished meal, swarmed from around the church, climbed the fences on either side of the Pike, men dropping at every step, and spread out into the clover. [16] Lawton's survivors streamed from the cornfield ahead, followed by the exultant enemy. Wofford and Law deployed their brigades quickly amid the backwash of battle.

Rufus Dawes, a soldier in the 6th Wisconsin, was among the pursuing Yankees. He never forgot the next few minutes: "A long and steady line of rebel gray, unbroken by the fugitives who fly before us, comes sweeping down through the woods around the church. They raise the yell and fire. It is like a scythe running through our line." [17] Hood ordered, "Fix bayonets! Charge!" The Rebel Yell rose over the din; the enemy, stunned by the sudden appearance of reinforcements and the devastating volley of musketry, fell back at a run, the Rebels after them.   Welch wrote, "like a hurricane we swept over the land." [18]   The Federals were chased back into the tall corn, the stalks shattered now by the bloody reapers of modern warfare.

The combat in Miller's Cornfield, from all reports, was some of the fiercest in the history of organized killing.   Perhaps somewhere, maybe at Cannae, the Catalonian Fields, Verdun, or the Bulge in the Ardennes, there was carnage to equal it, but for sheer gut-busting, heart-wrenching combat, the fighting in Miller's forty acres perhaps stands alone.   It was a Miltonic nightmare in which small groups of men wrestled with entire regiments; in which one glimpses through the smoke the unspeakable havoc of artillery blasting at close range clustered groups of yelling fiends, "with hideous ruin and combustion. . . . "

As Hood's division surged forward, Wofford rode at the center of the Texas Brigade line.   Looking left, as they entered the corn, he saw Hampton's Legion and the 18th Georgia, though loading and firing steadily, had slowed in their charge and were obliquing left.   He rode over to urge them on in proper alignment.   The enemy artillery and rifle fire around him surpassed any of his former experiences.   Private Welch wrote, "I never saw rain fall faster than the bullets did around us." [19] Sandie Pendleton, who had ridden forward at Jackson's behest to find Hood, remembered: "Such a storm of balls I never conceived it possible for men to live through.   Shot and shell shrieking and crashing, canister and bullets whistling and hissing most fiendlike through the air until you could almost see them . . . " [20] Wofford was surprised he did not see the missiles sheeted over the ground.   After speaking to Colonels Gary and Ruff, shouting over the din to be heard, he peered through the cornstalks and battlesmoke; he saw two Federal regiments maneuvering toward the left front and flank of his line.

He rode over to the First Texas and ordered it to "move by the left flank to their relief, which they did in a rapid and gallant manner." [21]   Afterwards, the First Texas moved by the right flank to the north end of the field, 200 yards in advance of the Brigade, stopping only when three Union batteries opened on them with double canister. As the iron balls ricocheted into the Texans, two companies were completely destroyed. "A Union officer saw a shot strike home and 'an arm go 30 feet into the air and fall back again . . . It was just awful . . .' " [22] The First Texans were soon on the verge of annihilation with fire coming in front and in rear from infantry on their right. Colonel Work sent three couriers to Wofford for aid; none made it - two were killed, the other lost a leg. The First Texas had to withdraw, leaving its flags in the confusion. [23]

Wofford, in the meantime, rode back to the left where he found "the fragment of the 18th Georgia in front of the extreme right battery of the enemy, located on the pike. . . . " [24] The Georgians were busy shooting down battery horses and gunners. "The 18th had advanced to within a few yards of the enemy's battery which had been playing on its ranks with terrible effect, and had silenced the guns, when the long dark line of the enemy was seen sweeping round to its left, threatening to cut it off. Two-thirds of its men had already fallen." Lieutenant Lemon saw a single shell knock down a squad of his men. [25]

Hampton's Legion, Wofford saw, reduced now to a few squads, was also engaged with the battery near the 18th Georgia. "We rushed," wrote Welch, "to within 50 or 60 yards of their battery and the grape and canister tore immense holes through our ranks . . . Never have I seen men fall so fast and thick. . . . " [26] Colonel Gary also saw the new Union battleline at this time on his left and pulled his survivors back into the corn on Wofford's order.

On the right of the Texas Brigade, the Fourth Texas faced impossible odds in the corn, but pushed the Federals back upon their batteries where canister crucified the Texans. The Fifth

Texas moved diagonally to the right and mixed with Law's men. They fought doggedly in the East Woods. After repulsing three counterassaults, in which "every man had expended his last cartridge, besides rifling the dead and wounded comrades' cartridge boxes," the Fifth grudgingly pulled back. [27]

Wofford, realizing that with the overwhelming enemy reinforcements already in view, coupled with his lack of support and horrendous casualties, rode back through the decimated, bloody corn to find Hood. Meeting Sellars, he pointed out the desperate straits of the Brigade. As they talked, he saw his men giving way and so ordered them to retire along the Pike to the Dunkard Church. As the division disengaged, Hood ordered the Fourth Texas to the left of the Turnpike to hold off Federal units threatening to flank the brigades from beyond the road. [28]

Wofford was livid at the lack of support. Many officers and gallant men, he wrote, had been "sacrificed for want of proper support. . . . " [29] Colonel Work of the First Texas was more specific:

> If required to carry strong positions in a few more engagements, and, after carrying them, hold them unaided and alone, this regiment must soon become annihilated or extinct without having accomplished any material or permanent good. [30]

General Hood, broken-hearted at the immolation of his division, passed his subordinate's concerns to Longstreet with words forcibly restrained:

> . . . the major-general commanding is aware of the number of messages received from me asking for reinforcements, which I felt were absolutely required after seeing the great strength of the enemy in my front, and I am thoroughly of the opinion had

General McLaws arrived by 8:30 a. m. our
victory on the left would have been as
thorough, quick, and complete as upon the
plains of Manassas on August 30. [31]

His division had lost nearly 1000 men, 50%, in his words,
"mowed down in heaps to the right and left." [32] The Hampton
Legion, First Texas, Fourth Texas, Fifth Texas, and the 18th
Georgia were mere shades. Their men lay on the clover field,
amidst the corn, among the trees, mangled and torn. Six Legion
colorbearers lay shot down; eight of the color guard of the First
Texas were down with their flags. A Fifth Texas survivor wrote,
"The Captain of my Company and his entire command cook
and eat out of one skillet, just five. One Company is entirely
annihilated, not a man left in it." [33] Robert Gould Shaw of the
Second Massachusetts marched over the scene of the vicious
fighting shortly afterward:

> . . . in half an hour, the brigade advanced
> through a cornfield in front, which, until
> then, had been occupied by the enemy; it
> was full of their dead and wounded, and
> one of our sergeants took a regimental
> colour there, belonging to the Eleventh
> Mississippi [Law's Brigade]. Beyond the
> cornfield was a large open field and such a
> mass of dead and wounded men, mostly
> Rebels, as were lying there, I never saw
> before; it was a terrible sight. [34]

The Texas Brigade rested behind the church and refilled
cartridge boxes. The men had plugged Lee's line of battle at
tremendous cost. Hungry, ragged, and tired, they had done all
that they could against overwhelming odds. Old Stonewall
knew Hood's men had done their utmost. When he ordered the
cavalry to arrest stragglers, he gave additional instructions to

leave Hood's men alone; "they had done enough fighting for one day, even by Old Jack's iron standards." [35]

Heros Von Borcke of Stuart's staff paid tribute to them: "It was astonishing to see men without shoes, whose lacerated feet often stained their path with blood, limping to the front to conquer or fall with their comrades." [36]   Shockley of the 18th reflected afterward: "I think it was a draw fight." [37] So it was. Hood's division had been bled white with nothing to show for it but ghastly casualty lists. "Our dead lay in rows upon the ground, where they had fought a fruitless fight," stated another. [38]

The Army of Northern Virginia stayed on the field on the 18th, offering to fight again if the enemy was up to it. McClellan wisely was not; he had been traumatized quite badly, too, with casualties at least as great as Lee's. The Confederates saw to the wounded, buried the dead, collected stragglers, and retreated the next day into Virginia. As the Texas Brigade crossed the Potomac, the men of the 18th Georgia "were compelled to assist the teamsters in gaining the heights on the south bank of the river, the mud being too deep for the half-worn down animals to drag their loads through . . . " [39]

As the men rested near Culpepper Court House that fall, the army was reorganized into two corps under Lieutenants-General Longstreet and Jackson. President Davis had approved the change the day after the Sharpsburg battle. [40] Brigades were also realigned to have regiments from the states together. Under this rubric, the 18th Georgia left the Texas Brigade and became a part of Brigadier General T. R. R. Cobb's Georgia Brigade. General Hood paid eloquent tribute to Wofford's men:

> Under the unfortunate organization of brigades by States, I lost the Eighteenth Georgia and Hampton's Legion, to both of which commands I, as well as my Texas troops, had become warmly attached. The former had served me longer than the

> latter, and in every emergency had proved
> itself bold and trusty; it styled itself, from a
> feeling of brotherhood, the Third Texas. [41]

There is no record of Wofford's reaction to this switch, but Milton Barrett of the 18th left little doubt of his feelings: "i don't like this Brigade as wel as I did texas." [42]

Wofford received distressing news from home in October; his wife Julia, in the latter stages of pregnancy, was having trouble physically. He requested leave of absence for November 1862 and returned to Cassville. [43] Supervising the farm and caring for the household had apparently caused Julia, with advanced pregnancy, to exhaust herself into prostration. Wofford arranged for her comfort and superintended the harvest. On November 30, Julia was delivered of a baby girl, whom they christened Martha Louise. [44]

Ever concerned about the welfare of the soldiers, Wofford noticed that many of the families of his men were beginning to feel the economic pinch of the war. The Conscription Act of the spring was taking many of the small farmers into the ranks, leaving their families in extremis. A Gwinnett County farmer had written as early as May 25, 1862, to his family:

> It is no use fur you . . . to depend on us,
> we are all in fur the ware and this damd
> old Jinrel woant give you a furlow or a
> discharge til you are dead ten days and
> then you have to prove it tha all hate him
> as bad as the devel he keepes a gard all the
> time and it is a fine thing fur he would be
> very apt to come up missing. [45]

In his own regiment, unknown to Wofford, Private Shockley of Jackson County, a volunteer in 1861, never received a furlough during the war; he was afraid to ask since he had been sick so much of the time and did not want to be called a slacker or "playing off." [46] To help aid these families, Wofford purchased interest-bearing bonds from Bartow County, the proceeds of the sales of which would help the indigent dependents of the soldiers. [47]

On November 24, 1862, he counseled one of his young officers who had been wounded at Second Manassas:

> Lieut John Hardin
> Your letter directed to me at Winchester Va did not reach me until since I arrived at home. I am much gratified to hear that you are able to walk but your wound which must have been a very painful one will be sore for some time yet and you can remain at home until you feel yourself fully able for duty. I should like to see you very much. the last time I saw you was on the battlefield with the captured colors in your hand. I had no time then to pay you the compliments your gallantry so truly merited. My wife who's illness brought me home is quite unwell. my last letter from the Regt was dated the 13th instant. [48]

Christmas 1862 was spent by Wofford at home with his family. Because of the birth of Martha, he had gotten extended leave of absence. Julia was progressing well after the birth under the care of Dr. J. S. Beazley, the family physician. Wofford's aging mother was well; the slaves were healthy, so the Colonel had every reason to rejoice. Then, tragedy struck the family. Shortly after New Year's Day 1863, Mary, their sprightly two-year-old, contracted diphtheria. After a week of suffering, she died on January 10. The deep religious faith of the parents kept them from despair, but the void would always remain.

The funeral was held January 11 at the Methodist Church in Cassville, Reverend J. W. McGehee presiding. The following hymn was sung in tribute:

> Why do we mourn departing friends?
>   Or shake at death's alarms?
> 'Tis but the voice that Jesus sends
>   To call them to His arms.
>
> Why should we tremble to convey
>   Their bodies to the tomb?
> There the dear flesh of Jesus lay
>   And left a long perfume.
>
> The graves of all His saints he blest,
>   And soften'd every bed
> Where should the dying members rest
>   But with their dying Head?
>
> Thence He arose, ascending high,
>   And show'd our feet the way:
> Up to the Lord our flesh shall fly,
>   At the great rising day. [49]

The effect of Mary's death upon Wofford was to be dramatic. In the great battles of Chancellorsville and Gettysburg, he was almost reckless in his lack of concern for his own personal safety.

Chapter 5

High Tide

Wofford returned to his command, encamped near Fredericksburg, Virginia, in late January 1863, after receiving the welcomed news that he had been promoted to brigadier general on January 23, to rank from January 7. [1] His new command was the former brigade of T. R. R. Cobb to which the 18th Georgia had been attached. At the Battle of Fredericksburg, December 13, 1862, Cobb had been killed in the defense of the famous stone wall at the foot of Marye's Hill. The 18th had proven itself then to its new colleagues by firing all its ammunition and fixing bayonets to repel the next assault. As Private Barrett wrote, "Our regiment shot 200 rounds [each] . . . " [2]

The other regiments in the brigade were the 16th Georgia, 24th Georgia, Phillips' Legion, and Cobb's Legion. They were veteran units all, having fought through every major campaign of 1862, incurring losses that were being made up slowly by conscripts and volunteers. Wofford was not long in endearing himself to the men with his concern for their welfare. "He was very different from the Cobbs," wrote a veteran of the 24th Georgia, "And soon gained the love of the men, something the Cobbs failed to do." [3]

By March, the men had exhausted the firewood supply in their camp. On March 3, Wofford moved the brigade "southwest one mile for a better wooded camp." [4] The winter was still very severe on the men. "Meat is a giting perty carse. we git 1/4 of a pound per day. beef has plade out. we git a little sugar. . . . " [5] To ease this problem, Lee sent Longstreet's corps, minus McLaws' division of which Wofford's was a part, to the Suffolk, Virginia area to forage for supplies. Wofford, while strict on foraging, allowed his men to hunt game to supplement their fare.

About this time, Wofford received orders from headquarters to establish for his command a special battalion or corps of sharpshooters, composed of "one commandant, eight commissioned officers, ten non-commissioned officers, one hundred and sixty privates, four scouts, and two buglers, specially drafted . . . " from each regiment in the brigade. [6] Armed with the latest Enfield rifles and the famous Whitworth sniper rifle, these men were specially trained for skirmish duty and for sniper harassment of the enemy. To increase the elan and promote the elite nature of these units, the "scouts" as they were known, were exempt from all onerous camp duty. They "messed and slept together and were never separated in action." [7] Deployed, they were on the right of the line, in battle at the front, and in retreat, the rear guard.

Wofford chose Lieutenant Colonel R. H. Patton, Company E, 18th Georgia, to command the Third Georgia Sharpshooters, as the scouts were officially designated. The men were thoroughly trained in marksmanship, stealth, and small unit tactics. By the end of April, 1863, Wofford's Brigade could boast an elite spearhead to lead his already casehardened veterans.

During this winter encampment, the men took a deep interest in matters spiritual. The terrible blood-letting of the 1862 campaigns, coupled with the obvious attrition of resources and consequent hardships on soldiers and families, began to tell on the men. They sought comfort in revivalism. Campmeetings sprang up in the camps. Preachers from home came in to preach and otherwise help the sorely pressed chaplains who were never numerous enough to care for the soldiers adequately.[8] Wofford, deeply spiritual himself, cooperated with these evangelists fully, attending services as much as possible, and suspending all but absolutely necessary work on Sundays.

In April of 1863, Union General Joseph Hooker, who had replaced Burnside as head of the Army of the Potomac, began an ambitious plan to flank Lee's army and cut him off from his supply lines and Richmond. Lee was still on the heights outside Fredericksburg where he had virtually destroyed Burnside's assault columns the previous December. His Confederates were spread thin along a wide front. Jackson's corps stretched from Hamilton's Crossing to Port Royal; McLaws' division held the line from Bank's Ford to Hamilton's Crossing, covering the old battlefield.   Major General R. H. Anderson's division was further west, helping Stuart's cavalry guard the upper fords of the Rappahannock.   62,000 Rebels were on hand to face whatever Hooker would throw at them.

The Union commander's scheme was simple and deadly, if it worked. He sent General Stoneman's cavalry on a sweep toward Richmond to destroy communications and force Lee to siphon off troops to watch him. Then, with Major General John Sedgwick feinting at Fredericksburg with two corps, Hooker would march upriver to Kelly's Ford, cross three corps under Major General John Slocum, and descend with vengeance on Lee's left flank at or near Chancellorsville, a small village located in a place appropriately called the Wilderness. He had 125,000 men, including cavalry, to perform this feat. Against any other Confederate commander, it might have worked; Hooker was contending, however, with the likes of Robert E. Lee and Stonewall Jackson. [9]

Private T. M. Mitchell of Phillips' Legion recorded in his diary for April 29, 1863: "long roll at six a. m. form a line of battle just below Fredericksburg . . . At Five P. M. marched down to the breastworks just west of Deep Run Creek worked on Breastworks until Eleven Oclock P.M. The Yankees having crossed the river this morning . . . just below the mouth of Deep Run Creek." [10] Wofford's men, incredulous at the rumor that Lee had been surprised by the Yankees, moved out that morning hungry but looking for a fight. "Many left for the battlefield without anything to eat, but cheerfully and quickly they were in line, all ready to meet the invader . . . singing, laughing, and shouting. . . . " [11] The next morning, Wofford sent a detail to the banks of Deep Run to cut down trees and clear a field of fire. [12]

By then, Lee learned from Stuart's couriers that all this hurrah near Deep Run was a sideshow of the big show coming off above Fredericksburg near Chancellorsville. Hooker had crossed heavy columns at Kelly's Ford and United States Ford and was descending on Lee's exposed left flank. Anderson had deployed his division to dig in and confront the turning column, but he was hopelessly outnumbered. McLaws' division was sent up the Plank Road past Fredericksburg at 12:30 A.M., May 1. [13] Mitchell recorded: "At one a.m. left the breastworks and marched on Plank Road towards Chancellorsville to reinforce Gen Anderson. We arrived on the field about ten a.m., formed a line of battle on the right of the road. . . . " [14] General Jackson then arrived with discretionary orders from Lee to do whatever was necessary to repulse the advance. Historian Ernest Furguson wrote of Jackson's decision: "Stop digging and pack up, he ordered. McLaws would take a column straight down the Turnpike toward Chancellorsville." [15]

McLaws did as ordered and was soon in contact with enemy skirmishers. [16] He deployed from column into line, Semmes' Brigade on the left of the road, then on the right, Mahone, Wofford, and Perry of Anderson's division. Wofford's men spread out in the dense thickets. They could hear heavy infantry fighting on Semme's and Mahone's front but only their own skirmishers firing in the trees ahead. [17] On May 2, Wofford moved his men to reinforce Mahone on his left. McLaws ordered his brigades to hold position during the day, waiting for Jackson to complete his march to the exposed right flank of the enemy. He was to probe with reinforced skirmish strength to keep enemy eyes off Jackson. Late in the evening of the 2nd, McLaws ordered an advance. [18]

Wofford's Third Georgia Sharpshooters pushed ahead, very nearly capturing a battery: "General Wofford led a charge of his battalion of sharpshooters on horseback, a thing very seldom done but often necessary to infuse the proper spirit into the soldiery." [19] The brigade followed, and, in McLaws' words, "became so seriously engaged that I directed him to withdraw, . . . his men in good spirits after driving the enemy to their entrenchments." [20]

In the meantime, Jackson struck the Federal right with overpowering force. Wofford's men could hear, six miles away, the vast cannonading and infantry firing, which was "so heavy as to seem as if the very hills were blowing up. . . . " [21] Shockley of the 18th wrote: "the ball did not open in earnest til Saturday evening old Jackson attacked them in the rear . . . the cannon fired so fast you could not distinguish them. . . . " [22]

Early next morning (the third of May), McLaws advanced the division to maintain pressure on the enemy. Wofford, his battle blood pulsing, was everywhere, encouraging his men onward. One wrote, "The General seemed to set at defiance the skill of the best marksmen in the Yankee army. . . . He seems to bear a charmed life and seems to be permitted to live to show friends how to fight and Yankees how to die." [23] His regiments were terribly cut up as they attacked the well-fortified enemy works. The 18th Georgia struck an angle of the fortifications and lost heavily in a front and enfillade fire. [24] Two 16th Georgia color-bearers were shot down in the enemy abatis, and the regimental flag was left leaning against a tree. "It was the regular Confederate flag-stars and bars," wrote the Yankee Colonel D. G. Bingham of the 64th New York, whose men, firing buckshot at close range, had stopped Wofford's men cold. [25]

Wofford, watching the Yankees with his fieldglass as his men regrouped, saw the enemy waver - now was the time. A correspondent of the *Richmond Sentinel* described the action:

> The position was to the right of the old turnpike nearly opposite the large brick house. Our brave commander was seen along the lines, from time to time, cheering the men, despite the crashing shower of shot and shell that was poured into our ranks - He was always greeted by his men with a shout that almost rent the air. At length the time came to charge; and the

Private William W. Beard, Company D, Danielsville Guards, 16th Georgia Regiment.

Courtesy of Charlotte Bond Collection, United States Army Military History Institute.

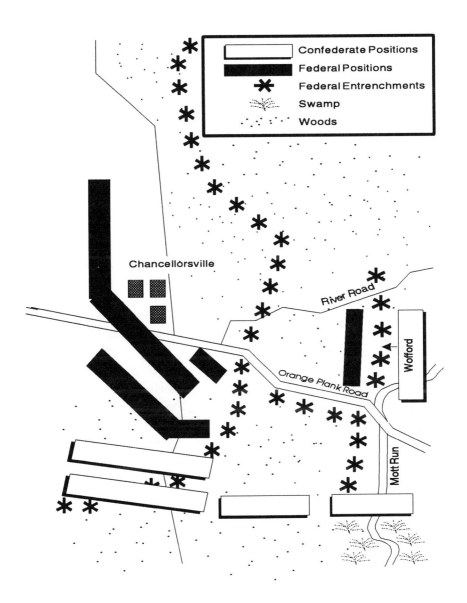

Wofford's Brigade at Chancellorsville, May 3, 1863.

Courtesy G. Judson Smith, Jr.

clear ringing voice of our well-beloved
chieftain was heard above the din and roar
of battle - "Fix bayonets, forward, march."
On they went in their impetuous charge of
death - the brave General leading the
charge with his hat in hand and cheering
until within twenty yards of the
breastworks; his iron voice was heard
again, "Charge them with a will!" "Whip
them back, take their breastworks!" They
took the breastworks. [26]

Mitchell of Phillips' Legion noted the time: "The enemy
retreated from behind their breastworks about ten a.m., we
gained a desided victory and taken many prisoners." [27] The
16th Georgia reclaimed its flag. As the Federals streamed back
toward the Chancellorsville ridge, Wofford led part of his
brigade in a circuitous route that placed his command between
the ridge and the retreating foe. On McLaws' order, Wofford
sent a flag of truce calling on fugitives of the 27th Connecticut to
surrender, which they did. McLaws reported of this incident:
"I think General Wofford is entitled to the most credit for their
capture." [28]

About noon of the 3rd, McLaws was ordered by Lee to
turn back toward Salem Church; the Federals under Sedgwick
had broken the Confederate line at Fredericksburg and were
advancing up the Plank Road. McLaws turned his division
around and marched to intercept the enemy. He told Wofford
to halt and watch the Mine Road for any enemy flanking
attempts and continued to Salem Church. Later, Wofford was
ordered up to reinforce Semmes and Wilcox whom the Federals
had attacked around the church. By the end of the day,
Sedgwick was hemmed in on three sides against the
Rappahannock at Bank's Ford, after vicious fighting.

As Wofford's Brigade rested that night, some of his men wandered over the battlefield. Colonel Robert McMillan, 24th Georgia, visited Salem Church, the focal point of the fight of the afternoon:

> The scenes of death and carnage witnessed here, no human tongue or pen can adequately describe. After the house was filled, the spacious church yard was literally covered with wounded and dying. The sight inside the building, for horror was perhaps never equalled in so limited a space. Every available foot of space was crowded with wounded and bleeding soldiers. The floor, the benches, even the chancel and pulpit, were all packed almost to suffocation with them. The amputated limbs were piled up in every corner almost as high as a man could reach; blood flowed in streams along the aisles and out at the doors; screams and groans were heard on all sides, while the surgeons, with their assistants, worked with knives, saws, sutures, and bandages to relieve or save all they could from bleeding to death. [29]

Others of Wofford's men collected souvenirs, as did Lieutenant Marcus Green of Phillips' Legion:

> I got some things out of Yankees pocket . . . I taken a pocket knife and looking glass out of ones pocket, a nice needle case out of another, $10.00 in greenbacks out of another, a ladies ambrotype another and taken a gold ring off one's finger. [30]

On the 4th, Wofford moved his men to Brigadier General Joseph Kershaw's right in a dense cedar thicket near Hazel Run about a mile east of Salem Church and a mile or so from the Plank Road to the northwest.   McLaws' and Anderson's divisions were to wait for Early's attack nearer Fredericksburg. The Yankees were in an obviously bad spot and if pressed, early enough, could perhaps be smashed.   But the hours passed. Wofford "was chafing like a furious charger" at the delay. [31] At 6 P.M. orders finally came for Wofford to advance against the Plank Road.   He called his men to attention and made the following speech, as recorded by a member of the 24th Georgia:

> Soldiers, they have put it on me to charge the Yankee battery in our front and run them out of there. . . . Now boys, I am going to tell you how it must be done. Just go right on up to them and when they see you will not stop they will run. Once you get them on the run don't give them time to turn around. Keep them going. All I ask of you is to keep in line with the Eighteenth but don't let the Eighteenth get off from you and get cut up. Men, I am sure you will do your duty. When you hear the words, doublequick, raise the yell, and go for them!

He then rode out in front and bellowed "Attention! Battalion! Forward! March!" [32] The men surged forward with a yell. Wofford urged them on with total disregard of his own safety. The enemy battery, as he had said, limbered up and pulled out barely ahead of his hard-charging men.

Coming to a dwelling, they captured 30 Federals, including a Colonel. The owner volunteered to guide Wofford to Banks Ford. The brigade "pressed on in the charge through a terrible pine and cedar thicket . . . " to the River Road, within a half mile of the enemy's pontoons. Wofford fired rockets to mark his position and sent a courier to McLaws to tell the Confederate artillery not to fire on the south bank for fear of hitting his men. McLaws in turn sent a courier to ask Wofford what he was doing "so far in advance of the line." Wofford sent back the message, "If I had fifty thousand Georgians I would not stop this side of Washington city!" [33]

Without support, the Rebel assault ended at midnight. Wofford could go no further. With support, his men believed, as one wrote to the *Atlanta Southern Confederacy*, "we could have captured this body of twenty thousand men at Banks Ford, as a matter of course we should have got their bridges, over which our victorious army could have passed, cut off Hooker's retreat, captured or thoroughly dispersed the whole grand army of the Potomac, secured all his supplies, and had Washington City at our own disposal." [34]

This was exactly what Lee had wanted to do, crush Sedgwick and cripple Hooker further, perhaps destroy him. The paralysis in his command, which was to cost him victory at Gettysburg, had begun to be manifest in the closing hours of the Chancellorsville campaign. Had Early and company attacked earlier on May 4, as Wofford saw, and Lee wanted, Lee's hopes would have been justified. Wofford's star was rising however. McLaws had seen first hand his subordinate's role in the campaign. Hood, in earlier reports, had lauded Wofford's abilities. John Coxe of Kershaw's Brigade also wrote, "Many also thought that the only other officer who could have fitted into Jackson's shoes was Wofford." [35] This was high praise indeed, considering the officer corps of the Army of Northern Virginia.

Brigadier General B. G. Humphries intimated to McLaws in a postwar letter about Wofford: "we all know that he was too prone to go forward . . . even into disaster." [36] On first glance, Humphries' statement smacks of an indictment until it is remembered that one of Jackson's many virtues as a military leader was audacity. The same proclivity to move too far in advance, as Humphries said of Wofford, is exactly the cause of Stonewall's tragic wounding and subsequent death. Yet it was also this audacity which made Jackson so effective as a tactician and so dangerous to the enemy.

On May 5, Wofford moved his command to the river at Banks Ford, "to prevent the Yankee cavalry from attacting our right flank." [37] The debris of the battle lay all around. "The wounded lay in all directions, calling for help and heaping curses upon their friends who had abandoned them in their distress. Guns, tent flies and cartridge boxes were packed up by the wagon loads." [38] In a driving rain that lasted all day, Wofford gathered his casualty figures while the men rested: Four officers killed; seventy men killed; thirty-one officers wounded; 448 men wounded. [39]

On the 11th of May, Wofford's Brigade moved back to its former camps nearer Fredericksburg. The next day, the sad news of Jackson's death on the 10th was announced to the army. Private Mitchell recorded in his diary: "the troops speak of his death with a mournful countenance." [40] His death was a loss that any army could ill afford. Within two months, at a place called Gettysburg, he would be tragically missed by the Army of Northern Virginia.

The next few weeks were spent drilling and refitting. The ranks were strengthened by the return of the sick and wounded who had recovered. Conscripts also filled vacant spaces in the lines. General Lee suspended all furloughs and reorganized the army into three corps: First Corps under Longstreet; Second Corps under Lieutenant General R. S. Ewell; and Third Corps under Lieutenant General A. P. Hill. "The troops of Lee were now at the zenith of their perfection and glory." Morale was at perihelion. Dr. Erwin J. Eldridge, one of the surgeons in the 16th Georgia, wrote his wife on June 3, 1863: "We are just on the eve of a march & leave in two or three hours. We do not know yet to where we are going. . . . Feeling full confidence in Genl. Lee we are ready to go any where he orders. . . . command is in fine health and spirits." [41]

On June 3, the First Corps led the army from the Fredericksburg area, reaching Culpepper Court House on the 5th. [42] On the 9th, the Brigade, with the rest of McLaws' division, marched toward Brandy Station to reinforce Stuart's cavalry. The enemy had crossed the Rappahannock at Kelly's Ford and attacked the Confederate horsemen. [43] Colonel Franklin Galliard of Kershaw's Brigade expressed the opinion of the infantry: "The whole affair was more like a sham battle and has rendered cavalry in my opinion more contemptible than ever when it comes to services upon the field of battle. If I were in that service I would quit it." [44]

On June 15th, the Brigade began its long trip into the North - Lee's second invasion. Mitchell of Phillips' Legion recorded their progress:

> Monday the 15th
> Marched west of Culpeper one mile and camp. with orders to cook three days rations to be ready to march in the morning at two o'clock
> Monday (sic) the 16th
> Marched at four a.m. pass through Woodville and to north of Spearsville one mile and camp having marched about twenty miles
> Wednesday the 17th
> Marched at Four o'clock a.m. keep down the south side of Blue Ridge Mountain pass Gains Cross roads about eight miles and camp.
> Thursday the 18th
> Marched at Five this morning camp near Piedmont Station on Manassas Gap RailRoad

Friday the 19th
Marched at Seven A.m. pass Piedmont
Paris at South foot of Blue Ridge Mountain.
Cross the Mountain at Ashby Gap, camp at
western foot of the mountain near the
Shenandoah River.
Saturday June the 20th 1863.
Leave Camps at four P.M. cross over the
west side of the River and camp. Enemy
said to be advancing from the east of the
Mountain and that our cavalry is falling
back.
Sunday the 21st
At two p.m. commenced to throw up breast
works on west side of the River. The
Brigade passed us going to meet the enemy
on East side of the Mountain. Our cavalry
is passing here in disorder.
Monday the 22nd
I crossed the river this morning to go to the
Brigade. find them in line of battle about
two miles east of Paris. At four p.m. the
Brigade moved back toward the River. I
am left behind to help burysome dead.
Stay all night at a house near by.
Tuesday the 23rd
I recrossed the River this morning and
found the Brigade in the old camp, received
orders this evening to be ready to march in
the morning.
Wednesday the 24th
Marched at four p.m. pass through
Millwood and Berryville cross the
Winchester and Harpers Ferry Rail Road at
Summer Point and camp.

Thursday the 25th
Marched at eight a.m. pass through
Smithfield. Clarkeville and Martinsburg,
about two miles and camp.
Friday the 26th
Marched at six a.m. cross the Potomack
River into Maryland at Williams Port.
Camp at Hagerstown
Saturday June 27th
Leave hagerstown at Seven a.m. cross into
Pennsylvania at Middleburg it being five
miles north of Hagerstown pass through
Greencastle camp at Marion.
Sunday the 28th
Moved six miles to Chambersburg and
camp. [45]

The march was long and hard on the men. Galliard of Kershaw's Brigade wrote his sister on the 28th from Chambersburg, describing sunstroke, lack of shoes, and attendant difficulties. But, he added, "Our army never was in better health and spirits." [46] Wave Ballard of the 16th Georgia recorded in his diary the same day:

Lying on the bank of a large creek - Black
and dirty. Low spirited - thoughts
wandering far away to those I love so much
at home. How strange it makes me feel to
see so many faces and not one familiar or
friendly one among them. I often think and
say to myself, only suppose the Northern
army should pass through our own
country, our dear old homes, our property
and everything we hold most dear,
destroyed by a craven foe. . . . [47]

Ballard was more prophetic than he could ever have imagined!

An inveterate forager, Marcus Green of Phillips' Legion was in a better mood.   At Chambersburg, the same day, he made the following diary entry: "I got plenty of good brandy and chickens, butter, loaf bread, cherry last night." [48]   In all truth, Wofford's men had been having a high time for themselves in the fertile, lush farmlands through which they were passing.   As Green indicated, they were consummate scroungers, despite Lee's orders to the contrary.   A member of the Third South Carolina in Kershaw's Brigade wrote almost wistfully of his compatriots from Georgia: "Last night (June 27) Wofford's Brigade of this div. stole so much that they could not carry what rations they drew from the commissary." [49]

The Brigade passed through Fayetteville on the 30th and camped near the Caledonia Iron Works owned by Thad Stevens of the United States Congress. Mitchell recorded: "I saw them burned to ashes today." [50] Surgeon Robert Myers of the 16th Georgia visited nearby Graffenburg's Springs, a resort in South Mountain: "I came across bathing houses, on quite an extensive scale - a ten pin alley, and flying horses (of wood) also several summer Houses studded over the grounds which had been prettily laid off with gardens and pathes . . . It rained all the afternoon." [51] It is well the good doctor had some recreation, for he would presently have all the business he could possibly handle.

Early on July 1, Wofford's men received orders to cook three days' rations and be ready to march. [52] After reaching the Chambersburg Pike, they had to wait until 4 P.M. for Ewell's wagon trains, fourteen miles long, to pass. They then marched to Marsh Creek near Gettysburg, arriving at midnight. [53] The next morning they loitered about while Lee and Longstreet debated assault plans.   Lee insisted that Longstreet's corps attack the Federal left, guiding on the Emmettsburg Road. [54] The latter finally got his men moving: McLaws' division had to wait again, this time for Hood's division to pass by and take the lead since he would form the right wing of the assault. Then, to avoid detection by Union signalmen on Little Round Top, Longstreet countermarched in a long circuit. After hours used up in what Lieutenant Lemon of the 18th Georgia considered as useless wandering, the First Corps at length deployed parallel to the Emmettsburg Road, tired and thirsty. [55]

Wofford's Brigade - 1,400 men - rested in Pitzer's Woods at the southern end of Seminary Ridge in reserve 150 yards behind Barksdale's Mississippi Brigade. "Both Longstreet and McLaws knew Wofford well, and that in a 'tight pinch' he could be relied on for succor. Hence on that day they decided to hold his splendid brigade in reserve. . . . " [56] The alignment of Wofford's regiments has been a mystery, but most probably they lined up as was customary: from left to right - Phillips' Legion, Cobb's Legion, 16th 24th, and 18th Georgia, with the Third Georgia Sharpshooters out front. [57]

Wofford scanned the distance in his field glasses. On the immediate right front were the Warfield and Snyder farmhouses and the guns of Cabell's artillery battalion. He saw "a field three-quarters of a mile in width, then a skirt of woods, two to three hundred yards wide, and then another field and woods, before reaching the base of the mountain. A quarter mile from the position where our line of battle was formed, and parallel with it ran the Emmettsburg Road, just beyond which was a dwelling, a barn, and a large peach orchard." [58] A farm road ran from his right flank, crossed the Emmettsburg Road at the orchard, and extended east into the distance toward the "rocky hill" or Little Round Top. Wofford made a mental note that this road would be a natural guide for an advance of the brigade. His orders from McLaws were to support Barksdale against the Peach Orchard. Kershaw and Semmes would attack on the right of the division's position. [59]

The orchard area, all the way to the mountain, was crammed with enemy troops and artillery. In the forenoon, while Longstreet was marching around, Union General Dan Sickles had moved his Third Corps forward to the rising ground adjacent to the Emmettsburg Road. His batteries now began probing the wooded ridges in their front, making things uncomfortable for Barksdale's and Wofford's men. Tree bursts sent shrapnel and limbs among the huddled ranks. Elijah Sutton of the 24th Georgia saw a solid shot plow through a tree and ricochet along the ground behind him. [60]

Anderson Reese of the Troup Artillery, which was stationed near Wofford's position, watched the activity in his front:

> The skirmishers of both armies were actively engaged as we came into position, those of the enemy being some distance this side of the road and making a determined stand to hold it. Very soon, however, they were driven back across the road upon their supports, and almost simultaneously with their withdrawal, our batteries opened fire upon the force in the peach orchard and field. [61]

About 4:00 P.M., E. P. Alexander brought the full force of 54 cannon to bear on the Federal lines. "In the Peach Orchard," wrote Fairfax Downey, "bursting shells bloomed like malignant scarlet blossoms, fragments of metal splintered the trees, and men watered their roots with blood." [62] All over the Federal position along the Wheatfield Road, the Confederate artillery wrought awful destruction.

Around 5 P.M., Hood's division engaged on the extreme right, striking toward Devil's Den and Little Round Top. At six, Cabell's guns ceased their barrage, paused, and fired three distinct shots, the signal for McLaws to push in his men. [63] Kershaw's men leaped the stone wall in their front and deployed, immediately attracting the Union artillery. Anderson Reese wrote, "The firing was the most rapid I have ever witnessed, and the earth literally vibrated under the continuous roar. . . . " [64] Barksdale's Brigade was supposed to attack the orchard angle simultaneously with Kershaw's advance. Wofford, watching intently, saw Kershaw's lines move forward but noted no corresponding move from the Mississippians. In fact, Barksdale's drummers were just then beating assembly instead of advancing. Wofford watched through the smoke as Kershaw's men engaged. As expected, the Union cannon in the orchard - guns which should have been occupied with Barksdale - followed the left wing of Kershaw and laid down a killing enfillade on the 2nd South Carolina. Colonel Galliard watched helplessly:

> The consequences were fatal. We were, in ten minutes or less time, terribly butchered. A body of infantry to our left opened on us and as a volley of grape would strike our line, I saw half a dozen at a time knocked up and flung to the ground like trifles. In about that short space of time we had about half of our men killed or wounded. . . . There were familiar forms and faces with parts of their heads shot away, legs shattered, arms torn off, etc. . . . [65]

As historian Miers wrote: "But somewhere the timing has gone awry. Kershaw is left alone, forced to split his brigade into two columns to cover the left flank that Barksdale has left exposed." [66]

The Mississippians were finally ordered forward upon Barksdale's repeated requests to McLaws and Longstreet. [67] In closed ranks, they slammed into the Union positions in the Orchard, relieving some of the pressure on Kershaw. The Federals fought manfully, their reinforcements coming down from Cemetery Ridge to engage the furious Rebel assault. Barksdale's men, excellent shock troops, caved in the salient, and pressed toward the Trostle Farm.

One of Wofford's "reckless fellows," Private Jesse M. Pendley, Company C, Phillips' Legion, was wounded at Gettysburg.

Courtesy of Ira Pendley.

After watching anxiously for a time, Wofford, according to one source, went to McLaws to get permission to advance. [68] Apparently some time had elapsed, for Kershaw's men grappled with the enemy in a seesaw battle for about an hour before retreating to the vicinity of the Rose farm in their rear. Semmes' men had also gone into the melee. [69] At last, Wofford was told to advance his men. The Georgians, impatient and spoiling to fight, moved over the ridge and deployed. At Wofford's command, they double-quicked into the fields that bordered the Emmettsburg Road. As they passed the Confederate batteries, the 24th Georgia had to break formation around the cannon. According to McLaws, they "were temporarily delayed in extricating themselves . . . and did not get out to join the brigade until it had gone about one hundred yards." [70]

Wofford saw the problem and rode over to urge them on, waving his hat at them. As he did so, he received an ovation from an unexpected source: "Hurrah for you of the bald-head!" he heard, shouted by Captain W. W. Parker, commanding the Virginia battery through which his men were passing. The cannoneers took up the shout and the brigade pressed forward, jumping the low stone fence in front of the guns, emboldened by the "thousand cheers from full and admiring hearts." [71] Lieutenant Lemon recorded that "the men at the guns cheered us gaily as we passed through. . . . " [72] Parker wrote to the *Richmond Sentinel*: "Oh he was a grand sight, and my heart is full now while I write of it . . . Long may General Wofford live to lead his men to victory." [73]

The men of the 24th caught up with the rest and in perfect order the brigade advanced toward the orchard. General Longstreet rode for a while in front, urging the Georgians to "cheer less" and " fight more." [74] A rabbit bounded suddenly ahead of the men; "Wofford's men, reckless fellows as they were, raised a shout, and about fifty shots were fired at the rabbit." [75] They missed. No matter - They would presently have bigger game for their gunsights. The Georgians then came

under long-range enemy artillery fire as they closed on the
orchard. Colonel Goode Bryan of the 16th Georgia remembered:
"a shell exploded and killed and wounded 30 men leaving only
7 men and one officer." [76]

Wofford, his units closely grouped in a line some 400
yards wide, guided on the Wheatfield Road, moving eastward.
This caused his troops to oblique away from Barksdale toward
the right. [77] The Georgian's right wing elements overlapped the
orchard, entering the wood on the right of the Wheatfield Road.
His center and left swept through the wreckage of the orchard
on both sides of the crossroads, mopping up the debris of
Barksdale's impetuous advance. [78] Private Reese observed:
"The Yankee dead lay thick around their guns and dead and
wounded horses literally cumbered the ground. . . . " [79]

The Federals who had punished Kershaw's left wing
were suddenly flanked by Wofford's fast-moving line. The
South Carolinians who had taken cover in the Rose Woods from
a terrific Federal pounding were the recipients of a welcome
surprise. Veteran Coxe recorded:

> We fought in that position for nearly half an hour,
> when to our surprise the thunder and roar of the
> Federal cannon and musketry in our front
> suddenly stopped, and the next moment we heard
> a tremendous Rebel cheer, followed by an awful
> crash of small arms, coming through the woods on
> our left front and from the direction of the peach
> orchard. Then one of our officers shouted and
> said: "That's help for us! Spring up the bluff,
> boys!" And we did so. Meanwhile the crashes of
> small arms and Rebel yells on the left increased.
> As we reached open ground over the bluff we saw
> the Federal artillery we had charged deserted and
> an almost perfect Confederate line of battle just

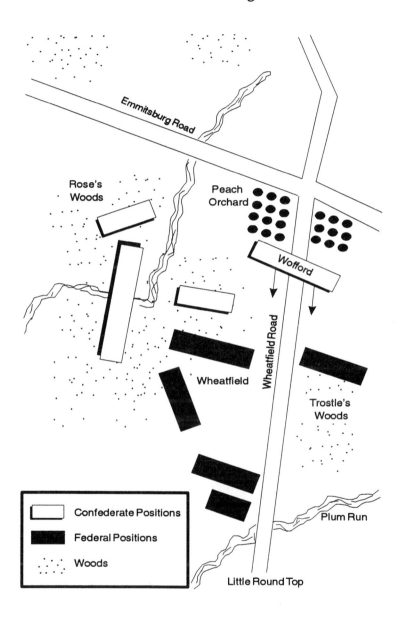

Wofford's Brigade at Gettysburg, July 2, 1863.

Courtesy G. Judson Smith, Jr.

>entering the woods, hotly engaging and
>driving the Federal infantry . . . an officer
>galloped from the right of the advancing
>line and ordered us to join his right and go
>forward. And that officer was Brig. Gen.
>William T. Wofford. [80]

It was one of the dramatic moments of the war. General
Kershaw never forgot the sense of relief he felt: "On emerging
from the wood as I followed the retreat, I saw Wofford riding at
the head of his fine brigade, then coming in . . . " [81]

As Kershaw's men linked up with Wofford's right, the
Georgians and South Carolinians swept over the stony hill, or
bluff, routing the enemy, and, cheering and yelling as they
loaded and fired, debauched from the woods upon the flank of
the Federal units in the Wheatfield. "The enemy," wrote
Kershaw, "gave way at Wofford's advance, and, with him, the
whole of my left wing advanced to the charge, sweeping the
enemy before them, without a moment's stand, across the stone
wall, beyond the wheatfield, up to the foot of the mountain." [82]

Union Brigadier General J. C. Caldwell reported, "The
enemy in great numbers came in upon my right flank and even
in my rear, compelling me to fall back or have my command
taken prisoners." The soldiers of the Fourth Michigan, under
Colonel H. H. Jeffords, stationed in the Wheatfield, suddenly
heard the rattling of cups on canteens and the "heavy tread of
rebel infantry" in their rear, fifty yards away. [83] It was a bad
situation indeed. The 140th Pennsylvania saw them coming
through the dense smoke from the area of the orchard and
presumed them to be Federals. A devastating volley from the
Georgians disabused them of that notion, however, and flanked
as they were, they had to retreat. [84]

Surprise notwithstanding, the Yankees fought
stubbornly as they fell back toward Cemetery Ridge and Little
Round Top. "Numbers, however would halt and give desperate
battle, in which the sword and bayonet were used. Portions of

Cobb's and Phillips' Legions had several hand-to-hand struggles over the enemy's colors, which they succeeded in capturing, and now have two stands in their possession." A soldier in Phillips' Legion wrote of one such encounter:

> We went into them with our bayonets and clubbed them with our guns. It was here that I went after the flag; and after shooting one man, and clubbing five others, I was in the act of reaching for the flag when a fellow named Smith jumped in ahead of me and grabbed it. I came very near clubbing him, but he put up such a pitiful mouth about having a family of small children that he wanted to see so bad, I let him have it so he could get a furlough. [85]

During this melee, Federal Colonel Jeffords heroically saved the flag of the Fourth Michigan but was mortally wounded by Wofford's men. Indicative of the savage fighting, one of the Georgians wrote of the incident: "A Federal officer attempted to use his sword, which one of the men wrenched from his grasp and thrust his bayonet into him." [86]

Even as they fought for their lives, the Yankees marvelled at the appearance of the Georgians: "They were moving obliquely, loading and firing with deliberation as they advanced, begrimed and dirty-looking fellows, in all sorts of garb, some without hats, others without coats, none apparently in the real dress or uniform of a soldier." Appearances can be deceptive, however, for the Federals admitted that the Georgians gave them all they could ask for and more. "The Confederates appeared to have the devil in them," said another. [87]

All along Wofford's front, the Federal line crumbled. In the Wheatfield, the well-directed volleys of his men shattered the Blue ranks, making a Tophet of the trampled grain. Union

General A. G. Ayres' Regulars met the Georgians and elements
of Kershaw's and G. T. Anderson's Brigades in the center of the
field, but retreated before the onslaught, leaving 900 of 2,000
men casualties. Wofford's exultant soldiers veered to the left of
the Wheatfield Road, through Trostle's Woods, into Plum Run
Valley. Lieutenant Lemon wrote: "We drove them down a
slope, captured a battery (Walcott's) to our left and pushed
across a small creek. . . . " [88] Wofford's men then struggled up
the mountain with desperation, but there they "met a terrible
volley; the enemy had, after being driven a mile, gained their
Gibralter and made a stand." [89] Colonel Galliard on Wofford's
right remembered that the bullets "literally came down upon us
as thick as hailstones." [90]

The 16th Georgia, according to its Colonel, Goode Bryan,
reached the farthest of Wofford's Brigade:

> No troops went so far as my 16th Georgia
> . . . there was no enemy either in front or on
> our right to cause us to fall back. . . . I was
> ordered to fall back by a courier from Gen
> Longstreet . . . Seeing Longstreet some
> short distance to my rear I went to him, and
> requested him not to order us back . . . His
> reply was I order you to fall back . . . [91]

Perhaps it was two of his men who provided the Yanks with
some comic relief on an otherwise grim day:

> The Confederates came charging into our
> lines and we captured many of Wofford's
> Brigade. . . . One tall, handsome first
> sergeant was being hurried over our
> prostrate bodies as we were settling into
> our last position. . . . "Going to the rear,
> Johnny?" asked one of our boys - "Yes and
> right glad I am to get to the rare," came the

quick response. As the smoke lifted, one solitary, individual "Johnny" appeared suddenly in front of, and almost near enough to, the Eighteenth Massachusetts to touch some of them with his gun, for he was charging "full tilt." The spectacle was so ludicrous, that many of the regiment broke out into a laugh, and they shouted, "You are not going to capture us alone, are you, Johnny?" and he immediately surrendered. [92]

As the firing sputtered out, Wofford's Brigade fell back through Trostle's Woods. Wofford was wrathy as he followed his men out of the trees, pistol in hand, abandoning their hard-earned gains. He told McLaws who rode up that he saw no need of the withdrawal and demanded to know who had ordered it. McLaws had not done so but he assumed that it came from Longstreet and hence had to be obeyed. Wofford told McLaws that since the brigade had been successful in the charge, the withdrawal might be "misconstrued." [93] Wofford grudgingly withdrew his men to the stonewall at the near end of the trampled, blood-soaked Wheatfield.

His men had reason to be proud of their evening's work. They had driven a numerically superior enemy for a mile or more, inflicting massive casualties while sustaining proportionately small damage themselves. Whether they could have gone further with more daylight and support is a moot point now. Goode Bryan, however, went to his grave believing that the Brigade indeed could have had ultimate success: "I have always thought," he wrote in 1877, "that if Gen L [ongstreet] had not ordered us to fall back we could have won the day. . . . " [94]

McLaws' part of the battle had been fought on the brigade level, inspired and sustained by the brigadier generals - Kershaw, Wofford, Barksdale and Semmes, the last two fatalities. Timing of brigade participation, as erratic and costly as it was for the lead units of Kershaw, actually worked in favor of Wofford. He led his regiments in when the enemy was discomfited and preoccupied. Guiding on the Wheatfield Road, his men had crumpled up the Federal units in domino fashion. Darkness alone had stopped him. His losses were 30 killed, 192 wounded, and 112 missing. [95] Now in the shambles of the battlefield, with the dead and wounded all around, Wofford could hear the axes of the Federals on Little Round Top as they dug in and fortified. He established a picket cordon near the creek. These outposts exchanged shots with those of the enemy but the latter did not advance - they had had enough for one day. [96]

Parties from each regiment went over the gory field to gather the wounded. Thomas Oliver, a lieutenant in the 24th Georgia, pulled a wounded Federal of the 140th Pennsylvania from the wheat. Long after the war, the Yankee, Lieutenant J. J. Purman, introduced Oliver, then mayor of Atlanta, to President Theodore Roosevelt. [97]

Hundreds more had traveled the last long mile of the way. Daylight revealed the horror of the battle in an unforgettable picture:

> In every direction among the bodies was the debris of battle - haversacks, canteens of tin and wood, every kind of rifle or musket, blankets, cartridge-boxes, and bayonet-scabbards, all strewed the ground. Caps and hats with the Maltese cross were mixed with the broad sombrero of the Texans; every conceivable part of the equipment of a soldier of the blue or grey mingled with the bodies of Yankee and rebel, friends and foes, perchance father and son. . . . Corpses strewed the ground at every step. Arms, legs, heads, and parts of dismembered

> bodies were scattered about, and sticking among the rocks, and against the trunks of trees, hair, brains, and entrails and shreds of human flesh still hung. [98]

Enough said about the intensity of the fighting on July 2 on the Confederate right.

At daylight on July 3, Wofford advanced the Third Georgia Sharpshooters into Trostle's Woods, the area they had vacated the previous evening. They soon engaged the enemy's skirmishers, so much so that Wofford advanced the Brigade "under cover of the woods," and formed on the right of the scouts, lest the enemy should attack in force. [99] As Wofford walked his lines, two distinguished visitors rode up to him, Generals Lee and Longstreet. Lee asked Wofford about the fight of the day before and the prospects of renewing it. "I told him," wrote Wofford later, "That the afternoon before, I nearly reached the crest. He asked if I could go there now. I replied, 'No, General, I think not.' He said, quickly, 'Why not?' 'Because,' I said, 'General, the enemy have had all night to intrench and reinforce. I had been pursuing a broken enemy and the situation was now very different.' " [100]

At that time, Lee was considering using all of Longstreet's corps to assault the Union center on July 3rd. [101] Longstreet convinced him that the "troops that had fought with me the day before were in no condition to support Pickett, and, beside, they were confronted by a force that required their utmost attention." [102]

During the great cannonade which preceded the Pickett-Pettigrew-Trimble charge of the afternoon of the 3rd, Wofford's men were idle. Unable to see what was happening on their left, they lay in the trees waiting. As the cannonade dragged on, a curious lethargy crept over them. Dickert of Kershaw's Brigade described it: "The men who were not actively engaged became numbed and a dull heavy sleep overcame them as they lay under this mighty unnatural storm . . . " [103]

After the bloody repulse of the Confederates in the center, McLaws' division was withdrawn to Seminary Ridge and deployed to receive an expected Federal counterattack. All the next day, they lay in line of battle while Lee sent an immense wagon train of wounded toward the Potomac. At one A.M. on the 5th, Wofford's Brigade left the battlefield in a westerly direction to North Pass in South Mountain near Fairfield, Pennsylvania. The skies opened on them in torrents. "It was pouring rain and as dark as Erebus," wrote Reese. [104] The roads liquefied under the thousands of marching feet. On the 6th, they crossed into Maryland and camped near Hagerstown. Moving to Williamsport, they camped on the grounds of St. James Medical College on the 7th. [105] They remained there for several days, building breastworks.

The brigade skirmished with Federal cavalry on the 10th through the 13th. On the 10th, Cobb's and Phillips' Legions with the Sharpshooters and the Troup Artillery "held the Yankee Army in check the whole day, engaging and driving the skirmishers back upon their reserves, and thereby deceiving and preventing their ascertaining the position of our Army." [106] On the 14th, they crossed the Potomac and reentered Virginia. One of the Georgians wrote to the *Athens Southern Watchman*:

> We crossed the Potomac the morning of the 14th inst. I tell you I felt good when I got back on Virginia soil once more. Gen. Lee, old grand pa, as the boys call him, was on his horse on the Virginia side, superintending the crossing of his army in person, most of the boys cheered him as they passed him. He looked as cool and as calm as a frosty morning. [107]

On July 22, at Chester's Gap in the Blue Ridge, enemy cavalry attempted to shell Lee's wagon train. Wofford's Brigade was sent to drive them off. The *Southern Watchman* correspondent described the action:

> As soon as our wagons came in range of their cannon they fired at them. Wofford's Brigade was ordered out to attack them, which we did about ten o'clock A.M. and charged them, Gen. Wofford, with his hat off in front . . . we made them skedaddle in a hurry . . . [108]

For once, the brigade had center stage and an audience. Lee, Longstreet, and others watched from the top of the mountain. Firzgerald Ross, accompanying them, recorded:

> We had a magnificent view, and could distinguish every figure in the fight which took place far below us. The Confederate Brigade - I think it was Wolford's [sic] - threw out skirmishers first, but presently, as the Yankees, who had dismounted, fell back towards their horses, the whole body advanced in line of battle over a broad open space. . . . As soon as they were on their horses the guns limbered up, and all trotted off together. [109]

Wave Ballard wrote in his diary of this affair: "charged through mud and water up to my knees, over fences and rock walls for 1 1/2 miles, after which we returned and camped for the night in Chester's Gap." [110]

The next day, the brigade led the division in line of march toward Culpepper. Whether they were being thus honored to be first in line, which was not their customary position, is unknown but the men took it as such. [111] From the 24th of July to August 3, the army rested near Culpepper where they received rations, supplementing them with blackberries which grew in abundance in the countryside.   Revivals also began again in the camps. [112]

On the 3rd, they moved over the old Cedar Mountain battlefield to Raccoon Ford on the Rapidan where they camped until August 22nd.   During the stay there, Wofford received very sad tidings from home - his infant daughter Martha Louise had died on the 9th of August, the second child to die within the year. [113] He doted on his children and was a devoted family man, so one can only imagine his anguish at such news.

On September 8, the corps marched to Hanover Junction and on the 11th boarded trains for Richmond. Many rumors flew about that they were headed for Georgia to reinforce Bragg's Army of Tennessee.   "All jubilant over the thought . . . ," wrote Ballard. [114] Indeed, they were destined to be part of the largest mobilization of troops in the brief history of the Confederate States of America.   Over rickety railroads, they were moving south, infantry, artillery, everything - a whole army corps. Ambitious for a much better supplied nation, it was phenomenal for the Confederacy to attempt such a feat. Rolling stock and tracks were by then decrepit and dangers abounded, but do it they did.   Colonel Asbury Cowan of Kershaw's Brigade wrote:

> These overcrowded trains were made up mostly of box cars to carry the troops. The men were packed in so tightly that there was no room to sit down and many stood from Virginia to Georgia with no chance to stretch cramped muscles except at wayside stations, where the train stopped for a few minutes. . . . some made their beds on the roofs of the cars and many lost their lives by being swept off by overhanging branches, road bridges and other obstacles. [115]

Diaries and letters of Wofford's men do not record any such fatalities, however, as his Brigade trundled along the rails. Mitchell of Phillips' Legion recorded their progress in his journal:

> Friday 11th
> Get aboard the cars this a.m. and left the Junction at eleven am arrived in Richmond about one p.m. leave Richmond at nine p.m. arrived in Petersburg about eleven p.m.
> Saturday 12th
> Left Petersburg at eleven p.m.
> Sunday 13th
> arrived in Weldon N.C. at six a.m. leave at nine a.m. arrive at Goldsboro at seven p.m.
> Monday 14th
> arrived at Wilmington N.C. at nine a.m. I saw today at this place the largest cannon I have ever seen . . .
> Tuesday September 15th 1863
> Left Wilmington at eleven p.m. crossing the Cape Fear River in a steam boat left on the cars from Westside as soon as we could get aboard arrived at Florence at eleven p.m.
> Wednesday 16th
> Left Florence at three am. arrived at Charleston, S.C. at one p.m. Left at six p.m.
> Thursday 17th
> arrived at Savannah Geo at four a.m. Left at eight a.m.
> Friday 18th
> arrived at Macon at two a.m. left at eight a.m. arrived in Atlanta at seven p.m.

> Saturday 19th
> Left Atlanta at eight a.m. Arrived at Dalton
> at Seven p.m. Train stayed at Dalton about
> three hours . . . Train arrived at Green
> Wood Station about eleven p.m. we get off
> the cars and camp
> Sunday 20th
> marched at eight a.m. pass through Ringold
> considerable cannonading in front. Camp
> about five miles west of Ringold.
> Monday 21st
> Marched through yesterdays battle field it
> being on and near Chicamauga Creek. we
> camp north side of the creek. [116]

Private Shockley of the 18th Georgia, and no doubt many others, were pleased when the trains stopped in Augusta, Georgia. While there for a rest period on the 17th, they received much-needed clothes from the Georgia Hospital and Relief Association. Headquartered in that city, that noble association supplied clothes, food and medical supplies to the Confederate armies throughout the war. Shockley received pants, drawers, and a shirt. [117]

Wofford's Brigade did not arrive in time to participate in the battle at Chickamauga Creek, September 19-20. His men joined in the pursuit of the defeated Federals, bottling them up in Chattanooga. The Georgians encamped on Missionary Ridge, a part of the besieging force. Milton Barrett wrote from there on the 24th: "we did not git hear in time to take a part in the battle last Sat and Sunday. i past over the Battlefield last Monday. it was a terable slauter. the dead lay thick for a bout three miles. . . . " [118] Shockley was not impressed with the area around Chattanooga - "there is more dust here than there are cherrys in Pennsylvany. . . . " [119]

Back in Virginia, General Lee received disturbing news from the battlefield: Hood was feared dead; Wofford was reported killed in action. Lee wrote Davis on September 23: "I fear also from the accounts, that General Wofford is dead; he was one of Georgia's best soldiers. I am gradually losing my best men . . . " On the 27th, he wrote the President again: "I am much obliged to your excellency for the information contained in your dispatch of last evening in reference to Generals Hood and Wofford. It has given me great relief." [120]

Wofford was very much alive but not well. The physical labors and pressures of two major campaigns, including the battles of Chancellorsville and Gettysburg, in addition to forced marches and vagaries of weather that were endured, had sapped his physical strength. The news of the death of a second child added a near impossible emotional burden. All of this broke him down during October. He went on sick furlough the first of November. [121]

The situation on the home front, Wofford learned as he convalesced, had deteriorated dramatically since the spring of the year. Although Governor Brown had appropriated a large amount of money through the Legislature, the largest portion of which was distributed to families in Bartow and adjacent counties, the picture was distressing indeed. As close as Marietta, a Confederate supply train was hijacked in April 1863 by "28 women, drawn up across the road - most of them armed with knives and pistols . . . " [122] In the view of the *Atlanta Southern Confederacy*, "These 'women seizures' [were] . . . a preconcerted movement among very wicked and ignorant women, generally instigated thereto and led by rascally individuals who aim at plunder and robbery." [123] Moreover, the Confederate Congress passed a tax law on April 24, 1863, that was in theory aimed at the wealthy but hurt most of all the families of the soldiers. The bill included an internal revenue, a license tax, and a tithe law which demanded one tenth of the crops raised on the farms. [124] Impressment was also being used to gather food and stock for the armies, with little regard for the people. A North Georgia farmer complained:

> The army wagons and parts of command of
> cavalry of our army is taking our produce
> our horses cattle sheep and hogs and very
> seldom pay anything when they do it. . . .
> they go into the cornfields and load their
> wagons and goes off and dont let a person
> know anything about it. [125]

Although Wofford as a Confederate general apparently
suffered little in this regard, he was as ever concerned with the
needs of the populace. He viewed with alarm and dismay also
the rapid growth of bands of renegades - deserters and
Unionists - who were terrorizing the citizens of northwest
Georgia. He learned of one guerrilla in particular with whom he
would have future dealings - John P. Gatewood. A deserter
himself, this man led a band of guerrillas who preyed on
Confederates and Unionists alike:

> In time, he formed a cadre of fellow
> deserters, bushwhackers, and criminals; a
> band that usually numbered fifty to one
> hundred men. Although he had no official
> status, Gatewood "claimed to be Southern
> in his sympathies," and between 1863 and
> 1865 he "scoured the country with his band
> of irresponsibles, pillaging, ravaging,
> plundering and killing." . . . His
> murderous reputation rapidly spread, and
> throughout the region Gatewood was
> known as the "longhaired, red-bearded
> beast from Georgia." [126]

Wofford was aware that Governor Brown had already
written to President Davis about assigning Wofford to Georgia
to combat these guerrillas. General Lee had demurred,
however, when Davis broached the subject to him: "I regard

2222

him as one of the best brigadiers in the division in which he is serving, and I do not see well how his services can be spared. . . ." [127]

Unionism was seen also in more peaceful circles than guerrilla bands. Wofford knew well of his friend Brown's poor showing in the October 1863 gubernatorial election. Brown's fourth victory at the polls was resounding statewide, but Wofford saw an alarming thing when he studied the tallies for the northern Georgia counties: Joshua Hill, an avowed antisecessionist and one suspected of collusion with the Union, "won in Bartow, Clayton, Carroll, Cherokee, Forsyth, Heard, Paulding and Hall Counties." [128]

In fact, this latent Unionism of the upcountry of Georgia would become more and more active as Sherman moved into the state the following year. At least two regiments in the Union army were made up of men from Pickens and adjacent counties. [129] It is also true that Union authorities saw Unionism in the South as a fifth column to be exploited: "During the war, the value of recognizing and encouraging small cells of Unionists behind Confederate lines seems to have been recognized by the Federal government as a part of war strategy." [130] Whatever, Wofford could see around him that the war was having dire effects on his neighbors and county. The end of all this was yet out of sight, but the trends were not hopeful.

Wofford's Brigade, in the investing lines around Chattanooga, was experiencing hard times. Supplies and rations were not being delivered to the troops except in driblets. Allen Jordan of the 24th Georgia spoke for all in a letter to his father, October 22, 1863:

> Please send me one vest, one pair of socks, one pair of galloses, one peck of potatoes, one little bucket of butter, one quart of molasses, one bottle of that brandy that Mother has been saving for me so long . . .

> and some apples, something to eat is the
> thing to please me. Father and Mother I am
> going to tell you what we have to eat here.
> We have corn bread and beef and it is so
> poor that it isn't fit to eat, when they bring
> them in here on the cars they are hardly
> able to travel to the pen where we kill
> them . . . [131]

Longstreet ordered his men, many of whom were shoeless, to make moccasins, Indian-style, from the animal hides. Wave Ballard recorded that his company received 12 cowskins, 6 calf skins, 1 hog skin, 2 goat skins, and a horse hide. [132] E. P. Alexander remembered that Longstreet also ordered his be-moccasined troops to swap their makeshift footgear perforce for the better shoes of Union prisoners. The prisoners took all of this in stride, wrote Alexander, figuring that their shoes were also p.o.w.'s, thus spoils of war. [133]

The shortage of supplies and food, in addition to the inclement weather, was to make the winter of 1863-64 the worst that Wofford's men encountered in the whole of the war. To exacerbate this already bad situation, Longstreet and Bragg decided that a Federal force under Burnside in East Tennessee should be interdicted before it could reinforce Chattanooga. To do this, Longstreet was to take his corps northeast toward Knoxville and blithely bag Burnside's force lock, stock, and barrel. [134]

For Wofford's Brigade, the campaign started on a sour note. On November 4, the soldiers marched to Tyner's Station where they boarded a train. Private Mitchell noted: "got aboard the cars at six p.m. it has been raining for the two last days and we had to get in stock cars with about three inches of soft manure on the floor . . . it is the filthiest place I was ever in . . . " [135] The men obviously spent the night standing. To make matters worse, the train also derailed later, but none was hurt.

Burnside retreated into the defenses of Knoxville as the Confederates moved up over the next two weeks. On the 29th of November, after several lurches and starts, Longstreet launched a disastrous assault against Fort Sanders, a huge redoubt on the outskirts of the city. The Brigade, commanded by Colonel Ruff in Wofford's absence, moved forward in column of regiments, led by Phillips' Legion. Ice and manmade obstacles, such as telegraph wires stretched over the ground, slowed the attackers. Manfully, they strove to get inside the fort. Lieutenant Lemon cut footholds in the frozen earthen rampart to climb to the top where he was shot and captured. [136] Colonel Ruff was killed on the parapet. Colonel H. P. Thomas of the 16th Georgia was killed inside the fort. [137] Many others were lost. It was an unmitigated disaster. Mitchell commented: "I was not hurt but got very bloody. . . ." [138] Surgeon Myers of the 16th Georgia summed it up with poignancy:

> . . . we returned to camp where all was quiet and sad. the feeling just after a battle is very depressing - the excitement intense at the time but after its all over and you get into camp and look around & miss so many familiar faces it makes the stoutest heart quiver. [139]

On December 4, Longstreet lifted, or gave up on, the siege of Knoxville and moved to near Russellville, Tennessee, where the corps set up winter camp. [140] "That winter was the coldest of the war. From the last few days of 1863 until the middle of January, 1864, the temperature hovered around zero degrees Fahrenheit in east Tennessee." [141] Into the teeth of these elements, the men were called out time and again to march to this or that place where the enemy was rumored to be. With the eye of a surgeon, Myers observed the effect of all this on the men: "Many of the troops are poorly clothed. very few if any with overcoats & some without blankets. they suffer terribly. . . ." [142]

Wofford returned to duty on January 10. [143] He was disturbed at the vicissitudes of his men but was subject himself to the vagaries of a rundown transport system which kept much-needed supplies from reaching the army. When the rail service was repaired, however, the corps did receive 3000 pairs of shoes. [144] If anything more could be gained by his personal presence, Wofford would do that, too. He visited his men often in their rude huts to talk with them. [145] They felt that they could count on him for help. For example, Shockley of the 18th Georgia wrote his wife from a Newnan, Georgia hospital about the prospects of a furlough: "If I could see Gen Wofford I might stand a chance but do not think it would do for me to write to him as he would know nothing only what I told him and he might think I was playing off. . . . " [146]

Some tragedies, however, could not be averted even by the best of commanders. Some men of the 16th Georgia were captured in early February in one of the numerous forays the Brigade made that winter. Unknown to Wofford, these men met with an undeserved fate in an incident which characterized the wretched conflict as a whole:

> On the tenth of that month a large number of
> soldiers fell into the hands of the Federals at
> Russellville, Tennessee and soon smallpox
> broke out among the prisoners. Becoming a
> burden to their captors, they were abandoned
> and left behind in the small Lost Creek
> Baptist Church near Newmarket, Tennessee
> . . . where they died. [147]

When the weather permitted, Wofford had regular drill and inspections to keep his men in fighting trim and no doubt also to keep their minds off their manifold troubles. Even this was undermined by the system of supply when in late March, while in camp near Greenville, Tennessee, orders came down that rations were to be cut to "two thirds of a pound of flour not bolted and 1/3 a pound of bacon." [148] After several days of this starvation, the men had taken about all that they could stand. Milton Barrett wrote:

> We all a greede to go to the genral (Wofford)
> and if he did not give us moar rashings to
> charge the comasary an take by force. He
> had us a extray days rashins ishued and got
> us all sorty pasafied. We could buy a little
> flour by going eight or ten miles after it. [149]

As early as March 20, rumors flew that Longstreet's corps would be returning soon to Virginia. [150] On the 28th of the month, the brigade moved to Bristol, Tennessee, arriving on the 31st. On April 13, the men boarded a train for Charlottesville, Virginia, where they camped until the 17th. On the 18th, they entrained for Gordonsville where they received at last good food and clothes. "All felt as if we were returning to our old home. . . . " [151] Colonel Galliard wrote, "The feeling of delight is universal with the Corps and is heartily reciprocated . . . The Virginia people know how to entertain and animate the soldiers." [152] A veteran in the 11th Georgia, encamped adjacent to Wofford's men, wrote home: "We air . . . seeing a fine time . . . getting plenty to eat sugar and coffee, rice and peas. . . . " [153]

The Corps enjoyed a grand review by General Lee on the 29th of April. Drawn up by brigade and division in a large field near Gordonsville, the tattered men, done up as best they could appear, buttons polished, weapons burnished, marched by their beloved chieftain, who raised his hat in solemn tribute as each unit passed by. The regimental bands blared "Hail to the Chief," an air later to be reserved for the presidents of the reunited nation. The artillery battalion attached to the corps fired salute after salute. The day was a gala one for all. After it was over, Lee left for his headquarters, knowing perhaps that soon, full soon if anyone had known, these same men would be trotting into harm's way at his call. [154]

Chapter 6

Wilderness to Guard Hill

In the spring of 1864, the Union armies had a commander who was new to the war in the east, having served until then in the western theater. He was General U. S. Grant, hero of Fort Donelson and Vicksburg, now in overall command of the Union forces in the field. Assigning General W. T. Sherman to campaign in Georgia against the Army of Tennessee, Grant decided to travel with the eastern army, still under the immediate command of General George Meade. Grant had never faced Lee and the Army of Northern Virginia, a fact that might have cowed anyone else in the Union officer corps. But Grant was not disposed to view Lee, or anyone else this side of heaven, with reverence. He did, however, realize one thing: to defeat the Confederacy, he must defeat the famous army of Lee and that was what he proposed to do. There could be no more retreating to refit and replan as his predecessors had done. Lee could not be given any respite. [1]

In Virginia, in late April, the Union host crossed the Rapidan near Chancellorsville and "marched along narrow country paths, through the dense blanket of thickets, matted underbrush, stunted pines, oaks, sweet gum and cedars, and tangled vines known . . . as the 'Wilderness.' " [2] General Lee, knowing of the Union advance, planned to attack Grant where the might of the enemy would be most mitigated, in the vast stretches of that forest. He accordingly ordered General Ewell's II Corps to move along the Old Turnpike toward Chancellorsville. General Hill's III Corps marched laterally along the Orange Plank Road. While they engaged the enemy, Longstreet was to proceed around the left flank of the enemy via the Catharpin Road. [3]

Private Mitchell noted in his diary on the evening of May 4: "Leave camp at 4 p.m. Cross the Virginia Central R. R. just south of Milton's Siding Camp about nine p.m. near Ellises

Mill." [4] The next morning they broke camp at 3 A.M. and marched to Richard's Shop on the Catharpin Road where they stopped for the night, eight miles from Spottsylvania Court House. Their march was delayed during the day by Union cavalry which after stubborn fighting retreated before General Thomas Rosser's horsemen. [5] The men heard sounds of cannonfire off through the woods on their left. It was an ominous noise indeed.

Wofford's Brigade was in the rear of McLaws' division, now commanded by General Kershaw. The Georgians were guarding the immense wagon train of the I Corps. [6] No doubt many of them chafed at being in the rear. Wofford's thoughts are unknown, too, but his star was about to rise to its zenith in the action which was to unfold the next day. At headquarters that night, he learned that Hill had struck the enemy hard and gotten punished in turn. At dark on May 5, Hill's men were spread out perpendicularly to the Plank Road some three miles north of Parker's Store. Lee was with them at the farm of Widow Tapp, a rare bit of open high ground in the forest. It was imperative that Longstreet reinforce them at that point as soon as possible. To do so required the I Corps to discontinue its flanking movement on the Catharpin Road, turn left along available routes, and strike the Plank Road at or near Parker's Store. Wofford returned to his brigade with orders to move out at 1 A.M., May 6. [7]

According to Mitchell's diary, the men started at 2 A.M., due no doubt to its being the rear guard. [8] As the division reached the Plank Road, and turned right toward the Tapp Farm, heavy firing broke out ahead. Federal General W. S. Hancock launched at 5 A.M. a heavy assault on Hill's Corps, striking the divisions of Heth and Wilcox. These units began to waver and finally break under the weight of the attack. [9] Longstreet urged his divisions, Field's and Kershaw's (Pickett's was absent), into double-time. Field's men trotted up the left of the Plank Road while Kershaw's quickstepped on the right. As the clearing of the Tapp Farm came into view, Longstreet's men had to dodge through the remnants of Hill's divisions. The time was 8 A.M. [10]

The Army of Northern Virginia had faced critical moments before in its brief history - at Sharpsburg, for instance - and would face more before the final curtain at Appomattox Court House. Perhaps none was as dramatic and menacing, however, as this at the Tapp Farm. As Bruce Catton wrote in memorable prose:

> And there was a moment, here by the Tapp homestead, with dawn coming up through the smoke and the Northern advance breaking out of the trees, when the authentic end of the war could be glimpsed beyond the ragged clearing. If Hancock's men could go storming on for another half mile . . . [11]

But it was not to be. "At this critical juncture," wrote Colonel William Poague, whose artillery battalion stood lonely in the Tapp yard, "Gregg's Texans (Field's men) came in line of battle at a swinging gait from the rear of our position." [12] As they deployed on the left of the road, Kershaw's men spread out in the trees on the right. Wofford's Brigade, coming up last, assumed position on the right of the division, with Anderson's of Fields' division on his right. [13] Shockley wrote, "our brigade went in without time to take a long breath. at first we drive the enemy . . . " [14]

The countercharge of the I Corps stopped the Union advance dead in its tracks and after vicious combat, often hand-to-hand, the enemy was forced back. One of Wofford's men reported to an Atlanta newspaper, "forming under a terrific musketry fire, [we] advanced against the triumphant and elated enemy, not only checking their advance but driving them back beyond their first line of fortifications and recovering the ground from which Hill had been driven that morning." [15] Mitchell

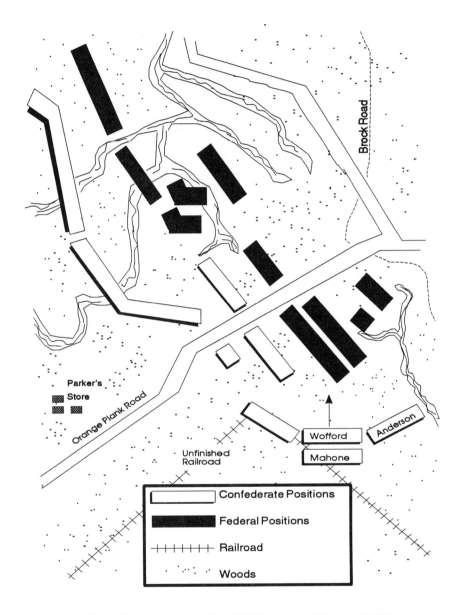

Wofford's Brigade at The Wilderness, May 6, 1864.

Courtesy G. Judson Smith, Jr.

recorded, "Our Div drawn in line and charge the Enemy driving the Enemy back at every Point." [16] Wofford narrowly escaped a mortal wound: "A minie ball struck him in the breast, penetrated his overcoat, glanced upon a button and dropped into the lining of his vest . . . " [17]

As the firing died out, Wofford rested his troops and realigned them. The enemy in his front had several lines of fortifications and reinforcements to boot. He could see that his task was not over. The Third Georgia Sharpshooters who had been scouting the area reported to Wofford that the enemy's extreme left was very near, hanging as it were in the air. In addition, they had found the grade of an unfinished railroad which almost paralleled the Plank Road. [18]

Wofford and staff rode back to find Longstreet. General Kershaw joined him at their commander's side. Wofford explained to them the situation and requested permission to move his brigade to the far right via the railroad grade, swing left and attack the Federal line in flank. As one veteran recalled, "Wofford discovered a chance to flank the enemy and applied for permission to make a charge." [19] Longstreet, already considering how best to flank the enemy, immediately granted permission. As Wofford prepared to leave, Longstreet had a second thought: If Wofford could do this with one brigade, why not use more muscle and achieve greater effect on the enemy? He ordered Anderson's Brigade to attack with Wofford, supported by Mahone's Brigade of Hill's Corps, both of which were in the area. To coordinate these units in the tangled woods, he sent along Colonel Moxley Sorrell, his chief of staff. [20] Kershaw was to press the enemy in front as soon as the flanking force was in position. [21]

Wofford led his brigade north via the railroad grade, followed by Mahone's men. Anderson was on the right of the grade. One of his men remembered: "We never saw any opening except where there was a right-of-way for a railroad that had been cut a few years before. . . . " [22] About a half-mile from the Brock Road, the force wheeled left and deployed into line, Wofford on the left, Anderson on the right, and Mahone in reserve. They had so far avoided detection from enemy pickets. Surprise was assured. It was near 11:45 A.M. [23]

The Federals were resting in bivouac on their extreme left, boiling coffee and no doubt discussing the events of the early morning. As at Chancellorsville the year before, their reverie was suddenly broken by a volley of musketry and the Rebel Yell. Federal Colonel Robert McAllister stated: "I heard firing on my left and rear. I soon discovered we were flanked. I immediately ordered a change of front to meet it . . . Held the enemy in front and delivered volley after volley into their ranks, but I soon discovered that they had flanked my left and were receiving a fire in my front, on my left flank and rear . . . At this time my line broke. . . . " [24]

The correspondent to the *Atlanta Southern Confederacy* recorded Wofford's assault:

> Wofford was soon hotly engaged, but his invincible veterans rushed forward with overwhelming impetuosity, driving the enemy panic stricken and in indescribable confusion from all his strongholds. He still pressed gallantly on, inflicting heavy losses upon his enemy and meeting with but little resistance until he reached the Plank Road - one mile and a half from where the enemy were first encountered. . . . After following the enemy a half mile beyond the Plank Road, Gen. Wofford ordered a halt, in order that his line might be reformed, and his troops, already exhausted by hard fighting and their long and rapid advance, might rest. . . . [25]

During this assault, Major J. M. Gurgan of Kershaw's staff, who had accompanied Wofford, rode back to report to his chief on the progress of the attack. En route, he met General Lee:

> As I was riding very rapidly he called to me to know what the matter was. "I am looking for General Longstreet and General Kershaw to report the success of General Wofford's flank attack, he is doubling the enemy's left back on the center," was my reply. General Lee placed his hand behind his ear and listening for a moment to the firing, said: "You are right. See General Longstreet and tell him to put his whole command in motion and we will drive the enemy across the Rappahannock." When I found General Longstreet there was a lull in the firing. His action was prompt and decisive, and in issuing orders to General Kershaw to take the initiative, he made a special point that Wofford's Brigade be placed in front thus recognizing its gallant services. [26]

Wofford's men had come within an ace of cutting the Germanna Ford Road which would have put them, properly supported, between the wings of Grant's host. The dense forest obscured their opportunity, however. Still, they had gravely hurt the enemy. A. C. Jordan of the 24th Georgia wrote to his father: "Father of all sights I ever saw this fight was it, more dead Yankees than I ever saw before." [27] A New York soldier, Darius Starr, wrote in his diary that evening: "Our lines have been awfully thinned. This is the hardest infantry fight that I ever saw." [28]

Wofford rode back along the Plank Road to find Longstreet, Kershaw and others elated at the results of the flank attack. Longstreet immediately ordered all units to attack the Union positions on the Brock Road, Wofford's leading, as Major Gurgan wrote. Wofford turned and rode back toward his position. [29] He heard an outburst of gunfire from behind. Riding back, he found Longstreet wounded and several officers killed, including General Micah Jenkins. [30] In a grievous mistake, a Confederate volley had cut down the old Warhorse and with that, the hope of the day. The delay subsequent to the wounding of Longstreet gave the enemy time to recover, reinforce, and entrench. [31]

At four P.M., Lee ordered the assault Longstreet had wanted at noon. It was too late and therefore unsuccessful, though courageously undertaken by the men. The enemy was ready this time. Federal Captain Henry Blake, in charge of the skirmishers in front of the Brock Road, heard the heavy tread of Rebel infantry coming his way, so close he could hear Rebel officers saying, "Forward! Guide right! Close up those intervals!" Then he heard the order, "Now, men, for the love of God and your country, forward!" [32] He ordered his skirmishers to retire into the waiting trenches of his men.

Wofford led his men forward against the troops of Hancock. The woods had caught fire and even the log breastworks of the enemy were aflame. His men strove valiantly, pierced the defenses, but could not hold their gains. [33] The old nemesis, no supports, haunted them again. In all truth, there was none, for Lee had flung everything he had on that part of the field in this desperate attempt to break Grant's left and center on the Brock Road. Wofford thus disengaged, put out pickets, and rested the brigade. [34]

Colonel Sorrell recorded in his Field Diary: "The attack resulted in no decided success the enemy not being dislodged night coming on the long days struggle is closed - the most wearisome, severe and exciting battle in which I have yet participated. . . . " [35] Indeed, it had been a day of battle in a Mephistophelian panorama: The tangle in the Wilderness, darkened further by billowing gunsmoke, the forest fires, the yelling and cursing, the crying and screaming, the crashing volleys of musketry, and above all, an invisible foe. It was unlike all other battles in its effect on survivors. A soldier of the 8th Georgia, Anderson's Brigade, remembered the Wilderness as the "battle that most tried my nerves." [36]

Saturday, May 8, was relatively quiet, both sides resting and reorganizing after the ordeal of the previous two days. Mitchell recorded: "Very little skirmishing today. Both Armies appear to be satisfied with yesterday's fighting." [37] Grant was, for a fact. He had had enough of the diabolical Wilderness, and having narrowly escaped the fate of Joe Hooker of the previous year, decided to move for Spottsylvania Court House on his left. Lee discovered this move on the afternoon of the 8th and sent Longstreet's corps, now under Richard Anderson, to intercept the enemy.

The road over which the corps was to travel, at night, had been cut by the engineers and was cluttered with stumps and debris which could have impeded a marching column in broad daylight. In addition, the forest fires started in the battle of the preceding day were burning furiously. It would be difficult to rest the men en route, so Anderson decided to start at 11 P.M. as ordered and push straight for Spottsylvania without stopping. This decision saved the army, as it turned out. [38] Kershaw's division led off into the smoking wasteland. Coxe of Kershaw's old brigade wrote afterwards: "Never before nor afterwards did I experience such a trying night march." [39]

Still, the men were in high spirits, happy to be leaving the Wilderness. Though not mentioned in their letters and diaries, Wofford's men participated in a wild outburst of the Rebel Yell which must have sounded hellish to the Federals moving parallel on the Brock Road. J. F. J. Caldwell recorded the phenomenon:

> Far up on the right of the Confederate line a
> shout was raised. Gradually it was taken
> up and passed down, until it reached us.
> We lifted it, as our turn came, and handed
> it to the left, where it went echoing to the
> remotest corner of Ewell's Corps.

Twice more the yell passed down the line. "The effect," wrote
Caldwell, "was beyond expression." [40]

Reaching the vicinity of Spottsylvania Court House on
the morning of the 9th, Kershaw's and Humphries' Brigades
supported General Fitzhugh Lee's cavalry in stopping the
enemy cavalry and General Warren's Federal infantry who had
also just arrived. Wofford's Brigade was ordered to move
around in the rear of the village to surround and capture
General J. H. Wilson's cavalry. Wofford led his men through
the dense woods undetected by the enemy. "He had nearly
reached the desired position, when a portion of Field's division,
knowing nothing of this movement, arrived in front of the court
house, and commenced advancing direct towards the
unsuspecting enemy. Upon the appearance of this force, the
Yankees faced right and thus eluded capture." [41] At 3 P.M. the
same day, Warren's 5th Corps furiously attacked the Rebel
position on Spottsylvania ridge and was repulsed with "great
slaughter to the enemy." [42] Wofford's Brigade was held in
reserve during this action and over the next four days.

The Confederate lines stretched north from Spottsylvania
Court House, once the whole army came up, forming at the
apex closest to the enemy a vast salient called the Mule Shoe.
On the morning of May 12, the Federals hurled a giant assault at
this bulge, overrunning it and capturing the larger portion of
the division of General Edward Johnson. In a dramatic moment,
General John B. Gordon of Robert Rodes' division led a savage
counterattack which stopped the enemy advance and pushed
them back toward the captured works. Rodes sent Scales'
Brigade to aid Gordon's left wing. Kershaw refused his right to

Private William W. Fitts, Company D, Danielsville Guards, 16th Georgia Regiment, killed at Spottsylvania Court House, Virginia, May 12, 1864.

Courtesy of Charlotte Bond Collection,
United States Army Military History Institute.

connect with Rodes in their entrenchments. Both then sent the brigades of Ramseur and Wofford to help plug the gap. [43] Wofford led his men into the melee. Seeing the exposed right flank of the enemy assault column, he took the 18th and 24th Georgia units out of line and moved by the left flank behind the rest of his hard-charging regiments. The two regiments formed perpendicular to the enemy and enfilladed their ranks, causing much disorder. Private Shockley wrote matter-of-factly: "Ramseurs and Woffords Brigs were ordered to charge them and retake the works we don so. . . . " [44]

Retaking the abandoned works, Wofford's men joined Rode's brigades in a driving rain until 2 A.M. in a terrible hand-to-hand struggle until they were recalled to a new line at the base of the salient. "We have killed about ten for every one we lost . . . ," wrote Shockley. [45] In truth, losses on both sides were horrendous. The combat surpassed all their former experiences in its nature and duration. To Caldwell, who came up with a reinforcing unit, the scene was Stygian:

> The trenches, dug on the inner side, were
> almost filled with water. Dead men lay on
> the surface of the ground and in the pools
> of water. The wounded bled and groaned.
> . . . The water was crimsoned with blood. . .
> The rain poured heavily and an incessant
> fire was kept upon us from front and rear.
> [46]

The Mule Shoe had earned a new and ominous sobriquet, "Bloody Angle." Wofford again had a close call when a Minie ball glanced off a rib. He was not incapacitated but badly bruised. [47]

After the 12th, Wofford's Brigade resumed its place in the Spottsylvania entrenchments. For the rest of the month, the men were constantly on the alert. Mitchell wrote on May 15th: "We have been under the fire of the enemy every day more or less since the 6th instant. We have met the enemy in all his movements. . . . He has been unsuccessful in all . . . " [48] Captain Charles Sanders of Cobb's Legion wrote to his sister: "Ever since the 4th of May we have been marching and fighting nearly the whole time. Our legion has lost many men, killed and wounded, and many of our command have been rendered unfit for duty." [49]

In late May, Grant moved toward Cold Harbor. Lee was quick once again to place the Army of Northern Virginia between his adversary and Richmond. As it happened, the two commanders were of the same mind at this point in time. Grant called up from the Peninsula below Richmond Major General W. F. Smith's 18th Corps to reinforce his badly depleted ranks. Lee, hurt almost as badly from the intense sparring with Grant, had Major General Robert Hoke's division come up also from the Peninsula. Grant wanted a last, all-out offensive that would knock the Army of Northern Virginia on its heels and open the door to the Confederate capital; Lee wanted nothing more in the world but to keep his adversary from doing that very thing. They met on an old battlefield of the war like two grizzlies, a fight to the death.

Hoke's men reached the Cold Harbor area on June 1 to link up with the First Corps. Hoke was supposed to place his command under Anderson, but for whatever reason, communications between them failed. Lee wanted an early reconnaissance-in-force to determine exactly where the Federal left flank was and to turn it if possible. When the movement began, Hoke did not show up and Kershaw's Brigade, led by Colonel L. M. Keitt, attacked alone. It was a disastrous affair, with Keitt getting killed and the brigade routed. [50] Kershaw's division fell back and with Hoke's men spread out and entrenched on a low ridge between Old and New Cold Harbor, straddling the road which connected the two hamlets. At the point where Kershaw's right met Hoke's left, a ravine bisected the ridge. This gully lay in a thicket of pines which jutted well out in front of the line with swampy ground and a stream that ran through the gully. Skirmishers and sharpshooters took position in these trees, but behind them the main line stopped on either side of the declivity. [51] Wofford's Brigade anchored Kershaw's flank; Brigadier General T. L. Clingman's Brigade was adjacent to him on the other side of the ravine. Thus a space of 50 to 70 yards presaged coming troubles.

Although there was disputation later over who was to cover the gap, Wofford or Clingman, the responsibility apparently was Hoke's. Clingman wrote later that he was informed by Hoke that Hagood's Brigade "would be stationed in front of my left and rear and cover this interval." [52] This is substantiated by Captain W. H. S. Burgwyn of the 35th North Carolina which occupied the left of Hoke's line, who recorded in his diary: "Our left was entirely unprotected by the moving of Hagood's Brigade (which had been till a short time previous in front of us and on our left). . . ." [53]

Except at the gap which with the gully, stream and undergrowth must have seemed impassable, Wofford's men dug in. "Picks and shovels were provided us (we knew what that meant), and we went to work with great enthusiasm to make our position more formidable." [54] Axemen cut down trees in front, letting them fall toward the enemy, forming a maze of abatis to impede attackers. At 5:00 P.M. the Federals attacked in massive formations. Along Wofford's front, they were slaughtered. Inevitably, however, the weak spot on Wofford's right was exploited. As E. P. Alexander wrote:

> Everywhere the enemy suffered severely and were driven back promptly and decidedly, except at the 50 yards gap . . . , through which flowed a small stream, bordered with woods and thicket. The enemy's dense column filled this wood, which sheltered them entirely from our view, and they penetrated the gap, and suddenly appeared on the flanks of the brigades on both sides. [55]

Private William T. Bailey, Company C, Hartwell Infantry, 16th Georgia Regiment, paroled at Hartwell, Georgia, May 18, 1865.

Private Henry M. Bailey, Company C, Hartwell Infantry, 16th Georgia Regiment, captured at Second Cold Harbor, June 1, 1864, died in Elmira, New York, Prisoner-of-War facility, February 13, 1865.

Courtesy of Georgia State Department of Archives and History.

The breakthrough produced a curious effect on Wofford's men, so involved were they with firing at the massed enemy in their front. A member of the 18th Georgia, Wofford's old regiment, remembered:

> . . . and through this gap the enemy came rushing, causing Company K to retreat precipitately. I had been firing so rapidly that my gun got hot, and the bullet could not be sent home. I was so intent in ramming the ball down that I did not hear any order to retire, neither did I hear any noise when our men left the works. All vanished as silently as spirits, and when I awoke to the real situation, looking toward Company K, I saw the Yankees clambering over the breastworks not twenty paces from me. . . . I sprinted away at breakneck speed. [56]

Captain Sanders of Cobb's Legion, on the left of the brigade, described the effect of the rupture thus:

> I was busy as a bee loading guns and giving out the cartridges to the men in front so that they might fire rapidly. During the intervals of the fight, the men were laughing at how many they had killed. On the right of our brigade, there was about a hundred Yanks or maybe three hundred in the line that was not occupied by any troops thus, though we did not know, and it was a great oversight on our part. We were fighting away, when all at once a perfect shower of bullets came from behind, for the Yankees were advancing in from the

> rear and a line of them was also advancing
> from the front. . . . We all saw that we had
> to get out of that place and that quick, too.
> The regiment on the right of our legion
> (Phillips' Legion) had already gone . . . The
> order for retreat was given and away we
> went . . . [57]

Mitchell of Phillips' Legion stated that they "fell back" 200 yards, but did not mention a rout. [58] Wofford, at the time of the breakthrough, was with Cobb's Legion on the left of the brigade, directing the defense. As his right-wing units retreated domino fashion, he had no recourse but to order the retreat of Cobb's Legion. He reformed the brigade some 200 yards behind the original line and began to organize a counterattack. He was clearly upset that his old regiment, the 18th, had broken; a veteran remembered: "I never heard such an excoriation as the regimental commander got on that occasion." [59]

It appears from available accounts that the breakthrough at the gap was just as surprising to the enemy as it was to the Rebels. Unplanned as it was and accompanied by the terrific slaughter on either side of the penetrating column, the Federals found themselves in the wooded gap before they knew it, thus their subsequent inability to exploit to the fullest the advantage gained thereby. One reason for this is explained by the topography: The woods were very thick on and around the ridge on which was the Rebel line. Behind the Confederates, the ground declined then rose gradually. It is not so strange then that the unhinged Rebel units could retire a hundred yards or so and rally before an enemy onslaught. The fact is, they could do so virtually unseen in the trees. Burgwyn wrote, for example, "The 31st North Carolina Regiment being behind the hill had not suffered as yet and had not seen the enemy owing to the hill and the very thick woods." [60]

General Kershaw reacted immediately to the threat, sending his old brigade, spearheaded by the 2nd South Carolina under Colonel William Wallace, from his extreme left to the rupture, with these orders, to "if I found a regiment of the enemy flanking his position, to charge them." [61] The South Carolinians, followed by the rest of the brigade and elements of Bryan's, arrived at the trouble spot and pitched into the enemy. After a furious fight, in which Wofford's men participated, the enemy was pushed back into the woods out of the gap. The latter retreated no further than the abandoned Confederate works in the trees, about 50 yards from Kershaw's line. [62]

Kershaw's Brigade, led by Colonel J. W. Henagan, occupied the left side of the ravine, assuming part of the works vacated by Wofford and stretching "at right angles to that on which we had fought that day, and the soldiers were ordered to fortify." [63] General Bryan, originally on Wofford's left, refused his brigade to connect with Henagan. General Kershaw sent the Virginia Brigade of Brigadier Eppa Hunton to retake the position vacated by Clingman on the other side of the gap. After severe fighting, Wofford bent his line to connect with Hunton on his right and Henagan on his left. General Kershaw then sent John Gregg's Texas Brigade to reinforce Hunton and Wofford. [64] The Rebel line now resembled a vast inward bulge, covering the gap but still weak. [65]

A section of Lieutenant Morgan Callaway's Pulaski (Georgia) Battery of Cabell's Battalion, was stationed at the knuckle where Henagan's line broke sharply to the rear. This lone Napoleon and crew under Second Lieutenant Robert Falligant masked the weakness of the line all the next day while a new line was being constructed several hundred yards behind Wofford's and Henagan's temporary position. [66] Fortunately for them, the enemy did not attack on the 2nd. The Rebels had time to dig in securely, with artillery emplacements, creating a vast crescent.

On the night of the 2nd, the temporary line was abandoned and the troops in them moved back to the new one. Kershaw, realizing the important work Falligant's section had rendered at the knuckle, did not want to sacrifice the gun and ordered it also to be withdrawn to the new entrenchment. Major Robert Stiles, adjutant of Cabell's Battalion, and Lieutenant Callaway began the arduous trip through the broken countryside in complete darkness, leading battery horses for the gun and limber of Falligant. As they passed behind Wofford's line, he stopped them and forbade the use of the horses because of the close proximity of the enemy - too noisy. He permitted them to proceed with twenty of his men. In Stiles' words:

> The gun was backed out of the little work, limbered up, and the ammunition chest replaced; some of the men took hold of the wheels and some of the tongue, and the piece was soon moving after us, almost noiselessly along the sassafras field toward Wofford's line. In a few moments we reached the goal, returning our thanks to the General . . . and the sturdy, gallant men they lent us; the horses were hitched up and we were rolling over the little bridges and up to the new line and the position selected for this now distinguished piece. [67]

Wofford's Brigade was then withdrawn to reinforce the new line, "just to the left of the old position. . . ." [68]

Grant, not satisfied with the brief breakthrough of June 1st, ordered a massive, all-or-nothing attack for June 3, a decision he regretted later. Brigadier General J. H. Martindale, whose 2nd Division of the 18th Corps was given the ravine as his objective in the attack, was ordered to deploy in column of brigades and mount a bayonet charge which would overwhelm the scanty Rebel patchwork line beyond the trees. He was ignorant of the preparations which had been made to receive his doomed men. "At precisely 4:30 on the morning of the 3rd of June Martindale's command moved down the stream, out of the woods, and against the earthworks." [69]

Except for sharpshooting, the Confederates held their fire so as many of the enemy as possible could enter the killing ground of the vast semi-circle of entrenchments. Waiting with anticipation for the enemy, Lieutenant Falligant never forgot that sight:

> What a magnificent battle scene! Through the gray dawn the lines of blue, tipped with steel, advanced in martial splendor. When the command ready! was given to the artillery, "Hold on, Cap!" shouted the Mississippians (three lines deep supporting us), "Let them come closer! Give us a chance!" A few moments later the royal welcome of the deep mouthed cannon and rattling musketry swept those in front from the face of the earth. [70]

Colonel E. P. Alexander, who had been present at some of the worst artillery bloodbaths of the war, wrote: "Then we turned loose on them, everything, infantry and artillery, canister, shot and shell. I think that at no point in the war, except at Bloody Angle, were the woods so torn up or the dead left so thickly strewn. . . . " [71] Wofford's men, in reserve, loaded rifles and passed them to those on the firing line.

For the next two weeks, the men sweated it out in the trenches at Cold Harbor. Captain Sanders explained to his wife:

> Sharpshooting is the order of the day, and a man can't look over the works without being shot at, so we have to keep close together to keep from being hit. At night one-third of the men have to keep awake all the time and the rest sleep with cartridge boxes on and their guns in their hands. . . . [72]

In this campaign at Cold Harbor, Grant had been drawing to an inside straight and had come up with one card too few, and he knew it. His adversary Lee, who had gambled often in that wretched war, had once again held the winning hand. The Union commander whereupon decided to fold his cards and leave the premises. In one of the truly great maneuvers of the war, he moved his army, unbeknownst to Lee, to the Peninsula, placing the Confederate capital in imminent and grave peril.

On June 13, the Army of Northern Virginia vacated its lines and moved once again to counter the Union threat. Wofford's Brigade moved through the old Frazier's Farm battlefield of 1862 and arrived in the Petersburg trenches on the 18th. Wofford's wound gave him much trouble in the heat of the trenches and the constant moving back and forth of the brigade. He was granted leave on July 3 for 30 days. [73]

Julia, expecting her third child, had taken the family to her father's home in Spring Place, Murray County, to be out of reach of Sherman's army as it moved toward Atlanta in May. On July 8, she delivered a baby girl; when Wofford arrived, she was christened Laura. [74] He found the family safe but heard distressing news about his house and office at Cassville: When the Yankees passed through in May, they had vandalized all the empty houses, insisting later that if the owners had not left, the soldiers would not have done it. [75] Wofford's mother was still in Cassville, too old and infirm to travel. He could not go to see her because of the enemy presence. He thus spent his furlough in Murray County.

During Wofford's leave, General Longstreet, recovering from his serious wounding of May 6, concluded some unfinished business regarding his subordinate. Always impressed with Wofford's behavior on and off the battlefield, he wrote the following recommendation to General Samuel Cooper and sent it through the channels:

I respectfully recommend Brig. General W. T. Wofford for promotion to the rank of Major General for conduct at the Battle of the Wilderness May 6th 1864. In the course of that action, I directed an attack to be made against the enemy's left by a portion of the corps under my command. Genl Wofford volunteered for the occasion and sought and attained for his Brigade the privilege of forming part of the flanking column. Much of the success attending that movement is due to General Wofford, who was distinguished by the energy and rapidity of his attack and the skill and gallantry with which he handled his Brigade. [76]

The recommendation was endorsed favorably as it passed through the red tape:

July 15, 1864 - Since I have had command of the Corps Genl Wofford has constantly exhibited superior zeal courage and ability and is altogether deserving of promotion RH Anderson Lt Genl

July 15, 1864 - He has since first taking command of his brigade always acted with boldness and judgment displaying great zeal and promptness in the execution of his duties I wish I had a division in this army to which he could be assigned RE Lee Genl. [77]

The recommendation for promotion went for naught, for there was no division, as Lee stated, for Wofford to command. It is significant, however, for this recommendation is as close as the high command of the Army of Northern Virginia came to admitting that it was truly Wofford who actually suggested the flank attack at midday of May 6. His men knew it, however, for as one of his officers wrote in the trenches at Petersburg most probably at the same time Longstreet was dictating his memo, "General Wofford merits a great deal of credit for the masterly manner in which this move [flank attack] was planned and carried into execution. . . . " [78]

The Brigade was near Chaffin's Bluff near Petersburg when Wofford returned to duty. On August 6th, Kershaw's division was ordered to reinforce General Jubal Early's force in the Shenandoah Valley. The destination was Front Royal on the Shenandoah River where they arrived on the 14th. [79] Two days later, Wofford was sent to the north side of the river to dislodge enemy dismounted cavalry from an eminence named Guard Hill. It was to prove the only tactical defeat of his Brigade. [80]

The hill was taken at small loss. Wofford, then, with cavalry guarding his flank, led the 24th, 16th, and Cobb's Legion across the river to drive back enemy reinforcements. The enemy in the meantime routed the cavalry and charged the infantry, while dismounted Federals poured a devastating volley into the closely aligned Georgians in the river. Private Floyd Jordan of the 24th Georgia described the disaster:

> . . . our boys got into a severe fight with the Yankie calvary on the 16th of this month in the evening about one hour before the sun went down, our boys charged the Yankie's calvary for about half a mile through an open corn field and got within 40 or 50 yards of them when there was a flank movement made and the enemy flanked around our left and got in our rear, and

> caused us to all fall back in a most confused
> condition . . . There was two hundred and
> fifty men taken in Waffords Brigade, . . .
> There was a force of Calvary posted on our
> left to protect and they gave a way at the
> sight of the enemy as usual, and caused all
> the Brigade to get flanked and taken
> prisoners but a few. That is there was only
> three Regiments ingaged . . . these are the
> portions of the Brigade that did what was
> done and hoped what was hoped but got a
> little the worst of it. [81]

Wave Ballard, colorbearer of the 16th Georgia, "rushed with the flag to a place within a few yards of the enemy's line. . . . Looking back, he saw his commander Col. (Edward) Stiles sinking to the ground. Not until then did he become aware of the falling back of the troops." [82] He ripped the flag from the staff and rejoined his friends.

In this debacle, Wofford's horse was killed under him, giving him a bad fall. Bruised and no doubt angry at the cavalry, he saw little humor in the joke made at Rebel headquarters that night: "Wofford swung his right and made a water-haul." [83] Strategically, however, this battle forced Union General Phillip Sheridan to withdraw his forces from the Valley for the time being. Wofford's attack had shown that Early's small army had received substantial reinforcements from Lee.

Wofford was more shaken by his fall than he first believed. He stayed with his command through September as it moved eastward to Gordonsville with Kershaw's division when Lee recalled them. Later, on September 26th, when the division was returned to Early, Wofford remained in Gordonsville, incapacitated by his wounds and the fall from his horse. On October 18, 1864, he was granted sick leave by a Medical Examining Board. [84]

Chapter 7

Department of North Georgia

Wofford reached Spring Place in the latter part of October. The Federals were still in Cassville, so he as a high-ranking Confederate officer dared not go there. He noted the conditions in Murray County. The war had not come there since Sherman had gone down the Western and Atlantic Railroad to the west, but Wofford saw the economic plight of the inhabitants and was greatly concerned by the lawlessness that prevailed. As a member of Confederate General Joe Wheeler's cavalry wrote in his diary:

> April 14, 1864 - I came on into Murray . . . and found many . . . glad to see us . . . The bushwackers are having everything their own way, and are taking any kind of property they want . . . Passed through Spring Place and found things in a very delapidated condition. [1]

The news from his hometown was of the worst: The Federals had burned the two colleges and many houses in reprisal for the murders of their men by guerrillas. One of the Federals recorded:

> October 12, 1864 - Last night while our train was passing through Cassville, a town four miles south of Kingston, an ambulance gave out and the driver unhitched and concluded to stay all night. That was some three miles from where we stayed. Nine stragglers also laid down beside the ambulance for the night. The 17th corps came through there today and found the

> driver dead, with a bayonet thrust through
> him and the traps of 9 men lying around.
> The horses and 9 men are missing. I heard
> tonight that the bodies of the 9 men have
> been found altogether. Our men burned
> the town. [2]

Wofford went to Cassville as soon as he could. He was
staggered by the devastation. All the houses were burned but
four, his own in ashes. The Negroes had followed Sherman's
soldiers. All store buildings, including his law office and
personal records, were gone. The enemy, to his relief, had
spared his mother's house, but she was very ill and alone - her
slaves had departed also. [3] He surveyed the intolerable
conditions that were prevailing in the area. The devastation of
the Union and Confederate armies which had passed through in
the spring during the Atlanta campaign was evident
everywhere. All farm stock and food had been confiscated by
both armies in turn. As one soldier complained, the only
difference between the two forces when they visited a house
was that the Confederates stole everything, as did the Yanks,
but the latter burned the place before leaving. [4]

Wofford reported to his friend Congressman Warren
Akin, also from Cassville:

> . . . bands of robbers are going through the
> country and taking anything they want and
> killing who they please . . . There is no law
> of any kind in that section. . . . There is
> corn on the Etowah River, in Cherokee
> County, but there is no way of hauling it.
> The horses are all gone, and nearly
> everything else, and the people are
> suffering much. [5]

The railroad had been destroyed by Sherman; farm vehicles had been confiscated by the armies. The people were near starvation.

Of special concern to Wofford as a military man was the heavy presence of deserters in the upper counties. Most of the deserters from both Confederate armies were Georgians, he was dismayed to learn, for the invasion of the state by Sherman had caused many Georgia soldiers to leave the ranks and return home to care for their destitute families. [6] He felt that if he could be given the authority, he could likely reclaim many of these men for the military. Such a command would also restore order and repress the guerrilla bands operating in the area. As noted earlier, Governor Brown had already mentioned this possibility to Davis in 1863, with no result. Now the situation was dire indeed.

After a month of observing conditions, Wofford decided to take the problem directly to the Confederate president. After caring for his family by moving them into his mother's house, he returned to the Brigade headquarters at Petersburg in late December. He visited with the officers and men for a last time and went on to Richmond to pursue his assignment to North Georgia. At George Washington Gretter's Boarding House, near the capitol, he went to the room of his friend Akin. The latter wrote to his wife on the following day, January 2, 1865: "Well, guess who slept with me last night? . . . Gen'l Wofford came to my room, and asked to board a few days, and I took him in my room and shared my bed with him. There was no other way for him to stay. . . . " [7]

The next day, Akin requested an audience with President Davis for he and Wofford to discuss the situation in Georgia. They also visited Postmaster General John Reagan about getting mail service restored to Cassville. [8] They met with Davis the following day, January 4th. Wofford was no stranger to the president who was well aware of Wofford's war record. Confederate Senator H. V. Johnson, Wofford's friend, had written to Wofford after the Wilderness campaign: "The

Herschel V. Johnson, Governor of Georgia 1853-57 and
Confederate Congressman, was Wofford's lifelong
friend and colleague.

Courtesy of Author's Collection.

president esteems you very highly. Your career has impressed
him very favorably toward you as a brave, energetic and skillful
general, and I am proud of you as a Georgian." 9 At the
conference, Wofford and Akin discussed with Davis the need of,
in Akin's words, "organizing a force in our section to protect
our people there against robbers and traitors. . . . " 10

On January 6, Wofford wrote to General Samuel Cooper,
Adjutant General, "I respectfully request that I may be assigned
to duty in North Georgia." 11 Major General Kershaw endorsed
it favorably on January 8 and forwarded it to Longstreet, who
approved it on the 12th with the notation that Brigadier General
Dudley Dubose would take over command of Wofford's
Brigade. On the 16th, Lee endorsed the request with the
following comment: "I do not know what duty is designed for
Gen'l Wofford. He is a brave and gallant officer & I regret to
part with him. If the duty in which he is to engage in is
considered of more importance than with his brigade I make no
objection." 12 On January 20, Special Orders #16-27 was sent to
Wofford: "Brig. Genl W. T. Wofford PACS is assigned to the
command of the Reserve forces of Northern Georgia and will
report to Major General Howell Cobb Command'g at Macon
Geo." 13

Wofford read the order with incredulity perhaps, for the
content did not square with his interview with the President.
He hurriedly sent a note to Davis on the 21st:

> I respectfully call the attention of the
> President to the enclosed order assigning
> me to duty in Georgia and my
> communication to General Cooper and ask
> that my orders may be made in accordance
> with his judgment as it is suggested that I
> misunderstood them at our interview. 14

On the same day, he wrote the following to Cooper:

> I respectfully represent that the object of the
> President in assigning me to duty in
> northern Georgia was for the purpose of
> organizing the large number of men in that
> portion of the state composed of skulkers,
> absentees, deserters and all other's liable to
> service, and for this purpose to take with
> me such number of supernumerary officers
> who live in that section as would be
> necessary and to have the command of
> such reserve forces as could be spared by
> Maj Genl Howell Cobb. [15]

The President revoked S. O. #16 in a note to General Cooper in
which he explained more fully the specifics of the matter and
added, "The order does not seem to me quite to cover the object
of his detached se-------." [16] New orders were issued on January
23, 1865:

> Special Orders 18/36
> He will proceed to Northern Georgia, with
> full power to collect such stragglers and
> deserters and to dissolve such illegal
> organizations as may be found in that
> section. He will place them in temporary
> orgn for immediate duty until they can be
> sent to their proper commands. He will
> also enroll all men liable to conscription
> who have thus far evaded the service. He
> is authorized to obtain from Maj Gen
> Howell Cobb such forces as may be
> necessary. [17]

Congressman Akin in the meantime had been lobbying
for Wofford's new assignment. He explained to his wife on
January 20: "I think Gen'l Wofford will be assigned to duty in

Northern Georgia. I saw the Secretary of War this morning and he recommended it." [18] Indeed, James A. Seddon, Secretary of War, had already received from an anonymous writer in Athens, Georgia, December 31, 1864, the following:

> General Wofford is a representative man, raised in upper Georgia, well-known through all that portion of the State. His high moral bearing, being a man of the strictest sobriety, and, indeed, of irreproachable moral character, eminently qualifies him to have the command of this portion of Georgia. His property was all scattered and destroyed by the enemy in Bartow County, and on a recent visit to this State on short furlough, and seeing the condition of the country, as I have attempted to picture it, he seemed to feel deeply the necessity of reform which we all believe so much needed. . . . I would cordially suggest the name of General Wofford. [19]

On January 23, Akin reported to his wife the successful conclusion of the matter: "He has gone to Northern Georgia to organize a force to protect the people there. I reckon his wife will rejoice when he gets home and will be near her all the time." [20] Wofford left Richmond on the 23rd and arrived at home within the week. After looking in on his family, he went on to Atlanta to begin his work.

He reported to General Cobb and began to put a staff together. Most of these officers were supernumeraries from his old Brigade: Captain J. T. Hackett, 16th Georgia; Lieutenant Colonel Thomas Elijah Winn, 24th Georgia; and Lieutenant Colonel Frank M. Ford, 18th Georgia. [21] Some of the men who joined him were furloughed home from the lines around

Petersburg but could not get back because of the disruption of transportation. Sherman was marching through South Carolina northward, and the Federals held East Tennessee. Mitchell of Phillips' Legion, for example, got a furlough in February, 1865, arrived home at Dalton, stayed 4 days, then walked 400 miles in 13 days to return to his unit in Virginia. "I have been gone just one month and have walked nearly four hundred miles and stayed at home four day." [22]   Others in Georgia who were ordered to report to Wofford in 1865 could not do so because of the shambles of Sherman's trek through the state in the previous November. Eliza Francis Andrews, for example, recorded in her journal that her brother had received orders to join Wofford's command in north Georgia in February. He was unable to do so. [23]

Wofford then began to gather the available forces in north Georgia. From the state militia, he got the 2nd, 12th, and 13th militia cavalry, about 1,500 men. [24] From the counties north of Atlanta were several detached local units which he mobilized: Colonel James Findley's 500; Colonel Ralston's 500; Colonel Ledger's 500; Colonel Simmons' 400; Colonel Baker's 400; Colonel Edmundson's 150; and Major Graham's 400. [25]

Brigadier General A. W. Reynolds, stationed in Athens, Georgia, had visited these commands in early January 1865 and reported to General Cobb:

> I regret to say that a large number of men comprising these organizations are within the conscript age and absentees from other commands. I am satisfied that a majority of them have been induced to join these regiments under the promise that they should not be disturbed, and have the privilege of remaining at home. These several commands are mostly unarmed. They should be made to assemble at some point where forage and provisions could be

obtained. There they should be organized,
disciplined, armed and drilled. [26]

Wofford ordered these units to rendezvous in Atlanta. He
immediately began a regimen of drill and discipline and sought
arms for them.

As the news of Wofford's force reached the Georgia
troops in the Army of Tennessee and Army of Northern
Virginia, many Georgia soldiers left their companies and set out
to join his men. General G. T. Anderson, commanding a
Georgia Brigade in Longstreet's corps, sent a complaint to corps
headquarters, March 25, 1865: "I believe that some at least of
the officers who have received permission to raise companies of
disabled men and non-conscripts, are abusing their authority
and offering inducements to our soldiers to . . . join their
companies." He added, "I do not pretend to say that Gen
Wofford encourages such conduct, but believe he would not." [27]
General Longstreet endorsed this complaint with one of his own
to Lee:

> The impression prevails among the Georgia
> troops of this command that persons at
> home, having authority to raise local
> organizations, are writing and sending
> messages to the men in the ranks here,
> offering inducements to them to quit our
> ranks and go home and join the home
> organizations. The large and increasing
> number of desertions, particularly amongst
> the Georgia troops, induce me to believe
> that some such outside influence must be
> operating upon our men. Nearly all of the
> parties of deserters seem to go home, and it
> must be under the influence of some
> promise . . . [28]

General Lee responded with General Orders #8, March 27, 1865, which warned all soldiers of the penalty of desertion or inciting to desert; copies were sent to Cobb and Wofford. [29] The latter was certainly guiltless of any collusion, but, in all truth, neither he nor anyone else could stop the steady hemorrhage of deserters who were concerned with their destitute families and who saw an excellent opportunity to be near home and still serve in the military.

Of greater concern to Wofford, however, was his responsibility to repress the guerrilla activity and restore law and order to the region. The state militia had tried valiantly to control the many bands of deserters, bushwhackers, and brigands who preyed on the populace. [30] Wofford, knowing of the depredations and the lawlessness, and cognizant of the militia's need for help, realized that the area needed a military presence, hence his desiring of a North Georgia command in the first place. His task, as his scouting parties reported in, was not going to be easy.

The list of lawless gangs was formidable: Colquitt scouts, Tate scouts, Aycock scouts, Baker scouts, Matt Moore's scouts, John Gatewood's scouts, John Prior's scouts, Woody's scouts, Lillard's scouts, McCollum's scouts, and Jordan's Gang. [31] These bands, all splendidly mounted on stolen stock, swept down out of their mountain lairs and plundered and killed at will. Indicative is the following occurrence in Murray County:

> . . . early one winter morning a raiding party came to the Fouts home and stayed four days. The invaders killed cattle and hogs, had the women cooking around the clock with no rest, took the beds, and crowded the fire, even burning the furniture. The men abused the children and finally hanged Soloman Fouts to a limb of a large oak tree in the yard. Following an argument, the group shot one of their

own men. . . . Finally the intruders decided
to leave but took all the livestock and
money they could, leaving only a calf and a
pig. [32]

Wofford's men, in March and April, scoured the hills
and valleys arresting such guerrillas and deserters. The terrain
being what it was and the territory to cover so large, it was
impossible to find them all. Their experience in searching was
not unlike that of the Georgia militia in the same task the year
before. Captain F. M. Cowan had led his State Line Cavalry to
Ducktown, Tennessee, to arrest Georgia deserters:

Cowan found that the timber had been
cleared in all directions, making surprise
impossible. "The ground," he added, "is
perforated with tunnels and they offer great
opportunities for a city of refuge in the
'lower regions' where this command 'goeth
not.'" No deserters were captured, but the
party did confiscate two "stolen" mules. [33]

Some semblance of order did return under Wofford's
disciplined approach. Governor Brown proudly told the
Legislature in April 1865 that "several hundred deserters had
been arrested in one week." [34] Some guerrilla leaders refused to
cooperate, however, and join Wofford's force. John Gatewood,
for example, was planning a raid on the Knoxville Railroad in
East Tennessee as late as May 2. Wofford reported this news to
Major General George H. Thomas, commander of the Federal
Department of the Cumberland in Nashville. These renegade
leaders were dangerous to Wofford's purposes, for above
everything else, he wanted to avoid a confrontation with the
Federal army. His force was too small and poorly armed to be
effective against the enemy's limitless resources; the area from
Atlanta to Dalton was already a wasteland, and open hostilities

would only make matters infinitely worse for the already impoverished civilians - whose welfare was his chief priority. To this end, he even ignored orders from Richmond to discomfit the enemy. [35]

On April 12, he went to Dalton under flag of truce to confer with Brigadier General H. M. Judah about feeding the people. Judah reported to his superior:

> Brigadier-General Wofford, C. S. Army came to my lines at Dalton today under flag of truce, and sent in a letter soliciting a personal interview for the purpose of obtaining consent to pass the grain wagons of the State of Georgia to such places near and in my lines as will enable Governor Brown to distribute the corn . . . to the northern counties. I had an interview of over two hours with General Wofford, in which he asserts his determination to force all guerrillas and independent organizations to Calhoun, where he is to establish his headquarters . . . I glean that he is acting in full concert with Governor Brown. He is said to ignore Confederate in favor of State authority. . . . He told me privately that steps were being taken to bring Georgia back into the Union. . . . General Judah is satisfied of General Wofford's sincerity. [36]

The Federal reply to Wofford's overture was cooperative enough, but he was requested not to move his main body of troops beyond the Etowah River without first notifying the Union commander. [37]

The destitution of the people was indeed staggering. In Bartow County alone, 5,181 persons of the county's population of 8,290 were destitute and on the verge of starvation. Larger counties such as Cobb were even worse. [38] In November, 1864, the Georgia Legislature had appropriated $800,000 to "purchase corn for the relief of the suffering and devastated counties." [39] By early March 1865, this corn was distributed to the counties near Atlanta. Brown also bought 50,000 bushels from the south Georgia counties and stored them in Marietta. Wofford was concerned, however, with distributing to the counties along the Western and Atlantic Railroad toward Chattanooga. He knew that in addition to the Marietta warehouses, corn was available south of the Etowah River and that impressment and tithe warehouses were full in many of the towns. [40] The railroad was out of action from Cassville to Dalton and the distribution had to be done by wagon train. These caravans had to be protected by armed escorts from the lawless element. The state, albeit that Lee had surrendered on April 9, was still Confederate until the Army of Tennessee surrendered. Wofford, then, had to coordinate distribution with his Federal counterpart in Dalton, hence his April 12th parley with Judah.

At this point, however, Federal cooperation with feeding the people became intermingled with the necessity of Wofford's surrender. Jefferson Davis and the Confederate government were in flight; Sherman had Johnston bottled up with the Army of Tennessee in North Carolina. The Confederate government of Georgia was in shambles. Why, then, should Wofford maintain an armed resistance when the Federal army could protect and feed the populace under a re-united government? On April 18, consequently, terms of surrender were sent to Wofford which were the same as Grant had offered to Lee. [41]

Wofford in the meantime had received Judah's dispatch of the 12th and responded by setting down plans for the delivery of the corn:

> First, I propose a cessation of hostilities
> for an indefinite period of time between
> the forces under my command and the

> Federal Army . . . Second, That I encamp
> my command in the neighborhood of
> Calhoun . . . [42]

He was not being obtuse or stubborn here. Communications
were slow between the armies and Wofford was in the saddle
most of the time, so he had not received the terms of surrender.
His desire for cooperation was manifest. On the 21st of April,
for example, he had received official word from General Cobb
that an armistice had been agreed upon by Sherman and
Johnston. He immediately sent a copy of Cobb's message under
flag of truce to Judah and allowed a Federal courier to pass to
Macon with dispatches for the Union commander there. [43]
   Judah responded angrily, however, to Wofford's request
of the 20th and repeated the need for immediate surrender.
Wofford responded with a remarkable letter which revealed his
raison d'etre as commander of North Georgia:

> Your communication of the 25th instant
> has been received, and I regret that my
> several propositions, which were
> intended alone for the protection of our
> suffering citizens, did not meet your
> approval. For the purpose of conferring
> with you upon the propriety and
> expediency of surrendering myself and
> the forces under my command, I propose
> to meet you at Resaca at 12 o'clock on the
> 8th of next month. I would have
> proposed an earlier day, but I am en route
> to one of the upper counties, where I have
> an appointment to meet some men who
> have been bushwhacking, to the terror
> and injury of our unfortunate people,
> with the hope of restoring law and
> order. . . . [44]

As seen here, Wofford was ready to remove any obstacle which stymied the distribution of food to the people. He indicated also his firm belief in the restoration of law and order. To that end, he surrendered at Resaca, Georgia, on May 2, 1865:

> I hereby surrender myself and the Confederate forces under my command to you upon the terms under which General Lee, C. S. Army surrendered to Lieut. Gen. U. S. Grant, U. S. Army, a copy of which is appended hereto. [45]

The formal surrender was set for May 12 at Kingston, to allow Wofford time to collect as many of his scattered force as possible.

As the Confederates gathered in Kingston, Wofford realized that many of them were on the verge of starvation. He requested Judah for help, and rations were issued. On the 12th of May, at the McCravey-Johnson House in Kingston, the formalities of Wofford's capitulation were conducted and the men paroled. Until the 20th of May, 4,000 came in from all over the area. A participant remembered:

> . . . so we made our way to Kingston and received our paroles. There was at that time a large number of soldiers at home, sick and wounded, besides a large number of others who had deserted and had been hiding out in the mountains. Some lived and slept in caves. Then there were a large number who claimed to be scouts, but they pillaged more than they scouted. The day of the parole, I saw the motliest crew I have ever seen before or since. These so-called scouts were strutting around with broad-brimmed hats, long hair and jingling spurs.

You could see the old "moss back" who
had crept out of his cave. You would find
groups of sad-looking men who had
followed Lee, Jackson, Johnston, and
Wheeler through the war. Some of them
carried the mud and dust of 5 or 6 states on
their old clothes. From all over north
Georgia and north Alabama they gathered
at Kingston. [46]

Any of them who wished to earn much-needed money were
given work on repairing the Western and Atlantic Railroad. [47]

Wofford's conduct and sincerity deeply impressed the
Federal command. General James Steedman, who received the
surrender, expressed to General Thomas at Nashville his "high
appreciation of the personal character of General Wofford, and
the belief that his earnest efforts had been used, and would be
under all circumstances used, to restore peace and quiet
submission to Federal authority in this part of the State. . . . " [48]
General Thomas knew an honest man when he saw one, and
responded to Steedman's communiqué with a noble gesture:

You may say to General Wofford that being
convinced of his sincerity and honorable
conduct I have asked to be permitted to
administer the President's amnesty oath to
him, thereby enabling him to use his full
influence to bring his people to a state of
peace and quiet at the earliest moment.
Should I fail, however, he must not be
discouraged, but by his future acts show
that he is worthy of such an act of clemency
on the part of the Executive, and I have no
doubt but that the amnesty will eventually
be granted him. [49]

High accolade indeed from the "Rock of Chickamauga," who was noted for his own sincerity and no-nonsense approach to matters military.

Thomas, true to his word, had also issued orders on May 3 to his forces that they "were assigned the honorable duty of protecting the defenseless, oppressed, and impoverished citizens of North Georgia, and enforcing the laws of the United States. . . . " [50] On May 12, Wofford telegraphed a further request to Thomas: "As it is important that a military force should remain here for a time, I beg that General Judah be authorized to leave a portion of his command. . . . " The request was instantly granted. [51] Thomas let it also be known unequivocally that those ex-Confederates in North Georgia who still maintained covert activity against the Union, would be branded as outlaws, hunted down and punished as such. [52]

Now that peace had been restored with Wofford's surrender of the last sizeable force of Confederate soldiery, the Union commanders in occupied Atlanta realized fully that Wofford knew exactly what he had said about the poverty and extreme hardship of the people. Union Colonel Ira Foster, Quartermaster General of Georgia, wrote to General Wilson in Macon, May 24:

> Cobb, Fulton, Clayton and contiguous counties in this State, by reason of both Northern and Southern armies having been quartered therein for several weeks, are totally destitute of the means for support only as supplies are shipped in from a distance. In these counties reside about 15,000 poor and penniless men, women, and children, who must, of necessity, starve unless the public shall supply their wants. The corn we have on hand cannot sustain life but a few days longer. We have no cheering prospects of getting more. Unless

you can afford relief, the human mind
cannot possibly comprehend the suffering
which must soon befall these sections. [53]

A Northern traveler, Whitlaw Reid, recorded, for
example, that in the midst of Atlanta's bustle, he saw "a poor,
half-starved half-naked white woman, gathering her little
children about her, . . . in dull wretchedness . . . " [54]

General Wilson ordered General Winslow, the Atlanta
commandant, to

Make such issues of rations to the poor
people of North Georgia as the welfare of
your command will permit, keeping in
view the fact that issues must be made only
to those in absolute want.   . . . Seize any
railroad iron or supplies you can find to
advance your work. The completion of the
railroad is our only means of escape. Push
everything to the utmost. . . . [55]

These measures were clearly not enough to alleviate the
destitution. In addition to the immediate need, not a seed was
under cultivation. 23,513 persons (4,910 families) in the counties
along Sherman's path north of Atlanta were raising nothing to
feed themselves in the long haul. [56]

Chapter 8

Postbellum Days

Wofford, once again a civilian, could not rest amidst the intolerable conditions of the populace. From Cartersville on June 29, he wired General Thomas: "The country through which the armies have passed, from Chattanooga to Atlanta, is without corn or money. If the Government could loan or sell on credit 30,000 bushels of corn it would prevent much suffering and enable the farmers to complete the cultivation of their crops." [1] Thomas acquiesced without question and also on Wofford's request, permitted people to "take and use the straggling government stock scattered over the county to help them farm." [2] Wofford also gave of his own meager resources to help the poor. "General Wofford was a very charitable man, as well as benevolent, and did more for the poor than he was really able to do, but it was his nature to disfurnish himself to relieve the distressed wherever he met them." [3] He could deny nothing to his former soldiers and their families.

Personal tragedy still haunted the Wofford family. On August 19, the General's daughter Laura died of diphtheria, the family scourge. Broken-hearted, the parents buried her beside her two sisters. Wofford, a deeply devout man, left no written comments about his sorrow, but to the end of his days, he carried the following poem, clipped from some newspaper, in his wallet:

Waiting

I have three little angels waiting for me,
On the beautiful banks of the crystal sea;
Not impatiently wait my darlings there,
For smiles light up their brows so fair;
And their little harps ring out so clear,
So soothingly sweet to faith's listening ears
And they live in the smile of the Savior's love
Who so early called my darlings above.

I have three little angels waiting for me,
On the beautiful banks of the crystal sea;
Forever free from sorrow and pain,
Spotless and pure from all earthly stain;
Never in erring paths to rove -
Safe in the bosom of infinite love,
Evermore, evermore walking in light,
Those beautiful angels robed in white.

I have three little angels waiting for me
On the beautiful banks of the crystal sea;
When my weary heart is throbbing with pain,
And I fain would clasp my darlings again,
I look away from this earthly strand
To the beautiful fields of the "Better Land,"
I will think of the beautiful angels there,
And offer to God a thankful prayer.

I have three little angels waiting for me
When I too shall stand on the crystal sea;
When the Great Refiner his image may trace
In the heart He has won by His saving grace
And in the robes of Christ's own righteousness dresst
My soul shall seek the home of the best--
On the beautiful banks of the crystal sea
My darlings, still waiting, shall welcome me.

On November 10, 1866, Helena, their fourth child, was born; she
alone survived to live a long and fruitful life. [4]

    Politically, as Wofford could see, the state was without a
governor since Brown was deposed. The new president of the
United States, Andrew Johnson, a conservative, appointed
James Jackson as interim leader of Georgia. The new governor
called a constitutional convention which was held in October
1865 to consider Johnson's reconstruction objectives: the states
should annul the secession ordinance, repudiate their war debts,

and free the slaves. [5] The Georgia convention drafted a new constitution which agreed to these conditions. November 15, 1865, was set as election day for state and national representatives.

Wofford was asked to run for U. S. Congress in the 7th District against H. G. Cole of Atlanta, an avowed Unionist during the war, and James P. Hambleton, candidate of the diehard ex-Confederates. Wofford, busy with finding means to combat the prevailing poverty and, no doubt, wrestling with personal grief, did not fill out a party card of eligibility; he did permit his friends to do so:

> General Wofford is not an extreme man in any sense. He is eminently conservative in all things. We need men in Congress in whose honor and integrity we can repose confidence, who will contend to the last for all we can now ask for in support of the policy of President Johnson, and who are as little obnoxious as possible to those in power. The reason for this is plain. We can expect little from those we so recently regarded as enemies.   . . . In General Wofford we have a man in whom all have confidence, the purity of whose motives no man North or South can question, upon whose record there is not a blot, and from whose influence we have more to expect than almost any man in the South. [6]

Wofford was elected almost unanimously. Charles Jenkins was elected Governor. At the December meeting of the state legislature, the 13th Amendment, abolishing slavery, was ratified. [7]

In January 1866, Wofford and the other southern representatives went to D. C. to assume their places in

Congress. It was not to be however, for Republican radical leaders won out in leading Congress to overturn Johnson's reconstruction plans. The southern men were refused their seats. [8] In all truth, despite the intensity of feelings and bitter memories, it would have been difficult for the men of the South to take the test oath prescribed for U. S. congressmen. This oath had the person to swear on his honor that he had not taken up arms against the nation, nor given aid to an enemy, nor voluntarily supported anything inimical to the Constitution. [9]

Wofford's reaction to this refusal is not known, but his priorities remained solid. While in Washington, he visited with Judge William Darrah Kelley, Representative of Pennsylvania, member of the powerful Ways and Means Committee and philanthropist. [10] Wofford explained to Kelley the horrible conditions of the people of all races and political bent in Northern Georgia. He outlined the efforts of the military to help alleviate the problems, but pointed out that much more was needed. Kelley, subsequently, "obtained much-needed food and supplies for his [Wofford's] district." [11]

Back in Georgia, Wofford wrote Governor Jenkins about the problem; Jenkins responded:

> Your letter of the 14th inst. is received. The Genl. Assembly have before them for consideration the subject of your communication. Of course I cannot say what they will do, and any State action concerning it must originate with them. Reports have been called for from the several counties. They come in slowly, but the number so far returned needing aid is appalling. [12]

In April, Wofford was appointed by the Legislature as chairman for the 7th District Distribution Commission, "to afford the greatest relief to the greatest number of the really deserving poor and suffering women and children." [13] His work was aided substantially when Kentucky sent 100,000 bushels of corn to the destitute area. [14]

He returned to Washington in May for more conferences. While there, he spoke with General Oliver O. Howard of the Freedman's Bureau and again with Kelley. General Thomas sent the following recommendation on behalf of Wofford's efforts:

> Wm. T. Wofford Esq. is at present in Washington D. C. on business connected with the destitute people of Northern Georgia. Mr. Wofford was a Brigadier General in the Rebel army and at the close of the War commanded troops in Georgia. Previous to his surrender of the troops under his command he transmitted for me dispatches to and from General Wilson; and at that time and subsequently he has exhibited a desire to alleviate all in his power the destitute condition of his people. Major General Steedman, General Judah, and Colonel Merrill at that time in Georgia called my attention to his services in aiding the military authorities in restoring order. He has acted with sincerity and any statement he may make from his knowledge of the condition of the people of Georgia can be relied upon. [15]

General Howard endorsed this letter thus: "I take great pleasure in endorsing this written statement - Mr. Wofford has often visited my office and I believe him to be a humane man and thoroughly interested in the cause of his poor and suffering people - " [16]

Wofford was truly making friends in high places on behalf of his district. Men of power such as Judge Kelley listened with much interest as Wofford explained his views on "the development of the diversified resources of the South." [17] One means to this end was the building of more railroads to facilitate the moving of commerce. On December 13, 1866, the Cartersville and Van Wert Railroad was incorporated to connect Cartersville with Pryor, Alabama. Wofford was named among the incorporators. When the company later leased convicts to lay track, however, he dissociated himself from it. [18]

Wofford, it must be understood, was not and never would be of the capitalist ilk. His longtime friend Joe Brown was to become quite wealthy in the post-war years, but Wofford could not be persuaded to aggrandize his own pockets at the expense of others. Railroads were to be used to move farm products, and otherwise facilitate commerce, rather than to be a means to a personal fortune. He opposed such Bourbon Democrats as Brown and John B. Gordon on this and other points as time went by. His net worth by 1880 reached $28,000.00 from his law practice, farming, and mercantile interests. [19]

Politically, during 1866, Wofford saw his state go from bad to worse. As historian Avery wrote:

> It is an epoch that baffles description. Neither war nor peace, marked by anarchy of war without its dignity and pretense of peace without its reality; ruled under a scorching travesty of law, alternating with bayonet despotism governed by a mob caprice. . . . It sported wantonly with every sacred axiom of civil liberty. Inspired by hate and operated with malice, it abortively retarded for a decade of years, the very object it claimed to seek, viz: a solid and fraternal

> rehabilitation of a sundered Union, and a
> warring people. It was the cruelest bit of
> political harlequinade ever practiced by
> an enlightened civilization. [20]

In November, the legislature refused to ratify the 14th Amendment which granted the Negro citizenship and suffrage. An enraged U.S. Congress, led by the Republicans, placed the Southern states under martial law. Georgia came under the Third Military District in March 1867. [21] An early advocate for Negro voting rights, Wofford was very concerned about this and helped form a committee of Bartow County's leaders to discuss the matter. Resistance to Congress was futile, they decided, and could only hinder the progress made in restoring stability to the area. The committee sent the following resolution to the state legislature:

> Resolved by citizens of Bartow, that in
> view of the recent action of the 39th
> Congress, in the passage of the Military
> Bill, and the amendments thereto, that the
> citizens of Bartow county, hereby express
> their readiness to comply with the
> requirements of said Bill and its
> amendments in the formation of a new
> Constitution and in the adoption of the
> constitutional amendments. [22]

On June 3, 1867, Wofford's mother died. He had her interred in the plot with his three children, then moved his family to Cass Station, having relocated his law office to Cartersville the previous year. He needed to be in an accessible location not only for this legal practice but also for his extraprofessional activities. His hometown, Cassville, was never to recover from its wartime devastation. Despite his unceasing efforts, the economic recovery in the rest of the county was agonizingly slow. The *Cartersville Express* commented July 10, 1868, "Times hard, money scarce, trade dull." A Union veteran and newspaper correspondent toured the area during this period and commented: "black ruins, old chimneys, broken bridges, and dilapidated fences . . . Ruin! ruin! ruin!" [23]

Wofford attended as an alternate delegate the state Democratic convention on July 23, 1868. At the county convention on September 9, he and P.M.B. Young were nominated to run again for Congress. The 7th District convention met in the Kingston Methodist Church on October 2nd. Both candidates spoke to the assemblage, both indicating their desire to abide by the wishes of the people. Wofford, remembering his own troubles with the test oath in 1866 and knowing that his younger colleague had had his political disabilities removed by Congress, graciously offered to step down. Young was nominated then by acclamation. [24]

Wofford's interest in railroad development remained undiminished. In 1870, the General Assembly had incorporated and granted state aid to the Atlanta and Blue Ridge Railroad Company; when some of the original incorporators left the state and the legislators determined that the public good was not being served, it amended the original charter and in 1871, named Wofford one of the new trustees. The track was run through Bartow, Cherokee, Dawson, and Lumpkin Counties. [25]

At the request of his friends, Wofford announced himself as a candidate for governor. He withdrew his name at the state convention, December 6, 1871, however, because he had somehow gotten associated with the corruption in the state. In a fiery letter to the editor, Alexander H. Stephens, of the *Atlanta Sun*, December 4, he denied any collusion. He denied that he had anything to do with a "ring" to elect L. N. Trammell President of the Georgia Senate, Colonel Norwood for U. S. Senator, and himself Governor. Second, he denied any interest in the lease of the Western and Atlantic Railroad. Thirdly, he

vehemently rejected the innuendo that he was a stooge of
Joseph E. Brown. He concluded with the following:

> Mr. Editor, I love peace, and I have charity
> for the errors of my fellow-man, but none
> for the willful and corrupt slanderer. I have
> borne these charges with too much
> patience; duty to myself, my relatives, and
> friends requires that I should silence the
> vile tongues of these would-be-assasins of
> my character. And for this purpose I
> denounce the man or men who have made
> these charges or circulated them to my
> prejudice, as base liars and cowards; and
> whenever I can find them, I will hold them
> personally responsible for their infamous
> falsehoods. . . . I have served my State in
> the Legislature, on the plains of Mexico,
> and in the hardfought battlefields of
> Virginia. For her, I have offered my life;
> and for evidence of my character for
> honesty integrity, and patriotism, I refer
> strangers to those who have known me
> from boyhood, at school, at the bar, in the
> Legislative halls, and as a soldier. [26]

During this time, Wofford was among a growing
number of Democrats who were disaffected with the corruption
of President Grant's national administration and the
machinations of the old line members in the Democratic Party
itself. On the national scene, many Republicans were veering
away from Grant's influence to post-Reconstruction thinking
and planning. In Georgia, persons like Wofford saw an
opportunity to make a "new departure," which would benefit
both parties and chart a course for the state's emergence from
Reconstruction and the unmitigated corruption of Republican

rule in Georgia which had become synonymous with Reconstruction. Wofford also saw that the Democrats had not been immune to graft, as he stated later in the 1877 Constitutional Convention: "since a democratic administration has been in power, as much almost of corrupt practices have been carried out as there were when we did not control Georgia." [27] New Departure Democrats thus decided to back Horace Greeley for President against Grant. [28]

The convention met in Atlanta, June 26, 1872. The "Greeleyites" won over the old-liners. Robert Toombs cried "Packed by God!" to no avail. [29] Wofford went to Baltimore as a delegate. Wrote one historian:

> The Democratic convention that met in Baltimore in July 1872 was one of the most bizarre in American political history. In sessions totaling only six hours, the delegates endorsed the decisions of the candidates and platform made at a convention one month earlier by the Liberal Republicans. . . . Key planks called for an end to reconstruction and complete amnesty for southern citizens, a return to a federal government with limited powers, civil service reform, and the halt of grants of public land to railroads and other corporations. [30]

Wofford in the roll-call voted for Greeley and B. Grats Brown on the first ballot. Seventeen of the twenty-two Georgia delegates did the same. [31] In the November election, Greeley carried Georgia, Louisiana, and Texas but Grant won hands down nationwide. [32] Wofford, designated an elector, went to Washington and cast his vote for Greeley and Brown. [33]

During the 1873 depression, Wofford, ever concerned with education, gave a parcel of land between Cass Station and old Cassville for the location of a public school. Over the next two years, voluntary funds were collected and a building was erected. Named for the General, it was called Wofford Academy, and he was elected a trustee. Until the turn of the century, it prospered, both as a public school during the week, and a church school on the weekends. [34] In 1877, the Legislature approved a bill to prohibit the sale of alcoholic beverages within a mile of the Academy. [35]

Wofford's last foray into national politics came in 1876 when he was again chosen as a delegate to the state Democratic convention. [36] The state party had followed Greeley's candidacy four years before, hoping that he would defeat Grant and lift the onerous Republican reconstruction measures. This did not happen, however, so in 1876, they looked to Samuel J. Tilden, Governor of New York, as a presidential candidate. Wofford went to St. Louis, Missouri, June 27-29, with the twenty-one other delegates and on the second ballot voted with them for Tilden. [37] At the national election on November 7, he was again designated an elector. He cast his electoral vote for Tilden, who had actually defeated Rutherford B. Hayes at the polls. [38]

The election, however, was disputed by the Republicans and thrown into Congress. An electoral commission was formed to decide the matter. Georgia was in an uproar. People talked of violence if necessary to seat Tilden. Joe Brown actually counseled such. [39] Southern Congressman, led by Benjamin H. Hill and John B. Gordon, worked a deal whereby Hayes, if inaugurated, would lift Reconstruction measures completely. This was done, and Hayes was the next president. Wofford was satisfied. [40]

Wofford's last major experience in state matters came in 1877. During the 1870's, the call for a new constitutional convention in Georgia came up again and again. The 1868 state document was tainted by the work of Republicans and their henchmen, said many in the state. Other pressing changes were also warranted if the state was to move comfortably into a new phase of prosperity. The homestead exemption had to be reduced if credit was to be restored; public schools should be protected; state support for railroads had to be re-examined, as it had long been a political toy. The gubernatorial office itself needed scrutiny. [41]

This need for a new constitution was eloquently expressed by the editor of the *Lumpkin Independent*:

> A new constitution can be framed and submitted for ratification then when wisdom and statesmanship may be employed in framing . . . will prove a splendid financial investment. One single change . . . will save enough money the first year to defray all expenses of a convention and will annually save over 50 thousand dollars. . . . One session of the legislature every two years would be quite enough, and, without any other reform, would save to us in ten years half a million dollars. We also want to see the number of judicial circuits reduced so that our Superior Judges will have enough work to keep them busy. . . . We want the homestead law revised . . . we want to see a . . . clause announcing the death and burial of illegally issued Bullock bonds with another clause . . . to forever prevent the granting of state aid to any corporation. [42]

The 1877 legislature called for a public referendum for June 12 of that year to test the public's desire for a convention. The vote was 48,181 for it and 38,057 against. [43] In Wofford's district, called by then "the bloody Seventh," only one county out of fourteen voted against the convention. [44] Wofford, who had for some time sympathized with his friends W. H. and Rebecca Felton in their Independent stance against the

Bourbons, was delighted in the mandate given him to represent his beloved northwest Georgia at the convention. He would use this forum to the fullest as his last opportunity to influence Georgia politics on behalf of the needs of the people. Governor Alfred H. Colquitt set July 11 as the date for the opening of the convention at the State House in Atlanta. [45]

That State House was itself a physical symbol of the need for a change in direction for the state. When the capitol moved from Milledgeville in 1868, H. I. Kimball had purchased the old opera house for the assembly hall. The edifice was, as Wofford alluded to in the Convention, "not fit for felons to live in, . . . without ventilation except upon one side . . . " [46] In the July heat of a Georgia summer, it is small wonder that tempers flared often in the Convention. The State House was thus emblematic in that its very presence reminded state leaders of the recent Reconstruction-Republican shenanigans, the troublesome public debt, and the need for stability, probity, and, above all, good sense in state government.

Wofford's stature in Georgia politics was underscored when he was placed on three of the 13 standing committees set up to frame resolutions: the Committee on the Executive Department, the Committee on the Cotton Tax, and the Committee on Finance, Taxation, and the Public Debt. The latter was called for by Wofford himself in the opening week when he presented the following resolution:

> Whereas, it is probable that a clause of prohibition of the further issuance of bonds or other indebtedness by the state of Georgia will be incorporated in the constitution; and Whereas, it is important that the present debt of the state be paid as rapidly as possible, that the people may be delivered of the enormous and ruinous rate of interest which they are paying; therefore Resolved 1st. That a committee of one from

each congressional district be appointed by
the President to inquire if the property of
the State can be made available for the
purpose of the payment of the public debt;
and Second. If it can be made so available,
to report such ordinance, or other measure,
as they may deem advisable. Third. That
the treasurer of this state report to this
house the precise amount of the public
debt, funded or floating. Fourth. Also, to
what extent the state is liable. [47]

The public debt was a scandal. The administration of
Rufus Bullock, rivaled in turpitude only by Grant's national
administration, had incurred a state debt of $6,500,000.00
through fraudulent Reconstruction bonds. By 1877, as Wofford
reminded the conventioneers, the debt was a whopping
$10,645,897.00, although the state had repudiated the Bulloch
bonds. [48]

On July 20, the ninth day of the Convention, Wofford
eloquently defended the rights of the farmers and ex-slaves of
the state against what he perceived was the blase smoothness of
the old plantation elite. The problem, as Wofford saw it, was
the requirement that all taxes had to be paid before a person
could vote. Times since the war had been especially hard on the
"little man" in Georgia. Wofford had seen first hand the
incredible poverty in his district:

A dollar is a very small thing in the eyes of
you gentlemen, but there are many to
whom it is a large thing. It is a hard thing
for gentlemen raised in the cities and in the
midst of wealth to understand the poverty
of the people. And I want to say to you
that when you adopt this clause you do an
injustice to hundreds of as pure patriots

and as good citizens as live in Georgia. . . .
We meet here as citizens of Georgia,
knowing no race, no class, no section, no
enemies, no friends. We meet here to
discharge a public trust, and not to carry
out our prejudices . . . I know parties in the
state of Georgia so unfortunate and so poor
that they haven't the means to pay their
taxes to the state now, and the debt
amounts to quite a sum. This provision
does not say that the voter shall only have
paid his poll tax. It is all taxes. [49]

Alexander R. Lawton, a prominent elitist, answered
Wofford's specificities with the generalization that all
constitutions everywhere required taxes paid before voting, that
persons must be taught their duties as citizens. Inherent in
Lawton's words was an unmistakable allusion to the freedmen:
"We are legislating for a people who have lately undergone
great political changes and it is our duty to teach the citizen that
he should discharge all duties imposed upon him by law. . . ."[50]
Wofford's warm concern for the unfortunate of any race
stood in stark contrast to Lawton's slick paternalism. Wofford's
eloquence on this subject went for naught, however, after it was
pointed out that he had voted for a poll tax in the 1861 Georgia
convention. Wofford did not rejoin the matter, no doubt
wondering if he was the only one who had witnessed the
terrible effects of four years of war - the person who could pay
his taxes in 1861 might very well have nothing in 1877 precisely
because of that war.
It should be noted here that Wofford was arguing for
principle, with a fundamental understanding of what a
constitution was essentially - a statement of principles which
protected all races, classes and peoples. If the document did not
work for everybody, it could not work for anybody. But, as
Coulter pointed out, most of the convention members argued

for a "collection of statutory laws . . . so fearful [they were] of letting any constitutional government fully rule over the people." [51]

In the session of July 21, Wofford took on no less a person than Robert Toombs, who as chair of the Committee of 26, continued the report on the Elective Franchise begun the previous day:

> Sec. 6. The general assembly may provide from time to time, for the registration of all electors, but the following classes of persons shall not be permitted to register, vote, or hold office: Those who shall have been convicted in any of the courts in this state of treason, of embezzlement of public funds, malfeasance in office, crime punishable by law with imprisonment in the penitentiary, or bribery, or larceny, idiots, or insane persons. [52]

Wofford moved to add "or of the U. S." after the word "state" in the article. To him, the article as read discriminated against Georgia citizens. "Why make it no bar to the criminal of another state that he should have been convicted of any of these crimes, and yet make it a bar to our own?"   Toombs dodged the question by replying that crimes were not the same in all the states and as Lawton had done, sought refuge in generalities. Wofford then offered the following to be added to Section Six: "Provided that the acts constituting the crimes of which the person shall have been convicted in other states shall be crimes by the laws of this state." [53] It was done.

Wofford's next speech was against the lobbyists who besieged the legislators at all times. In it, he mentioned one of the reasons for calling the convention in the first place: whether the state capitol should be in Atlanta or moved back to Milledgeville. He then spoke forthrightly:

> How did our debt accumulate? . . . Bribery
> and corruption put us here. Georgians
> helped to do it. . . . I assert that not less
> than $500,000.00 of money of the people of
> Georgia is in the hands of the lobbyists, and
> corrupt bribe takers and bribe givers. . . .
> The people demand honesty, and I, in the
> name of purity, demand for the people of
> Georgia safe-guards and protections
> against this corruption! [54]

His motion to draft safeguards against corruption of legislators
was laid on the table, not surprisingly perhaps.

Later, Wofford arose from his seat to defend the people
of Georgia from a slander that had within it the racism that was
to bring about the Jim Crow laws of a later date - the notion that
Negroes were uneducated savages and thus should have no
voice in the State's affairs. In a long, eloquent speech, he
basically reviewed the South's efforts primarily through the
Church to educate, uplift, and Christianize the slaves. Then he
added:

> . . . it is not for us to sit here and say there is
> no hope for them and that after two
> hundred years they are still savages after
> being trained by the people to Christianity
> and civilization. Georgia, by her legislature,
> has today given them equal educational
> privileges with the whites, and their college
> here in this city gets annually eight
> thousand dollars from the state. We are
> making an experiment and let us stand up
> to what is right. [55]

It is interesting that at least twice in this speech, Toombs
interrupted querulously to assert that the Negro was a savage.

During the discussion of the Bill of Rights section, Wofford broached another subject of concern which also dealt with the forgotten persons of the state - the convicts. In his January report to the Legislature, Governor James Smith had said: "last year [the number of convicts] was 1,108, of whom 114 were white, and 994 were colored. The number of convicts received during the year was 44, and the number of deaths 58 . . . The convicts were distributed among seven leasees. . . . " [56] Wofford was concerned that the lease system lent itself to abuse and thought that a state penitentiary would be more humane. The lease system, he said "is worse than any slavery the south ever had. Here our criminals are leased out and sold to leasees for twenty years without the power of the state to exercise that protection and care over them that humanity demands." He warmed to his task as he continued to describe the horrors of the leased convict, and added in poignant prose: "It is slow death. I charge it upon the system that it is a cruel stigma upon the people of Georgia. A slow death for the convicts; go to the records and see the death rate. . . . " [57] He concluded, "My proposition is to keep them in the penitentiary, and have enough of them established, and provide for their proper keeping and care." [58] His eloquent statement was remanded to the Committee on Public Institutions. The lease system, however, was to continue until its abolition in 1906. [59]

Wofford offered the following resolution regarding Confederate veterans who were crippled and widows and orphans of veterans: "The property of maimed and disabled confederate soldiers, and of widows and minor orphans of confederate soldiers, to the amount of four hundred dollars, be exempt from taxation, and that the next general assembly shall provide by law for carrying out this provision." [60] He then gave a moving speech on the veterans from his section, making especial reference to some of the convention by implication who had been exempted by the conscript laws:

... I am not surprised that these men who
were in bomb-proofs or who owned
negroes enough to be exempt under that
odious law of the confederate congress, the
conscript law - that law which took a man
who had eleven children and owned no
negroes to make a support for them in his
absence, and put him in the front of the
battle - and that they should not be angry
when this thing is asked of them. Be it said
to the disgrace of Georgia that when I rose
here yesterday to advocate the proposition
that she should recognize the patriotism
and valor of her dead confederate soldiers
and their wives, it created almost a row.
... I propose now, if this convention won't
recognize its obligations to these soldiers,
that they shall do something to recognize
the service of the disabled ones ... [61]

His reference to those who served in "bombproofs" because
they were exempted did not go unnoticed. His remarks on the
subject the previous day had made some angry; now, he really
struck a nerve. Wofford, however, remained unperturbed: "I
slandered no one." [62]

As a member of the public debt committee, he argued
that the proposed sinking fund for eliminating the debt should
not be raised by taxation and should not decrease aid for
education. In addition, the state had enough property to sell
which would raise funds for the debt, the Western and Atlantic
Railroad in particular. The motion was tabled and taken up
again before the close of the convention: "The increase of the
bonded debt of the State was prohibited, and its extinguishment
provided for by the creation of an annual sinking fund and by a
provision that the proceeds of the sale of all public property
should be applied to its payment." [63]

The convention closed on August 25; the new constitution was ratified on December 5. Wofford had done his best to make it a humanitarian and progressive document which would make room for all Georgians. As a contemporary wrote: "During the deliberations of that body he made an enviable reputation by his sensible and conservative course. Had he been permitted to have his way, many of the objectionable features in our present constitution would have been eliminated from it." [64]

As it turned out, the Populist movement of the century's turn actually implemented some of Wofford's ideas. The following excerpt from the 1892 Populist Platform is strangely reminiscent of his words in the 1877 Convention:

> The fruits of the toil of millions are boldly stolen to build up colossal fortunes for a few, unprecedented in the history of mankind; and the possessors of these, in turn despise the Republic and endanger liberty. From the same prolific womb of governmental injustice we breed the two great classes - tramps and millionaires. [65]

Wofford returned to his law practice and farm. On September 8, 1878, Julia died and was buried beside the three daughters and Wofford's mother. On October 2, 1880, he married Margaret Langdon of Atlanta. [66]

Normally a gentle, humble man, Wofford could be as bellicose as the next one. On September 15, 1880, during the electioneering of that year, he made a speech in LaGrange, Georgia, in which he made the following reference to J. W. Renfroe: "He called Renfroe a rogue and said that he would refuse his hand on the street for it was covered with crime." Renfroe challenged Wofford to a duel. J. M. Smith, an ex-governor whom Wofford did not support nor like either, carried the challenge to Wofford, who refused to accept it from Smith.

The affair was heating up to a showdown until Joe Brown and friends stepped in and, in Rebecca Felton's words, "United to calm down the 'raging sea.' " [67]

On May 22, 1884, General Wofford died peacefully in his sleep after a lengthy illness. His funeral was held on the 24th, a small graveside service at his request. Reverend Theodore E. Smith of the Presbyterian Church eulogized him. Wofford was then laid to rest beside Julia and his three "little angels" in the old Cassville cemetery. "The large concourse of sorrowing friends that followed his remains to their last resting place testified to the tender affection and high regard in which he was held by his fellow citizens." [68]

As John Bunyan wrote of Valiant-for-the-Truth, "So he passed over, and all the trumpets sounded for him on the other side."

Addendum

On Colonel William Wofford, the great grandfather of General William Tatum Wofford: In a book, *Boyer's French Dictionary*, which had passed down to him through the family, General Wofford, the subject of this biography, found an autobiographical statement written by his great grandfather:

> Wm. Wofford was born in the province, now State of Maryland, near Rock Creek, about 12 miles above the federal city, on the 25th day of Oct. 1728, then Prince Georges county, now in the ninety-third year of his age. Wrote without spectacles the 30th day of July, 1820.

With ancestral roots in England, William Wofford, the older of five brothers - the others being named Joseph, John, James, and Benjamin- migrated to Spartanburg County, South Carolina, before the American Revolution. He, in addition to being a leader of the community, erected the famous Wofford Iron Works which was subsequently burned by the British in the Revolution. He attained the rank of Lieutenant Colonel when hostilities broke out with Britain and served with great distinction in many of the campaigns against the British and Tories in South Carolina. At some point in the early 1790's, he moved to the Catawba River area and built a fort as a frontier outpost, naming it Fort Charles. Subsequent to the Revolution, he moved again, this time into Habersham County, Georgia, as mentioned in the beginning of this biography. He died in 1823, a venerable patriot and pathfinder of 96 years of age. Many of his descendants migrated in following decades to northwest Georgia, where today the Wofford name is honored.

Julia Adelaide Dwight's lineage was as distinguished as her husband's. With roots in England and New England, she could boast some very noted personages in her American line: The Reverend Doctor Timothy Dwight, a famous New England minister and educator; and collaterally, the Reverend Doctor Jonathan Edwards, a preeminent Puritan divine, scholar, and educator, whose writings still form a part of any serious anthology of American literature.

Her father, Samuel Broughton Dwight, was born on March 23, 1796, in Orangeburg District, South Carolina. He attended medical school in Philadelphia, returned to his home state, and married Mary Ann Jamison. He migrated then to Murray County in northwest Georgia where he established a medical practice and built Hopedale Plantation near Spring Place. He died in 1859. There is evidence that the Dwights and Woffords had had a long association in South Carolina and later in Georgia.

Footnotes

Chapter 1

[1] The LAVONIA TIMES AND GAUGE, February 23, 1934;   Carl Flowers, Jr., "The Wofford Settlement on the Georgia Frontier," GEORGIA HISTORICAL QUARTERLY 41 (Fall 1977), 258-267; Jane W. Hait, HISTORY OF THE WOFFORD FAMILY (Spartanburg, South Carolina: Reprint Publishing, 1993), 44-48.
[2] Lucy J. Cunyus, HISTORY OF BARTOW COUNTY (Easley, South Carolina: Southern Historical Press, 1976), 297.   Some sources list Wofford's birth year as 1824, including his grave inscription. On his Mexican War muster roll in 1847, he listed his age as 24, making 1823 the correct date (Wofford Papers).
[3] J. H. Austin, ABSTRACTS OF GEORGIA WILLS II n.p., n.d., 5.
[4] H. E. Kimzey, EARLY GENEALOGICAL AND HISTORICAL RECORDS OF HABERSHAM COUNTY, n.p., 1988, 228. Benjamin Wofford died in Cassville, March 2, 1836, and is buried in Bartow County.   There were at least two other Benjamins in the Wofford lineage, around Spartanburg and in Wofford's Settlement - one was the founder of Wofford College and a noted Methodist divine; the other was a Tory in the American Revolution.   See D. D. Wallace, HISTORY OF WOFFORD COLLEGE (Nashville, Tennessee: Vanderbilt University Press, 1951), 17-21.
[5] Adiel Sherwood, GAZETTEER OF THE STATE OF GEORGIA, CONTAINING A PARTIAL DESCRIPTION OF THE STATE, ITS RESOURCES, COUNTIES, TOWNS, AND VILLAGES (Atlanta: Richards, 1860), 40.
[6] James C. Flanigan, HISTORY OF GWINNETT COUNTY I (Hapeville, Georgia: Tyler, 1943), 95.
[7] Amanda Johnson, GEORGIA AS COLONY AND STATE (Atlanta: Cherokee, 1970), 430. ACTS AND RESOLUTIONS OF THE GENERAL ASSEMBLY OF GEORGIA, 1834 (Milledgeville, Georgia: Harrison, 1835), 150-151; 1835, 116-118. See also James C. Bonner and L. E. Roberts, eds., STUDIES IN GEORGIA HISTORY (Athens, Georgia: University of Georgia Press, 1940),

172-174. In 1831, a Society for Promoting Manual Labor in Literary Institutions was started in New York, "its members being under conviction that reform in our seminaries of learning was greatly needed, both for the preservation of health, and for giving energy to the character by habits of useful and vigorous exercise" (E. F. Stanton, "Manual Labor Schools," SOUTHERN LITERARY MESSENGER [March 1836], 15). In Georgia, this concept was coupled with an interest in teaching agricultural theory and practice. The Baptists and Methodists also founded manual labor schools in Eatonton and Covington. See also L. E. Roberts, "Educational Reform in Antebellum Georgia," GEORGIA REVIEW 16 (Spring 1962), 74-75, and Dorothy Orr, A HISTORY OF EDUCATION IN GEORGIA (Chapel Hill: University of North Carolina Press, 1950), 134 -149.

8   ATLANTA CONSTITUTION, May 24, 1884.
9   Lena Wofford Harley Letterbook, Wofford Papers.
10 E. M. Coulter, COLLEGE LIFE IN THE OLD SOUTH (Athens: University of Georgia Press, 1951), 48. Wofford is not listed in UGA alumni records.
11 This license is in the Wofford Papers.
12 CASSVILLE PIONEER, June 20, 1845.
13 Wofford Papers.
14 1850 Agricultural Census, Cass County, Georgia, microfilm.
15 James C. Bonner, A HISTORY OF GEORGIA AGRICULTURE (Athens: University of Georgia Press, 1964), 89.
16 Ralph Wooster, "Georgia Secession Convention," GEORGIA HISTORICAL QUARTERLY 56 (March 1956), 40; 1860 Cass County Census, 860#351. Wofford's mother had $2000 in real estate and $9280 in personal property in 1860 (860#352).
17 GEORGIA A SHORT HISTORY (Chapel Hill: University of North Carolina Press, 1947), 269. Samuel Small, BRIEF BIOGRAPHIES OF MEMBERS OF THE CONSTITUTIONAL CONVENTION 1877 (Atlanta: Constitution Publishing Company, 1877), 62-63.
18 Company muster roll in the Wofford Papers.
19 Ibid.

20 Ibid.; Lena Wofford Harley Letterbook.

21 Company muster roll.

22 Cunyus, 155; J. B. Mahan, Jr., "A History of Old Cassville 1833-1864," University of Georgia: Master's Thesis, 1950, 72.

23 Small, 62-63.

24 Ibid.

25 JOURNAL OF THE HOUSE OF REPRESENTATIVES OF THE STATE OF GEORGIA (Milledgeville: Orme, 1850), 201; hereinafter cited as HOUSE JOURNAL.

26 HOUSE JOURNAL 1850, 222.

27 Ibid., 234.

28 John W. Johnston, WESTERN AND ATLANTIC RAILROAD OF THE STATE OF GEORGIA (Atlanta: Stein, 1932), 44-45.

29 HOUSE JOURNAL 1851-52 (Macon, Georgia: Ray, 1852), 78. The owner of Cooper's Iron Works near Cartersville constructed a spur at his own expense from the main tracks   to his furnace, six miles distant. It is unfortunate that   Cassville did not do so, though when it burned in 1864, the   result was the same.

30 J. C. Ridpath, HISTORY OF THE UNITED STATES FROM ABORIGINAL TIMES TO THE PRESENT II (New York: Allen, 1876), 462.

31 Ibid.

32 HOUSE JOURNAL 1850, 485.

33 Ibid. 486. See also R. H. Shyrock, GEORGIA AND THE UNION IN 1850 (New York: AMS, 1968), 224-226, for discussion of the Proviso.

34 Eighty-one members voted against Wofford's amendment; forty-two voted in favor (HOUSE JOURNAL 1850, 487).

35 Horace Montgomery, CRACKER PARTIES (Baton Rouge, Louisiana: Louisiana State University Press, 1950), 33.

36 Lawton Evans, A HISTORY OF GEORGIA (New York: American Book Company, 1898), 259. U. B. Phillips, GEORGIA AND STATE RIGHTS (Macon, Georgia: Mercer University Press, 1984), 164-165.

37 Montgomery, 34.

[38] Coulter, GEORGIA A SHORT HISTORY, 309-310.   See also David Howe, POLITICAL HISTORY OF SECESSION (New   York: Putnam, 1914), 180-182, for discussion of the Georgia Platform.

[39] HOUSE JOURNAL 1851-52, 40, 56.

[40] "Journal of Joseph Addison Turner," Woodruff Library, Emory University.   Lawrence Huff, "Joseph Addison Turner's Role in Georgia Politics," GEORGIA HISTORICAL QUARTERLY 50 (March 1966), 3.

[41] CASSVILLE STANDARD, September 30, 1852.

[42] ATHENS SOUTHERN BANNER, September 23, 1852.

[43] GEORGIA A SHORT HISTORY, 310; Montgomery, 83 ff.

[44] CASSVILLE STANDARD, October 10, 1852; Mahan, 74. Some historians in referring to William Tatum Wofford as bringing out the "Tugalo Ticket," have confused him with his uncle William B. Wofford who was called "General Wofford" from his long connection with the Georgia Militia. In 1853-54, Howell Cobb refers to General Wofford from Carnesville, Georgia, and the Tugalo Democrats.   William Tatum was at that time "Captain Wofford" in reference to his Mexican War service. See R. P. Brooks, ed., "Howell Cobb Papers," GEORGIA HISTORICAL QUARTERLY 6 (1922), 38-39.

[45] According to John W. Burke's Diary, the selling of the STANDARD to his friend Wofford was politically motivated: Burke was a delegate to the 1852 convention also but was noncommittal in his newspaper as to specifics of political bent other than being generally Democratic. Being Southern Rights inclined, and a close friend of Wofford's, he sold the journal   to Wofford rather than risk damaging that friendship in the political heat that eventuated in the "Tugalo" faction   (Woodruff Library, Emory).

[46] ATLANTA DAILY INTELLIGENCER, September 10, 1860.

[47] CASSVILLE STANDARD, September 23, 1852.   In 1854, the General Assembly gave the town control over granting liquor licenses (ACTS AND RESOLUTIONS 1854-55, 118).

[48] Small, 63; House Roster, Wofford Papers.

[49] Wofford Papers.

50 Mahan, 50; Sherwood, 40.

51 HOUSE JOURNAL 1853-54, 118; Cunyus, 146.

52 Cunyus, 260-61; Sarah Temple, FIRST ONE HUNDRED YEARS: A SHORT HISTORY OF COBB COUNTY IN GEORGIA (Athens: Brown, 1935), 188.

53 Bonner, 131.

54 Ibid., 132; see also Roland Harper, "The Development of Agriculture in Upper Georgia From 1850 to 1890," GEORGIA HISTORICAL QUARTERLY 5 (1922), 3-27.

55 AGRICULTURAL CENSUS, 1860, 860#351. See G. B. Crawford, "Cotton, Land, and Sustenance: Toward the Limits of Abundance in Late Antebellum Georgia," GEORGIA HISTORICAL QUARTERLY 72 (Summer 1988), 215-247.

56 Herbert Wender, "The Southern Commercial Convention at Savannah," GEORGIA HISTORICAL QUARTERLY 15 (June   1931), 173.

57 Vicki C. Johnson, THE MEN AND VISION OF THE SOUTHERN COMMERCIAL CONVENTIONS 1845-1871 (Columbia, Missouri: University of Missouri Press, 1992), 96.

58 James D. B. DeBow, "The Rights, Duties, and Remedies of the South," DEBOW'S REVIEW 23 (September 1857), 235.

59 Johnson, 114, 118, 121, 141-3.

60 Wofford kept a list of his bondsmen in his papers; they were Sam, James, Amelia, Chance, Jim, Charlotte, Charles, Phoebe, Dick, Amanda, Caroline, Sally, Emily, and George.

61 Johnson, 144-45.

62 "Southern Convention at Montgomery," DEBOW'S REVIEW 24 (May 1858), 427.

63 "Late Southern Convention at Montgomery," DEBOW'S REVIEW 24 (June 1858), 574.   Note that DeBow had deleted "Commercial" from the title.

64 Ibid., 605.

65 Johnson, 97.

66 Mahan, 61-62.

67 Ibid., 122.

68 MURRAY COUNTY MARRIAGE RECORDS BOOK III, 89.

69 B. W. Dwight, HISTORY OF THE DESCENDANTS OF JOHN DWIGHT I (New York: Trow, 1874), 393.

70 I. W. Avery, HISTORY OF GEORGIA FROM 1850 TO 1881 (New York: Brown and Derby, 1881), 108.

71 GEORGIA A SHORT HISTORY, 315. R. P. Brooks wrote of Cobb's political woes: "He never recovered his popularity with the Georgia democracy. In 1860 the party refused to put his name before the Charleston convention for the presidency; and even at the Montgomery convention of the seceding states, the undying resentment of the southern extremists prevented consideration of his name for the first place in the new government" ("Howell Cobb and the Crisis of 1850," MISSISSIPPI VALLEY HISTORICAL REVIEW 4 [December 1917], 298).

72 Thomas F. Schott, ALEXANDER STEPHENS OF GEORGIA (Baton Rouge: LSU Press, 1988), 286. "Rarely in American history has there been a convention as tumultuous as the one that assembled in Charleston, South Carolina in April, 1860," "National Party Conventions," CONGRESSIONAL QUARTERLY 1976, 15.

73 POLITICAL HISTORY OF SECESSION, 410-411.

74 Cunyus, 163; John Wykle, editor of the CASSVILLE STANDARD and supporter of Douglas, said in October, 1858: "They (the State Rights men) are giving the Democracy trouble, and the sooner their places are filled by 'Simon Pure' Democrats, the better it will be for us."

75 TOWARD A PATRIARCHAL REPUBLIC (Baton Rouge: LSU Press, 1977), 14.

76 GEORGIA A SHORT HISTORY, 316.

77 "Autobiography of George Gilman Smith," Southern Historical Collection, University of North Carolina, Chapel Hill, 64. Price, Wofford's good friend, was a farmer with 26 slaves and a personal wealth of $22,800. Trippe, like Wofford, was a lawyer with 30 slaves and a personal wealth of $24,500. Trippe was oldest at 59; Price was 42; Wofford 39 (Wooster, 40).

78 Schott, 319.

79 JOURNAL OF THE CONVENTION AT MILLEDGEVILLE AND SAVANNAH 1861 (Milledgeville: Boughton, Nisbet, and Barnes. 1861), 37-39.   See also Walter McElreath, CONSTITUTIONAL HISTORY OF GEORGIA (Atlanta: Harrison, 1912), 92-93.

80 Percy S. Flippen, ed., "From the Autobiography of Herschel V. Johnson, 1856-1867," AMERICAN HISTORICAL REVIEW 30 (January 1925), 327.

81 "Obituary," ATLANTA CONSTITUTION, May 24, 1884.

82 Evans, 273.

83 Cunyus, 210-211.

84 Wofford Papers.

85 JOURNAL OF 1861 CONVENTION, 139.

86 United States War Department, OFFICIAL RECORDS OF THE WAR OF THE REBELLION Series 4, I (Washington, D. C.: Government Printing Office, 1889), 136. Hereinafter as OR.

Footnotes

Chapter 2

[1] Edwin Mims, SIDNEY LANIER (Boston: Houghton Mifflin, 1905), 46.

[2] Wofford Papers; ROME WEEKLY COURIER, May 3, 1861.

[3] "Journal of J. L. Lemon, Co. A 18th Ga.," 1; used by permission of Mark Lemon. See also J. M. Folsom, HEROES AND MARTYRS OF GEORGIA: GEORGIA'S RECORD IN THE REVOLUTION OF 1861 (Macon: Burke and Boykin, 1864), 12-13.

[4] Wofford Papers.

[5] Ibid.

[6] R. A. Quinn, "History of the Important Movements and Incidents of the Newton Rifles (18th Georgia)," CONFEDERATE LETTERS DIARIES AND REMINISCENCES 1860-1865 10 (Georgia Department of Archives and History), 5. Hereinafter as Quinn.

[7] THE CONFEDERACY IS ON HER WAY UP THE SPOUT: LETTERS TO SOUTH CAROLINA 1861-1864 ed. J. R. Heller III and Carolyn Ayres Heller (Athens: University of Georgia Press, 1992), 22. Hereinafter as Barrett.

[8] ATLANTA SOUTHERN CONFEDERACY, July 2, 1861; Lemon, 1.

[9] William S. Shockley to his wife, June 14, 1861, Duke University Special Collections. Wofford's Service Record, Wofford Papers.

[10] Ibid. AUGUSTA DAILY CHRONICLE AND SENTINEL, June 23, 1861.

[11] Wofford Papers.

[12] T. Conn Bryan, CONFEDERATE GEORGIA (Athens: University of Georgia Press, 1953), 81; W. A. Bragg, JOE BROWN'S ARMY: THE GEORGIA STATE LINE (Macon: Mercer, 1987), 5.

[13] FIRST HUNDRED YEARS, 240; Lemon, 2.

[14] Quinn, 6; Lemon, 2.

[15] Barrett, 25.

[16] Lemon, 2.

[17] Barrett, 29; Lemon, 2, called the place Camp Cedar.

[18] William Jeffrey, RICHMOND PRISONS (New York: Republican Press, 1893), 8; Folsom, 13.

19 William B. Hesseltine, CIVIL WAR PRISONS: A STUDY IN WAR PSYCHOLOGY (New York: Unger, 1964), 57.

20 Jeffrey, 21; Lemon, 2; Quinn, 6-7.

21 Quinn, 7; Lemon, 3; Folsom, 13.

22 Barrett, 31.

23 Mrs. Wofford to Colonel Wofford, November 12, 1861; she mentions seeing in the November 9th RICHMOND EXAMINER that the Regiment had returned to Richmond.

24 Wofford Papers.

25 Barrett, 30.

26 Ibid., 35.

27 Quinn, 8. Their mail, however, was sent from Akokeek, Virginia, not Dumfries (Ian Tickell, "An Uncommon Solder's Due Cover from Virginia," CONFEDERATE PHILATDELIST 40 [May - June 1995], 104-105).

28 HOOD'S TEXAS BRIGADE LEE'S GRENADIER GUARD (Waco, Texas: Texian Press, 1970), 72.

29 Wofford Papers.

30 Lemon, 3.

31 J. B. Polley, HOOD'S TEXAS BRIGADE: ITS MARCHES ITS BATTLES ITS ACHIEVEMENTS (Dayton: Morningside Press, 1988), 18 - 19. See also Don Everett, ed., CHAPLAIN N. A. DAVIS AND HOOD'S TEXAS BRIGADE (San Antonio, Texas; Principia Press, 1962), 78.

32 Shockley to wife, November 23, 1861; Lemon, 3.

33 Shockley to wife, January 4, 1862, and January 7, 1862, Duke University; A. J. Cone, "Georgians in Hood's Texas Brigade," CONFEDERATE VETERAN 19 (February 1911), 1.

34 "Spirit of 1861," (camp newspaper) December 25, 1861, Woodruff Library, Emory; also in Wofford Papers.

35 Burnett deserted January 29, 1864; White was captured at Saylor's Creek, April 6, 1865 (Lillian Henderson, ROSTER OF CONFEDERATE SOLDIERS OF GEORGIA [Hapeville: Longino, 1958], 617; 623).

36 "Spirit of 1861," Woodruff Library, Emory.

37 Ibid.

38 A SOLDIER'S LETTERS TO CHARMING NELLIE (New York: Meade, 1908), 18. Shockley to wife, January 4, 1862, Duke University.
39 Ibid.
40 Julia Wofford to Colonel Wofford, November 7, 1861; November 9, 1861; November 12, 1861. Sally Mae Akin, "Refugees of 1863," GEORGIA HISTORICAL QUARTERLY 31 (June 1947), 114.
41 Julia Wofford to Colonel Wofford, November 21, 1861. ACTS AND RESOLUTIONS 1861 (Milledgeville: Burke, 1862), 101.
42 The Cassville postmaster did use "Manassas, Ga." on his CDS for a time, but after the war the original name of Cassville, as listed in January 1861, was retained (Gerald J. Smith, "Manassas, Georgia," CONFEDERATE PHILATELIST 39 [November-December 1994], 223-224).
43 Richard McMurray, JOHN BELL HOOD AND THE WAR FOR SOUTHERN INDEPENDENCE (Lincoln, Nebraska: University of Nebraska Press, 1982), 34.
44 Douglas Southall Freeman, LEE'S LIEUTENANTS I (New York: Scribners, 1944), 154.
45 MR. LINCOLN'S ARMY in BRUCE CATTON'S CIVIL WAR THREE VOLUMES IN ONE (New York: Fairfax, 1984), 154.
46 CHARMING NELLIE, 18 - 19, 26; Shockley to wife, February 13, 1862, Duke University; John Bell Hood, ADVANCE AND RETREAT (New Orleans: Hood Orphan Memorial Fund, 1880), 20.
47 Valmor Giles, RAGS AND HOPE: RECOLLECTIONS OF VAL C. GILES (New York: Coward-McCann, 1961), 66.
48 Quinn, 8. In his HOOD'S TEXAS BRIGADE, Polley said they arrived on the 10th (20).
49 Shockley to wife, March 15, 1862, Duke University.
50 ADVANCE AND RETREAT, 19. Freeman wrote at length of Hood's discipline in LEE'S LIEUTENANTS I, 196-199, and implied that it was his discipline that brought promotion (198). That may be, but Hood was also a West Point graduate, which probably influenced the promotion more. Colonel Wofford, as

Shockley said, may have been tougher with his 18th Georgia in discipline and training.

51 William S. Hassler, ed., "Civil War Letters of William Dorsey Pender to His Wife," GEORGIA REVIEW 17 (Spring 1963), 65.

52 Polley, HOOD'S TEXAS BRIGADE, 21.

53 Ibid.

54 Quinn, 8; see also Lemon, 4.

55 Polley, CHARMING NELLIE, 30.

56 Lemon, 4.

57 Shockley to wife, April 12, 1862, Duke University; Quinn, 8; Giles, 72; Lemon, 4, says they entrained on the 11th.

58 Shockley to wife, April 20, 1862; Nicholas Pomeroy, "War Memoirs," Confederate Research Center, Hillsboro, Texas, 12.

59 Ibid.

60 ADVANCE AND RETREAT, 20.

61 Shockley to wife, May 18, 1862, Duke University; Pomeroy, 12.

62 CHARMING NELLIE, 33 - 34; Pomeroy, 13; Donald Henderson, "General Hood's Brigade," SOUTHERN HISTORICAL SOCIETY PAPERS 29 (1901), 300; ADVANCE AND RETREAT, 23; Giles, 77; Barrett, 63.

63 Lemon, 4.

64 Barrett, 63.

65 Lemon, 4. The men were issued Enfield muskets on May 15 (Lemon, 4).

66 CHARMING NELLIE, 38.

67 Lemon, 4.

68 Shockley to wife, May 16, 1862, Duke University.

69 Wofford Papers.

70 Ibid.

71 Mrs. R. H. Jones of Cartersville, ten miles south of Cassville, wrote to her husband on April 13, 1862: "The Yankees have got to Cartersville at last there was great confusion on yesterday morning the cars arrived at Big Shanty and when the passengers went in to breakfast there was some yankees come running out of the woods and got abord of the train and went a kiting they

had a firman along with them they came to Cartersville and passed through slowly so that some more Yankees could get on they had been one or two pilfering about here two or three days to see what he could see He got on the train with them whin they came through they said they were carring aminition to Beauregard told the bigest kind of lies Mr Madisc said he thought they were rether suspicious caricters.   They cut the telegraph wire in two or three places our people got (Yonah and Texas) train and put out after them they pushed them sotight they left the train and took to their heel and ran.   The cavilry company is after them now . . . " Dorothy Jones Morgan, ed., A VERY PERSONAL GLIMPSE OF THE CIVIL WAR ERA FROM 1849 TO 1863 (self-published, 1993), n.p.n.

[72] Temple, 244.

[73] William Hood to parents, February 22, 1862, Rebecca Hood Papers, Woodruff Library, Emory.

[74] Wofford Papers.

[75] Julia Wofford to Colonel Wofford, November 8, 1861; Harry Pfanz, GETTYSBURG THE SECOND DAY (Chapel Hill: University of North Carolina Press, 1987), 399.

[76] Wofford's reaction is unknown. McMurray, 34 - 35, discusses Hood and Wofford and concludes that the promotion over Wofford was attributed to Hood's West Point career, his relationship to President Davis, and the fact that a Texan was perhaps the best choice to lead a Texas brigade. McMurray wrote of Hood's colonels: "Wofford was the best of the lot" (36).

Footnotes

Chapter 3

[1] Barrett, 69; Quinn, 9; Pomeroy, 15.

[2] RICHMOND DISPATCH, June 9, 1862.

[3] RICHMOND WHIG, July 4, 1862.   Throughout the war, Wofford's men had to "toot their own horns" in order to gain public recognition for their services; Lemon, 5; Folsom, 14.

[4] Gerald J. Smith, ed. LETTERS, DIARIES, AND REMINISCENCES FROM THE UNION AND THE CONFEDERACY (Murfreesboro, Tennessee: Ambassador, 1996), 132-133.

[5] Shockley to wife, July 2, 1862, Duke University.

[6] McMurry, 51.

[7] Ibid., 52.

[8] William Fletcher, REBEL PRIVATE, FRONT AND REAR (Washington, D.C.: Zenger, 1985), 34.

[9] Ibid., 35-36.

[10] Shockley to wife, August 4, 1862, Duke University.

[11] LEE'S LIEUTENANTS II, 73-80.

[12] Pomeroy, 26.

[13] OR I, 12, pt 2, 604-606.

[14] Ibid.

[15] Folsom, 15.

[16] Pomeroy, 29.

[17] Lemon, 7.

[18] CHARMING NELLIE, 62-63. A. J. Cone of the 18th Georgia wrote of this incident in "Hanging a Federal Spy," CONFEDERATE VETERAN 10 (1902), 30, and gave his name as Mason. Cone also places the event a month later. W. H. Andrews agrees with Polley on location and date but not on particulars, FOOTPRINTS OF A REGIMENT A RECOLLECTION OF THE FIRST GEORGIA REGULARS (Atlanta: Longstreet, 1992), 55.

[19] Pomeroy, 29; ADVANCE AND RETREAT, 33.

[20] W. T. Hill, "The First Troops Through Thoroughfare Gap," CONFEDERATE VETERAN 23 (1915), 544.

[21] E. M. Law, "The Virginia Campaign of 1862," PHILADELPHIA WEEKLY PRESS, October 26 and November 2, 1887.

[22] CHARMING NELLIE, 63.

[23] James Longstreet, FROM MANASSAS TO APPOMATTOX (New York: Smithmark, 1994), 180.

[24] ADVANCE AND RETREAT, 33-34.

[25] Longstreet, 183.

[26] Theron Haight, "Gainesville, Groveton, and Bull Run," WAR PAPERS READ BEFORE THE COMMANDARY OF THE STATE OF WISCONSIN, MILITARY ORDER OF THE LOYAL LEGION OF THE UNITED STATES II (Wisconsin: Milvan, 1896), 364-365; Folsom, 15.

[27] OR I, 12, pt 2, 608.

[28] David Hamer, "One Man's War," Manassas National Battlefield Park Library, 16-19.

[29] ATLANTA SOUTHERN CONFEDERACY, October 11, 1862.

[30] Shockley to wife, September 2, 1862, Duke University.

[31] ADVANCE AND RETREAT, 34-35; Wofford's Report, OR I, 12, pt 2, 608.

[32] Pomeroy, 30; Giles, 127; Lemon, 8.

[33] Giles, 127; Pomeroy, 31.

[34] Davenport to family, September 5, 1862, Alfred Davenport Papers, New York Historical Society.

[35] Ibid.

[36] OR I, 12, pt 2, 609.

[37] ATLANTA SOUTHERN CONFEDERACY, October 11, 1862.

[38] Lemon, 9.

[39] Charles W. Cowtan, SERVICE OF THE TENTH NEW YORK VOLUNTEERS (NATIONAL ZOUAVES) IN THE WAR OF THE REBELLION (New York: Ludwig, 1882), 129.

[40] VOICES OF THE CIVIL WAR: SECOND MANASSAS (Alexandria, Virginia: Time Life, 1996), 134.

[41] OR I, 12, pt 2, 609.

[42] John W. Stevens, REMINISCENCES OF THE CIVIL WAR (Hillsboro, Texas: Hillsboro Mirror Print, 1902), 57.

[43] "Memoir, 1903," South Carolina Historical Society, Charleston, South Carolina.

44 Shockley to wife, September 2, 1862, Duke University.

45 OR I, 12, pt 2, 610.

46 ATLANTA SOUTHERN CONFEDERACY, October 11, 1862; Lemon, 6-7.

47 Fletcher, 42.

48 John Hennessey, SECOND MANASSAS BATTLEFIELD MAP STUDY (Lynchburg, Virginia: Howard, 1985), 461; 454.

49 Henderson, 306.

50 CHARMING NELLIE, 75.

51 Colonel P. A. Work's Report, OR I, 12, pt 2, 614.

52 OR I, 12, pt 2, 608-619.

53 Ibid., 547, 560.

54 OR, 19, pt 1, 929; ADVANCE AND RETREAT, 37-38.

55 CHARMING NELLIE, 78.

56 Wofford Papers; The State Legislature ordered a medal for T. H. Northcutt (ACTS AND RESOLUTIONS 1862, 265).

Footnotes

Chapter 4

[1] Stevens, 66.

[2] Barrett, 74.

[3] STEPHEN ELLIOT WELCH OF THE HAMPTON LEGION ed. J. M. Priest (Shippensburg, Maryland: Burd Street Press, 1994), 10.

[4] Stevens, 66.

[5] Shockley to wife, September 26, 1862, Duke University: Folsom, 15.

[6] ADVANCE AND RETREAT, 41.

[7] Wofford's Report, OR 19, 1, pt 1, 927; ATLANTA SOUTHERN CONFEDERACY, October 11, 1862.

[8] OR 19, I, pt 1, 927.

[9] Welch, 6.

[10] ADVANCE AND RETREAT, 42.

[11] Ibid., 41.

[12] Pomeroy, 38. Heros Von Borcke of General Jeb Stuart's staff recorded the following incident in MEMOIRS OF THE CONFEDERATE WAR FOR INDEPENDENCE I (New York: Smith, 1938), 236-237: I felt obliged to rebuke a Texan, who, only a few steps from me, had just rolled over, by a capital shot, a porker galloping across the street at sixty yards distance, for his wanton disregard of the rights of property. With a look of utter astonishment, he turned to me, and asked, "Major, did you have anything to eat yesterday? and, upon my answering in the negative, said, "Then you know what it is to be hungry; I haven't tasted a morsel for several days." I had nothing more to say. . . .

[13] Stevens, 74.

[14] Gerald Judson Smith, Jr., "'Satisfaction Wherever He Served' The Career of Alexander Robert Lawton 1818-1862," Georgia Southern University: Master's Thesis, 1994, 97-98.

[15] OR 19 I, pt 1, 923.

16 Welch, 6; Lemon, 10, is the only reference this writer has found in contemporary sources testifying to the anger of the men at having their breakfast interrupted.

17 Rufus Dawes, SERVICE WITH THE SIXTH WISCONSIN VOLUNTEERS (Dayton; Morningside, 1984), 245.

18 Welch, 6; Stevens, 74; Lemon, 10.

19 Welch, 8.

20 Quoted in LEE'S LIEUTENANTS II, 208.

21 OR 19 I, pt 1, 928.

22 Stephen Sears, LANDSCAPE TURNED RED: THE BATTLE OF ANTIETAM (New York: Ticknor and Row, 1983), 222.

23 Work, "The First Texas Regiment of the Texas Brigade of the Army of Northern Virginia at the Battles of Boonsboro Pass or Gap and Sharpsburg or Antietam, Maryland, in September, 1862," unpublished and undated manuscript (Confederate Research Center, Hillsboro, Texas), 3.

24 OR 19 I, pt 1, 928; see also Colonel S. Z. Ruff's Report, ibid., 929-930.

25 ATLANTA SOUTHERN CONFEDERACY, October 11, 1862; Lemon, 10.

26 Welch, 8.

27 Pomeroy, 40.

28 OR 19 I, pt 1, 929.

29 Ibid., 934.

30 Ibid., 938.

31 Ibid., 923.

32 ADVANCE AND RETREAT, 44.

33 Stevens, 77.

34 Robert Gould Shaw to parents, September 21, 1862, BLUE-EYED CHILD OF FORTUNE: LETTERS OF ROBERT GOULD SHAW ed. Russell Duncan (Athens: University of Georgia Press, 1992), 240.

35 Sears, 305.

36 Von Borcke, 234.

37 Shockley to wife, September 26, 1862, Duke University.

38 W. R. Hamby, "Hood's Texas Brigade at Sharpsburg," CONFEDERATE VETERAN 15 (1908), 20.

[39] Folsom, 15.

[40] OR 19, pt 2, 643.

[41] ADVANCE AND RETREAT, 43.

[42] Barrett, 92; Folsom, 16.

[43] Wofford's Service Record, Wofford Papers; letter to Lieutenant John Hardin, November 27, 1862, Confederate Miscellany, Woodruff Library, Emory; Dwight, 393.

[44] Dwight, 393.

[45] Henry Robinson to his wife, Henry Robinson Letters, Woodruff Library, Emory.

[46] Shockley to wife, January 12, 1864, Duke University; Shockley died in prison in 1865.

[47] LETTERS OF WARREN AKIN CONFEDERATE CONGRESSMAN ed. Bell I. Wiley (Athens: University of Georgia Press, 1959), 49.

[48] Wofford to Hardin, Confederate Miscellany, Woodruff Library, Emory.

[49] Wofford Papers; a copy of the hymn in Julia's hand was kept by Wofford the rest of his life.

Footnotes

Chapter 5

1 Wofford Service Record, Wofford Papers.

2 Barrett, 81.

3 E. H. Sutton, GRANDPA'S WAR STORIES (n.p.,n.d.), 25.

4 Diary of T. M. Mitchell, Company B, Phillips' Legion, March 3, 1863; with permission of Robert Thomas.

5 Barrett, 92.

6 John D. Young, "A Campaign with Sharpshooters," ANNALS OF WAR (Dayton: Morningside, 1988), 270. Young stated that these units were formed in 1864, but evidence shows 1863.

7 Ibid. See also "Sharpshooting in Lee's Army," CONFEDERATE VETERAN 3 (1895), 98.

8 Barrett, 96. See also Gerald J. Smith, SMITE THEM HIP AND THIGH: GEORGIA METHODIST MINISTERS IN THE CONFEDERATE MILITARY (Murfreesboro: Ambassador, 1993), 74-97.

9 Abner Doubleday, CHANCELLORSVILLE AND GETTYSBURG CAMPAIGNS OF THE CIVIL WAR (New York: Blue and Gray Press, 1955), 1-11.

10 Mitchell, 13.

11 ATLANTA SOUTHERN CONFEDERACY, May 19, 1863.

12 Mitchell, 14.

13 OR I 25, pt 1, 824.

14 Mitchell, 14; Lemon, 11.

15 CHANCELLORSVILLE 1863: THE SOULS OF THE BRAVE (New York: Knopf, 1992), 124.

16 OR I 25, pt 1, 825.

17 Mitchell, 14.

18 OR I, 25, pt 1, 826.

19 ATLANTA SOUTHERN CONFEDERACY, May 19, 1863.

20 OR I, 25, pt 1, 826; RICHMOND SENTINEL, May 28, 1863.

21 Mitchell, 15.

22 Shockley to wife, May 4, 1863, Duke University.

23 ATLANTA SOUTHERN CONFEDERACY, May 19, 1863.

[24] Folsom, 16.

[25] OR I, 25, pt 1, 341.

[26] RICHMOND SENTINEL, May 28, 1863. The waver which Wofford saw was actually the New York regiment pulling out to be replaced by another unit in the trenches. This exchange took place at a critical moment, when the Confederates were regrouping for another assault. The Yankees were barely in position when Wofford's men rolled forward a second time.

[27] Mitchell, 15.

[28] OR I, 25, pt 1, 826. The report of the 27th Connecticut mentions several officers and 57 men unaccounted for after the retreat on May 3 (OR I 25, pt 1, 332).

[29] "Memoir," Confederate Miscellaneous Personal Papers, Georgia Department of Archives and History.

[30] Diary of Marcus Green, Kennesaw Mountain National Military Park.

[31] ATLANTA SOUTHERN CONFEDERACY, May 19, 1863.

[32] Sutton, 35-36.

[33] Ibid., 36.

[34] ATLANTA SOUTHERN CONFEDERACY, May 19, 1863.

[35] "The Battle of Gettysburg," CONFEDERATE VETERAN 21 (1913), 436.

[36] Lafayette McLaws, "McLaws' Division and the Pennsylvania Reserves," PHILADELPHIA WEEKLY PRESS, October 20, 1886.

[37] Mitchell, 16.

[38] Augustus Dickert, HISTORY OF KERSHAW'S BRIGADE (Newberry, South Carolina: Aull, 1899), 223.

[39] OR I, 25, pt 1, 820.

[40] Mitchell, 17.

[41] Dickert, 223; Dr. E. J. Eldridge to wife, June 3, 1863, author's collection.

[42] Mitchell, 18; Eldridge to wife, June 3, 1863.

[43] Ibid., 19.

[44] "Franklin Galliard's Civil War Letters," Southern Historical Collection, University of North Carolina, 30.

[45] Mitchell, 19-21.

46 Galliard, 32; Folsom, 17.

47 Thomas Holley, RAMSEY VOLUNTEERS THE 16TH GEORGIA INFANTRY REGIMENT ARMY OF NORTHERN VIRGINIA CSA (Fernandino Beach, Florida: Wolfe, 1995), 21.

48 Marcus Green Diary, 6.

49 T. N. Simpson to Aunt, June 28, 1863, "FAR, FAR FROM HOME": THE WARTIME LETTERS OF DICK AND TALLY SIMPSON THIRD SOUTH CAROLINA VOLUNTEERS ed. Guy Everson and Ed W. Simpson, Jr. (New York: Oxford, 1994), 251.

50 Mitchell, 22.

51 Diary of Surgeon Myers, Eleanor Brockenbrough Library, Museum of the Confederacy, Richmond, Virginia, n.p.n.

52 OR I, 51, pt 2, 731.

53 McLaws, "Gettysburg," SOUTHERN HISTORICAL SOCIETY PAPERS 7 (1879), 71.

54 Pfanz, 29.

55 Lemon, 17.

56 Coxe, 434; Sutton, 40; "Kershaw's Brigade at Gettysburg," BATTLES AND LEADERS OF THE CIVIL WAR III, 333.

57 Stephen Dent, "With Cobb's Brigade at Fredericksburg," CONFEDERATE VETERAN 22 (1914), 550-551; Bachelder's map of July 2 (Pfanz, 497) aligns them from right to left as 16th, 18th, 24th, Cobb's Legion, Phillips' Legion, but gives no reason for doing so. A participant in Wofford's Brigade, however, aligned them in the customary way stated in the text (see RICHMOND DAILY ENQUIRER, August 5, 1863).

58 RICHMOND DAILY ENQUIRER, August 5, 1863; Coxe, 433; Jennings Wise, THE LONG ARM OF LEE: CHANCELLORSVILLE TO APPOMATTOX (Lincoln, Nebraska: University of Nebraska Press, 1991), 645.

59 McLaws, "Gettysburg," 69-70.

60 Sutton, 41; McLaws, ibid., 70.

61 John Stegeman, THESE MEN SHE GAVE: CIVIL WAR DIARY OF ATHENS, GEORGIA (Athens: University of Georgia Press, 1964), 92; Lucy D. Bryan, "James Fielding Dillard, Confederate Soldier," University of Georgia: Master's Thesis, 1940, 77-79.

62 THE GUNS AT GETTYSBURG (New York: Collier, 1958), 87.

63 "Kershaw's Brigade at Gettysburg," 334.

64 Stegeman, 92.

65 Galliard, 36.

66 Earl Schenck Miers and R. A. Brown, GETTYSBURG (New Brunswick: Rutgers, 1948), 156. The assault was to be en echelon, by steps, with brigades going in at intervals to keep the enemy occupied without time to reinforce weak points in the line. For some reason, Longstreet waited too long to commit the units. Thus, Hood's division fought alone for an hour at least before Kershaw went in. Barksdale should have committed closely on Kershaw. The Brigadiers realized this if their commanders did not.

67 McLaws, "Gettysburg," 73.

68 Coxe, 435; McLaws does not mention this in the SHSP or his other Gettysburg articles.

69 "Kershaw's Brigade at Gettysburg," 337.

70 "Gettysburg," 73; RICHMOND DAILY ENQUIRER, August 5, 1863.

71 Royall W. Figg, "WHERE MEN ONLY DARE TO GO!:" OR THE STORY OF A BOY COMPANY BY AN EX-BOY" (Richmond: Whittet and Shepperson, 1885), 140.

72 Lemon, 17

73 RICHMOND SENTINEL, July 27, 1863.

74 Frank Lawley, "Battles at Gettysburg," LONDON TIMES, August 18, 1863; MANASSAS TO APPOMATTOX, 372. The ubiquitous A. J. Fremantle of the Coldstream Guards reported that Longstreet led a Georgia regiment against a battery (THREE MONTHS IN THE SOUTHERN STATES [Edinburgh and London, 1863], 261). This may be, but it must have been one of Semmes' regiments, the only other Georgia brigade in McLaws' division. William Youngblood, riding with Longstreet as Wofford's men committed, stated, "Just as we rode from the timber . . . I noticed we were riding in front of Wofford's men . . . He (Longstreet) checked his horse and waited until Wofford's men had gotten in front of us . . . " ("Personal Observations at Gettysburg," CONFEDERATE VETERAN 19 [1911], 286). Diaries and letters of

Wofford's personnel do not mention Fremantle's observation. The good Englishman may have mistook Barksdale for Longstreet.

75 McLaws, "Federal Disaster." He mentions several lepus encounters on that eventful afternoon. If it was the same rabbit in each, the bunny must have been having a big day!

76 Letter to McLaws, December 10, 1877, Southern Historical Collection, University of North Carolina. Fairfax Downey attributes this incident (one wonders how what with all the iron and lead which were flying like hail all over the place) to Major John Bigelow's Ninth Massachusetts Battery (100). Bigelow recorded that after the war, a Georgia officer, perhaps Bryan, said to him: "Visit my Georgia home, and I will show you enough graves and one-armed and one-legged men to satisfy you a lifetime" (THE PEACH ORCHARD, GETTYSBURG, JULY 2, 1863 [Minneapolis, Minnesota: Kimball-Stoner, 1910], 53).

77 Bryan to McLaws, December 10, 1877.

78 Lemon, 17.

79 Stegeman, 92.

80 Coxe, 434-35. The RICHMOND DAILY ENQUIRER, August 5, 1863, describes this moment substantially as Coxe does. See also John Purifoy's "Longstreet's Attack at Gettysburg," CONFEDERATE VETERAN 31 (1923), 292-294. See also Wofford's statement in John Bachelder, "Gettysburg Campaign," III 175A, MS, Bachelder Papers, New Hampshire Historical Society.

81 "Kershaw's Brigade at Gettysburg," 337; McLaws, "Gettysburg," 73.

82 Lemon, 17. F. B. Williams, Jr., ed. "From Sumter to the Wilderness: Letters of Sergeant James Butler Suddath," SOUTH CAROLINA HISTORICAL MAGAZINE 63 (April 1962), 98-99. See also Kershaw's Report, OR I 27, pt 1, 369.

83 OR I, 27, pt 1, 380; Pfanz, 291.

84 Robert L. Stewart, HISTORY OF THE ONE HUNDRED AND FORTIETH REGIMENT, PENNSYLVANIA VOLUNTEERS (Philadelphia: Franklin, 1912), 291.

85 RICHMOND DAILY ENQUIRER, August 5, 1863; Richard Coffman, "A Vital Unit," CIVIL WAR TIMES ILLUSTRATED 20 (June 1982), 44.

86 Ibid.; see also Union Brigadier General James Barnes' report, OR I 27, pt 1, 602.

87 The Survivor's Association, HISTORY OF THE CORN EXCHANGE REGIMENT 118TH PENNSYLVANIA VOLUNTEERS (Philadelphia: Smith, 1888), 244; W. A. Swanberg, SICKLES THE INCREDIBLE (New York: Ace, 1956), 175.

88 Lemon, 18.   Fairfax Downey wrote: " . . . the 3rd Massachusetts Battery had been placed in position on rocky, marshy ground by one of Sickles' staff officers. General Charles Griffin, an old artilleryman, rode by and frowningly noted the poorly-chosen spot. 'Get that battery out of there,' he ordered. 'You can't live in that place five minutes.' Before the teams could come up it was too late. A Rebel charge swept forward. Lieutenant Aaron F. Walcott of the 3rd succeeded in spiking one of his pieces before the position was overrun" (117).

89 RICHMOND DAILY ENQUIRER, August 5, 1863.

90 Galliard, July 17, 1863 (36); Coxe, 435.

91 Bryan to McLaws, December 10, 1877, Southern Historical Collection.

92 Robert Carter, FOUR BROTHERS IN BLUE: A TRUE STORY OF THE GREAT CIVIL WAR FROM BULL RUN TO APPOMATTOX (Washington, D.C.: Gibson, 1913), 312-313.

93 McLaws, "Federal Disaster"; Lemon, 18. Coxe recorded a different story: "Wofford, seeing that night was near and that there were no supports on right or left or in the rear, and after surveying the hill through his field glasses ordered us to about face and fall back across the wheatfield . . . " (435). Marcus Green of Phillips' Legion stated in his diary: "Barksdale's Brigade gave way on our left and we had to fall back . . . " (6). Longstreet explained why he recalled them in "Lee in Pennsylvania," ANNALS OF WAR, 425-427.

94 Bryan to McLaws, December 10, 1877.

95 OR I, 27, pt 2, 363.

96 Lemon, 18.

97 Stewart, 425-429.

98 Carter, 324-325.

99 RICHMOND DAILY ENQUIRER, August 5, 1863.

100 Quoted in Doubleday, 188.

101 LEE'S LIEUTENANTS III, 144 ff.

102 "The Mistakes of Gettysburg," ANNALS OF WAR, 627.

103 Dickert, 246.

104 Stegeman, 95.

105 Mitchell, 21; RAMSEY VOLUNTEERS, 21.

106 RICHMOND DAILY ENQUIRER, August 5, 1864; Mitchell, 22; RAMSEY VOLUNTEERS, 21; Shockley to wife, July 13, 1863, Duke University.

107 ATHENS SOUTHERN WATCHMAN, August 5, 1863; OR I, 27, pt 2, 385.

108 Ibid; Folsom, 17.

109 CITIES AND CAMPFIRES OF THE CONFEDERATE STATES ed. Richard Harwell (Illinois: University of Illinois Press, 1958), 91. FROM MANASSAS TO APPOMATTOX, 431.

110 RAMSEY VOLUNTEERS, 22; Mitchell, 24.

111 Mitchell, 24.

112 "SMITE THEM HIP AND THIGH . . . ," 91.

113 Wofford Papers. It is not clear in his service record, which is fragmented, if Wofford returned home after hearing the news of his daughter's death. He was present with the Army in September when Longstreet's corps moved to Chickamauga (OR I, 29, pt 2, 711).

114 RAMSEY VOLUNTEERS, 24.

115 THE SOUTH CAROLINIANS: COLONEL ASBURY COWAN'S MEMOIRS ed. Natalie J. Bond and O. J. Coward (New York: Vantage, 1968), 83-84.

116 Mitchell, 25-26; Lemon, 19-20; OR I, 30, pt 4, 672.

117 Shockley to wife, September 18, 1863. See "SMITE THEM HIP AND THIGH . . . , " 60-69, for discussion of the Georgia Hospital and Relief Association.

[118] Barrett, 107; B. F. Redd of Phillips' Legion, in "McLaws' Division at Chickamauga," CONFEDERATE VETERAN 21 (1913), 585, stated that the Legion was in the fight of the 20th of September. Mitchell and Lemon do not confirm this in their diaries.

[119] Shockley to wife, September 26, 1863, Duke University.

[120] OR I, 29, pt 2, 743 and 753.

[121] Surgeon Myers' Diary, November 23, 1863.

[122] ATHENS SOUTHERN WATCHMAN, April 8, 1863. Peter R. Wallenstein, "From Slave South to New South: Taxes and Spending in Georgia From 1850 Through Reconstruction" (Ph.D. Dissertation, Johns Hopkins, 1973), 196-197.

[123] ATLANTA SOUTHERN CONFEDERACY, April 16, 1863.

[124] S. E. Ambrose, "Yeoman Discontent in the Confederacy," CIVIL WAR HISTORY 8 (September 1962), 261.

[125] Quoted in Steven Hahn, THE ROOTS OF SOUTHERN POPULISM: YEOMAN FARMERS AND THE TRANSFORMATION OF THE GEORGIA UPCOUNTRY, 1850-1890 (New York: Oxford. 1983), 127.

[126] Jonathan Sarris, "Anatomy of an Atrocity: The Madden Branch Massacre and Guerilla Warfare in North Georgia, 1861-1865," GEORGIA HISTORICAL QUARTERLY 77 (Winter 1993), 697.

[127] Robert E. Lee to Jefferson Davis, September 11, 1863, OR I, 29, pt 2, 711.

[128] Hahn, 130.

[129] R. S. Davis, Jr., "Memoirs of a Partisan War: Sion Darnell Remembers North Georgia, 1861-1865," GEORGIA HISTORICAL QUARTERLY 80 (Spring 1996), 93-116.

[130] Frank Klingberg, "The Southern Claims Commission: A Postwar Agency in Operation," MISSISSIPPI VALLEY HISTORICAL REVIEW 32 (Fall 1945), 196.

[131] "The Thomas G. Jordan Family During the War Between The States," GEORGIA HISTORICAL QUARTERLY 59 (1975), 137.

[132] RAMSEY VOLUNTEERS, 25.

[133] E. Porter Alexander, "Assault on Fort Sanders," BATTLES AND LEADERS III, 746.

[134] Ibid.; G. Moxley Sorrell, RECOLLECTIONS OF A CONFEDERATE STAFF OFFICER (Jackson, Tennessee: McCowat-Mercer, 1958), 199-200.

[135] Mitchell, 28.

[136] Lemon, 20; this gallant officer was later among the 600 Confederates who as prisoners of war were transported to Charleston, South Carolina, and placed deliberately in harm's way in 1864.

[137] Alexander, "Assault on Fort Sanders," 749.

[138] Mitchell, 30.

[139] Myers, November 29, 1863.

[140] Alexander, "Assault on Fort Sanders," 750-751; Mitchell, 32; Myers, December 4, 1863.

[141] Barrett, 114; Sorrell, 210; Folsom, 18; OR I, 31, 520.

[142] Myers, January 17, 1864.

[143] Ibid., January 10, 1863.

[144] Sorrell, 209.

[145] Myers, January 17, 1864.

[146] Shockley to wife, January 12, 1864, Duke University.

[147] James G. Flanigan, HISTORY OF GWINNETT COUNTY (Hapeville, Georgia: Tyler, 1943), 214. This tragedy is confirmed by the muster rolls of the 16th Georgia, Henderson II, 540-546.

[148] Barrett, 115; Galliard, March 27, 1863.

[149] Barrett, 116; the Federals also heard of the "Bread Riot" in Wofford's brigade (OR I, 33, 954).

[150] Shockley to wife, March 20, 1864, Duke University.

[151] Mitchell, 34-35; Dickert, 340.

[152] Galliard, April 24, 1864.

[153] John Everett, May 4, 1864, Confederate Miscellany, Woodruff Library, Emory.

[154] Dickert, 341; Mitchell, 35.

Footnotes

Chapter 6

1 BRUCE CATTON'S CIVIL WAR, 481-482.
2 Travis Hudson, "A History of the 59th Georgia Volunteer Infantry Regiment II," ATLANTA HISTORICAL JOURNAL 26 (Winter 1982-83), 20.
3 LEE'S LIEUTENANTS III, 346-347.
4 Mitchell, 35.
5 Ibid; "Sorrell's Field Diary," Ellen Brockenbrough Library, Museum of the Confederacy, June 15, 1864, 44.
6 OR I 36, pt 1, 1061.
7 "Sorrell's Field Diary," 45.
8 Mitchell, 35.
9 "Memoirs of Henry Heth II," CIVIL WAR HISTORY 8 (September 1962), 300-326.
10 Mitchell, 35; "Sorrell's Field Diary" stated " . . . a little after day" (45); Shockley to wife, May 16, 1864, stated " . . . about sunrise . . . " (Duke University).
11 BRUCE CATTON'S CIVIL WAR, 507.
12 GUNNER WITH STONEWALL: REMINISCENCES OF WILLIAM T. POAGUE ed. Monroe Cockrell (Jackson, Tennessee: McCowat-Mercer, 1957), 90.
13 Dickert, 345-346.
14 Shockley to wife, May 16, 1864, Duke University; Mitchell, 35.
15 ATLANTA SOUTHERN CONFEDERACY, June 15, 1864. Kershaw, in his report, OR I, 36 pt 1, 1061, stated that Wofford's Brigade was not involved in this counterattack. This does not square with the diaries and letters of Wofford's men. Wofford, unfortunately, did not leave a report.
16 Mitchell, 35. Hazard Stevens, "The Sixth Corps in the Wilderness," MASSACHUSETTS HISTORICAL SOCIETY PAPERS 4 ed. T. F. Dwight (Boston: Cadet Armory, 1895-1918), 197.
17 ACWORTH NEWS, August 28, 1887.

18 ATLANTA SOUTHERN CONFEDERACY, June 15, 1864. The writer of this article, unidentified, must have been one of Wofford's staff officers. His account of Wofford's suggestion of the flank attack is more detailed than Kershaw's in OR I, 36, pt 1, 1061. John Coxe of the 2nd South Carolina, in "Last Struggles and Successes of Lee," CONFEDERATE VETERAN 22 (1914), 356-359, stated that Wofford's Brigade, last in line as seen, actually advanced up the unfinished railroad grade after leaving the wagon train, thereby flanking the Federals early in the battle. This is not supported by other evidence. Also, from the maps, it is difficult to see how Wofford could have done it since the cut veered sharply away from the Federals at that point in the fight. Coxe's assertion has interesting possibilities, however, and in that tangled landscape, anything could have happened. If nothing else, Coxe lends credence to Wofford's knowledge of the railroad cut and his use of that information later that morning. E. A. Pollard, in HISTORY OF THE LOST CAUSE (New York: Treat, 1866), 392, states that late in the afternoon of that day, Wofford sought and obtained permission to flank the enemy and got in among the enemy's wagons. This is not supported. The one constant in all this is that it was indeed Wofford who suggested Longstreet's flank attack.

19 ACWORTH NEWS, August 28, 1887.

20 OR I, 36, pt 1, 1061.

21 LEE'S LIEUTENANTS III, 360-361.

22 Aurelia Austin, GEORGIA BOYS WITH STONEWALL (Athens: University of Georgia Press, 1967), 69.

23 "Sorrell's Field Diary," 42.

24 N. A. Trudeau, BLOODY ROADS SOUTH (Boston: Little, Brown, 1989), 101; Morris Schiaf, THE BATTLE OF THE WILDERNESS (Boston: Houghton Mifflin, 1910), 268.

25 ATLANTA SOUTHERN CONFEDERACY, June 15, 1864.

26 ACWORTH NEWS, August 28, 1887.

27 "Thomas G. Jordan Family," 138.

[28] "From Spottsylvania Court House to Andersonville: A Diary of Darius Stout," ed. Merton Coulter, GEORGIA HISTORICAL QUARTERLY 41 (June 1957), 181.

[29] "Sorrell's Field Diary," 46; Coxe, "Last Struggles and Successes of Lee . . . , " 357.

[30] Kershaw, OR I, 36, pt 1, 1062; Coxe, ibid., 356.

[31] E. M. Law, "From The Wilderness To Cold Harbor," BATTLES AND LEADERS IV, 126.

[32] Trudeau, 108.

[33] Alexander Webb, "Through The Wilderness," BATTLES AND LEADERS IV, 161.

[34] OR I, 36, pt 1, 1062.

[35] "Sorrell's Field Diary," 44.

[36] Hudson, 23.

[37] Mitchell, 35; "Sorrell's Field Diary," 43.

[38] LEE'S LIEUTENANTS III, 379-380.

[39] Coxe, "Last Struggles . . . , " 356.

[40] J. F. J. Caldwell, HISTORY OF A BRIGADE OF SOUTH CAROLINIANS (Philadelphia: King and Baird, 1866), 135-136.

[41] ATLANTA SOUTHERN CONFEDERACY, June 15, 1864; Shockley to wife, May 16, 1864, Duke University; "Sorrell's Field Diary," 44; OR 35, pt 1, 878.

[42] "Sorrell's Field Diary," 45; Webb, BATTLES AND LEADERS IV, 165.

[43] OR I, 36, pt 1, 1072; "Sorrell's Field Diary," 48.

[44] Shockley to wife, May 16, 1864, Duke University; ATLANTA SOUTHERN CONFEDERACY, June 16, 1864; FROM MANASSAS TO APPOMATTOX, 563.

[45] Shockley to wife, May 16, 1864, Duke University.

[46] Caldwell, 143.

[47] ACWORTH NEWS, August 28, 1887.

[48] Mitchell, 36.

[49] Richard Harwell, ed., "DEAR MOTHER DO NOT GRIEVE ABOUT ME. IF I AM KILLED, I'LL ONLY BE DEAD": LETTERS FROM GEORGIA SOLDIERS IN THE CIVIL WAR (Savannah, Georgia: Beehive, 1977), 296.

[50] Dickert, 370.

51 LEE'S LIEUTENANTS IV, 395.
52 A CAPTAIN'S WAR: THE LETTERS AND DIARIES OF WILLIAM H. S. BURGWYN 1861-1865, ed. H. M. Schiller (Shippensburg, Maryland: White Mane, 1994), 148.
53 Ibid.
54 A. J. Cone, "A Close Call," CONFEDERATE VETERAN 17 (1919), 372.
55 FIGHTING FOR THE CONFEDERACY: THE PERSONAL RECOLLECTIONS OF GENERAL EDWARD PORTER ALEXANDER ed. Gary Gallagher (Chapel Hill: University of North Carolina Press, 1989), 400-401.
56 Cone, 396.
57 Harwell, 297.
58 Mitchell, 35.
59 Cone, 396.
60 Burgwyn, 140; italics mine.
61 William Wallace, "Operations of 2nd South Carolina, 1864-65," SHSP 7 (1889), 129.
62 "Diary of the First Corps," OR I, 36, pt 1, 1060.
63 Dickert, 371.
64 "Sorrell's Field Diary," 56.
65 Ibid.
66 Gerald J. Smith, "Kershaw's Salient," MILITARY HISTORY TBA.
67 Robert Stiles, FOUR YEARS UNDER MARSE ROBERT (New York: Neale, 1908), 290.
68 Mitchell, 37.
69 W. F. Smith, "The Eighteenth Corps at Cold Harbor," BATTLES AND LEADERS IV, 225.
70 SAVANNAH MORNING NEWS, June 13, 1898.
71 FIGHTING FOR THE CONFEDERACY, 406.
72 Harwell, 298.
73 Wofford Service Record, Wofford Papers.
74 Dwight, 393.
75 Reid Mitchell, CIVIL WAR SOLDIERS (New York: Touchstone, 1988), 141.
76 Wofford Papers.

77 Ibid.

78 Folsom, 19. Folsom's HEROES AND MARTYRS is actually a compilation of regimental histories written by participants in each unit. They wrote while the events of the war were fresh; the writer of the 18th Georgia article had recently been in the Wilderness battle and knew what he was talking about.

79 Mitchell, 40.

80 Ibid.

81 "Thomas H. Jordan Family," 138-139.

82 RAMSEY VOLUNTEERS, 28-29.

83 F. W. Dawson, REMINISCENCES OF CONFEDERATE SERVICE 1861-1865 ed. Bell I. Wiley (Baton Rouge: LSU Press, 1980), 121.

84 Service Record, Wofford Papers. Wofford was not present at the disaster at Cedar Creek, October 19, 1864. He received payment for his lost bay the following January.

Footnotes

Chapter 7

[1] Quoted in MURRAY COUNTY HERITAGE compiled by the Murray County Historical Committee (Roswell, Georgia: Wolfe, 1987), 71.

[2] Charles Wells, ARMY LIFE OF AN ILLINOIS SOLDIER (Washington, D.C.: Neale, 1906), 112. Mahan, 120-125, discusses the situation fully.

[3] LETTERS OF WARREN AKIN, 64-65.

[4] Bell I. Wiley, "Confederate Letters of John W. Hagan," GEORGIA HISTORICAL QUARTERLY 38 (1954), 196.

[5] Akin, 65. According to Akin (61), Major General Howell Cobb had sent provisions to the affected counties. Whether Wofford approached Cobb about this is unknown, but such would have been consistent with Wofford's nature.

[6] NEW YORK TIMES, January 18, 1865. RICHMOND DAILY DISPATCH, January 26, 1865, quoted the ATLANTA APPEAL: "If one half the men of the Confederacy capable of bearing arms would cease to shirk their duty . . . and . . . come to the front we could expel the invaders from our soil within six weeks." See also Paul Escott, "Southern Yeomen and the Confederacy," MAJOR PROBLEMS IN THE CIVIL WAR AND RECONSTRUCTION ed. Michael Perman (Lexington, Massachusetts: Heath, 1991), 304.

[7] Akin, 148.

[8] Ibid., 66.

[9] ACWORTH NEWS, August 8, 1887.

[10] Akin, 66.

[11] Wofford Papers.

[12] Ibid.

[13] Ibid.

[14] Ibid.

[15] Ibid.

[16] Ibid.

[17] Ibid.

18 Akin, 86.

19 OR I, 49, pt 1, 977-978.

20 Akin, 93.

21 Henderson II, 519, 561; III, 30.

22 Mitchell, 51-52; CONFEDERATE MILITARY HISTORY 6 ed. Clement A. Evans (Atlanta: Confederate Publishing Company, 1889), 647.

23 THE WARTIME JOURNAL OF A GEORGIA GIRL ed. Spencer B. King, Jr. (Macon: Ardivan, 1960), 85, 130.

24 Bragg, 115.

25 OR I, 49, pt 1, 962-963.

26 Ibid., 962.

27 OR I, 46, pt 3, 1356.

28 Ibid., 1355.

29 Ibid., 1357.

30 Bryan, 140.

31 Cunyus, 243-244; George M. Bates, HISTORY OF ROME AND FLOYD COUNTY (Atlanta: Webb and Young, 1922), 205-209; OR I, 49, pt 2, 606; Bryan, 152.

32 MURRAY COUNTY HERITAGE, 77-78.

33 Bragg, 115.

34 Bryan, 155.

35 OR I, 49, pt 2, 456, 469. General George M. Thomas wished to avoid useless bloodshed also but was ready if need be. When he received a report on April 18, 1865, of a planned raid by Wofford, he replied: " . . . if he makes the attempt I will so despoil Georgia that 50 years hence it will be a wilderness" (OR I, 49, pt 2, 396). Thomas did not make idle threats. Wofford assured him it was rumor (Ibid., 456).

36 Ibid., 355. The Peace Movement in Georgia, 1864-1865, engineered by Alexander H. Stephens and Governor Brown, was a widespread attempt to, as Wofford intimated, bring Georgia back into the Union, regardless of Davis and the Confederate government. Historians have not been kind to Brown and Stephens about this. See E. M. Coulter, CONFEDERATE STATES OF AMERICA (Baton Rouge: LSU Press,

1950), 533-544; John E. Talmadge, "Peace-Movement Activities in Civil War Georgia," GEORGIA REVIEW 7 (Summer 1958), 190-203; Bryan, 172-173. For a cogent discussion of the impact of peace movements and religion on morale, see Richard E. Beringer, et. al., WHY THE SOUTH LOST THE CIVIL WAR (Athens: University of Georgia Press, 1986), 268-293.

[37] OR I, 49, pt 2, 380.

[38] Ibid., 1062.

[39] Temple, 368. " . . . the white women would come in Mother's yard in the broad daylight and steal peaches and apples . . . , " wrote a Rome citizen, March 11, 1865 (quoted in S. V. Ash, "Poor Whites in the Occupied South," JOURNAL OF SOUTHERN HISTORY 58 [February 1991], 53).

[40] Akin, 65; OR I, 49, pt 2, 963.

[41] OR I, 49, pt 2, 361.

[42] Ibid., 418.

[43] Ibid., 428, 463, 473.

[44] Ibid., 488.

[45] Ibid., 569-570.

[46] Wofford Papers.

[47] OR I 49, pt 2, 723-724. Robert MaGill, PERSONAL REMINISCENCES OF A CONFEDERATE SOLDIER BOY (Milledgeville: Boyd, 1993), 66.

[48] OR I, 49, pt 2, 605.

[49] Ibid., 768. Wofford signed the amnesty oath, July 29, 1865, one of the earliest Confederate officers to do so; a copy is in the Wofford Papers.

[50] Ibid., 591.

[51] Ibid., 736-737.

[52] Ibid., 485-486.

[53] Ibid., 492.

[54] AFTER THE WAR: A TOUR OF THE SOUTHERN STATES 1865-1866 (New York: Harper, 1984), 360-361.

[55] OR I, 49, pt 2, 493.

[56] Ibid., 1052.

Footnotes

Chapter 8

1 OR I, 49, pt 2, 1052.
2 ACWORTH NEWS, August 28, 1887.
3 Ibid.
4 Wofford Papers.
5 GEORGIA A SHORT HISTORY, 360-361.
6 Quoted in Sidney Andrews, THE SOUTH SINCE THE WAR (Boston: Houghton, Mifflin, 1971), 329-330. The NEW YORK TIMES, December 10, 1865, wrote that Wofford was " . . . a Union man at heart, a true friend, and a Christian gentleman."
7 GEORGIA A SHORT HISTORY, 361.
8 Ibid., 364; Avery, 351.
9 Reid, 436.
10 DICTIONARY OF AMERICAN BIOGRAPHY 5 ed. Dumas Malone (New York: Scribners, 1933), 299-300.
11 DAB 22, 44.
12 Wofford Papers.
13 CONFEDERATE RECORDS OF GEORGIA 4 (Atlanta: Byrd, 1911), 107.
14 GEORGIA A SHORT HISTORY, 349. See also J. B. McGehee, AUTOBIOGRAPHY (Buena Vista, Georgia: Weaver, 1916), 130-131. The years of 1865, 1866, and 1867 also saw disastrous crop failures in Georgia, exacerbating the poverty (Willard Range, A CENTURY OF GEORGIA AGRICULTURE 1850-1950 [Athens: University of Georgia Press, 1954], 84).
15 Wofford Papers.
16 Ibid.
17 Kelley to Wofford, March 14, 1880, Wofford Papers.
18 Cunyus, 169-170. This railroad, changed to Cherokee Railroad Commission in 1870, lasted until 1878, when it was sold at public auction. See also Mildred Thompson, RECONSTRUCTION IN GEORGIA (Savannah: Beehive, 1972), 86-87; 96-97.

19 Census, Bartow County, 1880.

20 Avery, 335.

21 GEORGIA A SHORT HISTORY, 364-365.

22 Cunyus, 249. The Amendment was ratified July 21, 1868.

23 J. C. Carter, MAGNOLIA JOURNEY (Tuscaloosa, Alabama: University of Alabama Press, 1974), 154.

24 L. M. Holland, PIERCE M. B. YOUNG: THE WARWICK OF THE SOUTH (Athens: University of Georgia Press, 1964), 118-119. See also Holland's "PMB Young and the Restoration of Sovereignty to Georgia," EMORY UNIVERSITY QUARTERLY 7 (June 1951), 143-150.

25 ACTS AND RESOLUTIONS 1871 (Atlanta: Hemphill, 1872). 183-184.

26 ATLANTA SUN, December 4, 1871.

27 Small, 114.

28 J. C. Edwards, "Georgia's Political Schism in 1872: Two Letters," GEORGIA HISTORICAL QUARTERLY 56 (Fall 1972), 432. See also Judson C. Ward, Jr., "The New Departure Democrats of Georgia: An Interpretation," GEORGIA HISTORICAL QUARTERLY 41 (September 1957), 227-236.

29 Edwards, 432. See also Michael Perman, "The Forked Road to Redemption 1873-1876," THE ROAD TO REDEMPTION: SOUTHERN POLITICS 1869-1879, 149-177.

30 "National Party Conventions 1831-1972," CONGRESSIONAL QUARTERLY (May 1976), 23.

31 Ibid., 133.

32 Edwards, 436.

33 Avery, 468.

34 Cunyus, 150-151.

35 ACTS AND RESOLUTIONS 1876 (Atlanta: Harrison, 1877), 331.

36 DICTIONARY OF GEORGIA BIOGRAPHY II, ed. Kenneth Coleman and C. S. Garr (Athens: University of Georgia Press, 1983), 1077.

37 "National Party Conventions," 134.

38 Ibid.

[39] AUGUSTA CHRONICLE AND SENTINEL, September 7, 1876; Derrell Roberts, JOSEPH E. BROWN AND THE POLITICS OF RECONSTRUCTION (Tuscaloosa: University of Alabama Press, 1973), 83-85; Francis B. Simkins, A HISTORY OF THE SOUTH (New York; Knopf, 1963), 232-294.

[40] Schott, 504-505.

[41] John Stevenson, "The Georgia Convention of 1877," (Unpublished paper, Western Carolina University, 1994), 23; W. P. Brandon, "Calling the Georgia Constitutional Convention of 1877," GEORGIA HISTORICAL QUARTERLY 17 (September 1933), 194.

[42] THE LUMPKIN INDEPENDENT, September 5, 1876.

[43] ATLANTA CONSTITUTION, June 28, 1877; SAVANNAH MORNING NEWS, September 2, 1876.

[44] Stevenson, 23.

[45] Evans, 315; Brandon, 203; Rebecca L. Felton, MY MEMOIRS OF GEORGIA POLITICS (Atlanta: Index, 1911), 174; Small, 103.

[46] Small, 102-103; Eugene Mitchell, "H. I. Kimball: His Career and Its Defense," ATLANTA HISTORICAL BULLETIN 3 (October 1938), 253.

[47] Small, 35.

[48] Evans, 310.

[49] Small, 65.

[50] Ibid.

[51] GEORGIA A SHORT HISTORY, 381.

[52] Small, 70.

[53] Ibid., 71.

[54] Ibid., 103.

[55] Ibid., 228 It is supreme irony that in the antebellum period, Toombs and company pointed out with pride how the South had actually civilized the Negro and rescued him from savagery ("SMITE THEM HIP AND THIGH . . . ", 15-16).

[56] AUGUSTA CHRONICLE, January 12, 1877.

[57] Small, 434.

[58] Ibid., 440.   Matthew I. Mancini studies the lease system in ONE DIES GET ANOTHER: CONVICT LEASING IN THE AMERICAN SOUTH 1866-1928, Columbia, South Carolina:

University of South Carolina Press, 1996.   See also Elizabeth Taylor, "Convict Lease System," GEORGIA HISTORICAL QUARTERLY 26 (March 1942), 113-128.

[59] GEORGIA A SHORT HISTORY, 398.

[60] Small, 296.

[61] Ibid.

[62] Ibid.

[63] Ibid., 319-321.

[64] ACWORTH NEWS, August 28, 1887.

[65] "National Party Conventions," 55.

[66] ACWORTH NEWS, August 28, 1887.

[67] LAGRANGE DAILY REPORTER, September 16, 1880;   Felton, MY MEMOIRS . . . , 273.

[68] ACWORTH NEWS, August 28, 1887;
ATLANTA CONSTITUTION, May 24, 1884.

BIBLIOGRAPHY

I.   Primary Sources

A.   Manuscript Collections

Confederate Research Center, Hillsboro, Texas
        Nicholas Pomeroy, Memoir, 5th Texas
        P. A. Work, Memoir, First Texas
Eleanor Brockenbrough Library, Museum of the Confederacy,
        Richmond, Virginia
        Robert Myers, Diary, 16th Georgia
        Moxley Sorrell, Diary, Longstreet's Staff
Duke University Library, Durham, North Carolina
        William S. Shockley, Letters, 18th Georgia
Emory University, Woodruff Library, Atlanta, Georgia
        John W. Burke, Diary
        Confederate Miscellany
        William Dobbins, Letters, Phillips' Legion
        John Everett, 11th Georgia
        Rebecca Hood, Papers, 18th Georgia
        B. L. Mobley, Letters, Cobb's Legion
        Henry Robinson, Letters
        "Spirit of 1861," Camp Newspaper, 18th Georgia
        Alexander H. Stephens, Letters
Georgia Department of Archives and History
        J. S. Beazley, M.D., Papers, Wofford's physician
        Joseph E. Brown, Letters, Governor
        Confederate Letters, Diaries, Memoirs:
                Robert McMillan, Memoirs, 24th Georgia
                R. A. Quinn, Memoirs, 18th Georgia
                J. J. O'Neill, Memoirs, 18th Georgia
        Wofford Family, Geneaology File
Kennesaw Mountain National Military Park
        Marcus Green, Diary, Phillips' Legion

Manassas National Military Park
    David Hamer, "One Man's War," 10th New York
National Archives
    "Letters Received by the Confederate Secretary of War
    1861-1865," Record Group 10785
New York Historical Society
    Alfred Davenport, Letters, 5th New York
New Hampshire Historical Society
    John Bachelder Papers
Private Collections
    Dwight Harley, Jr., Wofford Papers
    Mark Lemon, James Lemon Diary, 18th Georgia
    Robert Rybolt, Howell Cobb Letters
    Gerald J. Smith, E. J. Eldridge Letter, 16th Georgia
    Robert Thomas, T. M. Mitchell, Diary, Phillips' Legion
South Carolina Historical Society
    T. C. Albergotti, "Memoir," Hampton's Legion
Southern Historical Collection, University of North Carolina
    Franklin Galliard Letters, 2nd South Carolina
    LaFayette McLaws Papers
    George G. Smith, "Autobiography," Phillips' Legion

B.   Printed Sources

1.   Newspapers

ACWORTH NEWS
ATLANTA APPEAL
ATLANTA CONSTITUTION
ATLANTA SOUTHERN CONFEDERACY
ATLANTA SUN
ATHENS SOUTHERN BANNER
ATHENS SOUTHERN WATCHMAN
AUGUSTA CHRONICLE
AUGUSTA DAILY CHRONICLE AND SENTINEL
CARTERSVILLE EXPRESS
CARTERSVILLE TRIBUNE
CASSVILLE PIONEER
CASSVILLE STANDARD
LAGRANGE DAILY REPORTER
LAVONIA TIMES AND GAUGE
LONDON TIMES
LUMPKIN INDEPENDENT
NEW YORK TIMES
PHILADELPHIA WEEKLY PRESS
RICHMOND DAILY DISPATCH
RICHMOND EXAMINER
RICHMOND SENTINEL
RICHMOND WHIG
ROME (GEORGIA) COURIER
SAVANNAH MORNING NEWS

2.   Official Publications

ACTS AND RESOLUTIONS OF THE GENERAL
        ASSEMBLY OF GEORGIA 1834-1877
        (Various Publishers).
CONFEDERATE RECORDS OF GEORGIA.
        Atlanta: Bond, 1911.
JOURNAL OF THE CONVENTION AT MILLEDGEVILLE
        AND SAVANNAH 1861.
        Milledgeville: Boughton, Nisbet, and Barnes, 1861.
JOURNAL OF THE HOUSE OF REPRESENTATIVES OF THE
        STATE OF GEORGIA 1850-1877
        (Various Publishers).
ROSTER OF THE CONFEDERATE SOLDIERS OF GEORGIA
        6 Vols.
        Compiled by Lillian Henderson.
        Hapeville: Longino and Porter,
        1956-1960.
A STENOGRAPHIC REPORT OF THE PROCEEDINGS OF THE
        CONVENTION HELD IN ATLANTA, GEORGIA 1877.
        ed. Samuel Small. Atlanta: Constitution
        Publishing Company, 1877.
UNITED STATES BUREAU OF THE CENSUS.
        SEVENTH, EIGHTH AND NINTH
        CENSUS RECORDS.   1850-1870.
THE WAR OF THE REBELLION: A COMPILATION OF THE
        OFFICIAL RECORDS OF THE UNION AND
        CONFEDERATE ARMIES. ed. Robert N.
        Scott. Washington, D.C.: Government
        Printing Office, 1888.

C.   Other Printed Sources

1.   Articles

Akin, Sally Mae. "Refugees of 1863,"
        GEORGIA HISTORICAL QUARTERLY 31
        (June 1947), 114-115.
Alexander, Edward P. "Assault on Fort Sanders."
        BATTLES AND LEADERS OF THE CIVIL
        WAR III. eds. R. U. Johnston and C. C.
        Buell. New York, 1885-1887.
Anonymous. "Sharpshooting in Lee's Army,"
        CONFEDERATE VETERAN 3 (1895), 98.
Brooks, R. P. "The Howell Cobb Papers," GEORGIA
        HISTORICAL QUARTERLY 6 (1922), 35-84.
Cone, A. J. "A Close Call," CONFEDERATE
        VETERAN 27 (1919), 372. (18th Georgia)
_____ "Georgians in Hood's Texas Brigade,"
        CONFEDERATE VETERAN (1911), 1.
_____ "Hanging a Federal Spy,"
        CONFEDERATE VETERAN 10 (1902), 30.
Coulter, E. M., ed. "From Spottsylvania Court
        House to Andersonville," GEORGIA
        HISTORICAL   QUARTERLY 41 (June 1957), 177-190.
"Confederate Brigadiers in Congress,"
        CONFEDERATE VETERAN 10 (1897), 528-529.
Coxe, John. "The Battle of Gettysburg,"
        CONFEDERATE VETERAN 21 (1913), 433-436.
        (3rd South Carolina)
_____ "Last Struggles and Successes of Lee,"
        CONFEDERATE VETERAN 22 (1914), 356-357.
Davis, R. S., Jr. "Memoirs of a Partisan War: Sion
        Darnell Remembers North Georgia 1861-1865,"
        GEORGIA HISTORICAL QUARTERLY 80
        (Spring 1996), 93-116.
DeBow, James D. B. "Late Southern Convention at Montgomery,"
        DEBOW'S REVIEW 24 (June 1858), 574-606.

_____ "Southern Convention at Montgomery Alabama,"
DEBOW'S REVIEW 24 (May 1858), 424-428.

_____ "The Rights, Duties, and Remedies of the South,"
DEBOW'S REVIEW 23 (September 1857), 235-236.

Dent, Stephen. "With Cobb's Brigade at Fredericksburg,"
CONFEDERATE VETERAN 22 (1914), 550-551.

Flippen, P. S. ed. "From the Autobiography of Herschel V.
Johnson 1856-1867,"
AMERICAN HISTORICAL REVIEW 30
(January 1925), 311-336.

Gaines, Lizzie. "We Begged to Hearts of Stone:
The Wartime Journal of Cassville's Lizzie
Gaines," NORTHWEST GEORGIAN 20 (1988), 1-6.

Haight, Theron. "Gainesville, Groveton, and Bull Run,"
WAR PAPERS READ BEFORE THE   COMMANDARY
OF THE STATE OF WISCONSIN, MILITARY ORDER OF
THE LOYAL LEGION OF THE UNITED STATES II.
Wisconsin: Millvan, 1896.

Hamby, W. R. "Hood's Texas Brigade at Sharpsburg,"
CONFEDERATE VETERAN 16 (1908), 20-24.

Hassler, William S. ed. "Civil War Letters of General William
Dorsey Pender to His Wife," GEORGIA REVIEW 17
(Spring 1963), 57-75.

Henderson, Donald. "General Hood's Brigade,"
SOUTHERN HISTORICAL SOCIETY PAPERS 29
(1901), 300-301.

Heth, Henry. "Memoirs of Henry Heath II,"
James L. Morrison, Jr. ed. CIVIL WAR HISTORY 8
(September 1862), 300-326.

Hill, W. T. "First Troops Through Thoroughfare
Gap," CONFEDERATE VETERAN 23 (1915), 544-545.

Kershaw, Joseph. "Kershaw's Brigade at Gettysburg,"
BATTLES AND LEADERS III, 331-339.

Law, Evander. "From the Wilderness to Cold Harbor,"
BATTLES AND LEADERS IV, 118-144.

_____ "The Virginia Campaign of 1862,"
PHILADELPHIA WEEKLY PRESS,
October 26 and November 2, 1887.
Lawley, Francis. "Battles of Gettysburg,"
LONDON TIMES, August 18, 1863.
Longstreet, James. "The Campaign of Gettysburg,"
PHILADELPHIA WEEKLY TIMES November 3, 1877.
_____ "General Longstreet's Account of the Campaign
and Battle," SOUTHERN HISTORICAL SOCIETY
PAPERS 5 (1878), 54-85.
_____ "Lee in Pennsylvania," ANNALS OF WAR.
Philadelphia: Times Publishing, 1879, 414-446.
_____ "Lee's Invasion of Pennsylvania,"
BATTLES AND LEADERS III , 244-251.
_____ "Lee's Right Wing at Gettysburg,"
BATTLES AND LEADERS III , 339-354.
_____ "Letter From General Longstreet,"
SOUTHERN HISTORICAL SOCIETY
PAPERS 5 (1878), 52-53.
_____ "The Mistakes of Gettysburg,"
PHILADELPHIA WEEKLY TIMES, February 23, 1878.
Mclaws, LaFayette. "The Battle of Gettysburg,"
PHILADELPHIA WEEKLY PRESS. April 21, 1886.
_____ "The Federal Disaster on the Left,"
PHILADELPHIA WEEKLY PRESS, August 4, 1886.
_____ "Gettysburg," SOUTHERN HISTORICAL
SOCIETY PAPERS 7 (1879), 64-90.
_____ "McLaw's Division and the Pennsylvania
Reserves," PHILADELPHIA WEEKLY
PRESS, October 20, 1886.
Purifoy, John. "Longstreet's Attack at Gettysburg,"
CONFEDERATE VETERAN 31 (1923), 292-294.
_____ "The Splendid Valor Shown at Gettysburg,"
CONFEDERATE VETERAN   34 (1926), 17-19.
Redd, B. F. "McLaws' Division at Chickamauga,"
CONFEDERATE VETERAN 21 (1913), 585-586.
(Phillips' Legion)

Sanders, C. C. "Chancellorsville," SOUTHERN HISTORICAL
    SOCIETY PAPERS (1921),166-172. (Cobb's Legion)
Stevens, Hazard. "The Sixth Corps in the Wilderness,"
    MASSACHUSETTS HISTORICAL SOCIETY PAPERS
    4 ed. T. F. Dwight. Boston: Cadett Armory, 1895-1918.
Todd, G. T. "Recollections of Gettysburg,"
    CONFEDERATE VETERAN 8 (1900), 240. (18th Georgia)
Webb, Alexander. "Through The Wilderness,"
    BATTLES AND LEADERS IV, 152-169.
Wallace, William. "Operations of 2nd South Carolina 1864-65,"
    SOUTHERN HISTORICAL SOCIETY PAPERS 7 (1889),
    128-131.
White, M. E. "The Thomas G. Jordan Family During the War
    Between The States," GEORGIA HISTORICAL
    QUARTERLY 59 (1975), 134-140. (24th Georgia)
Williams, F. B., Jr. "From Sumter to The Wilderness:
    Letters of Sergeant James Butler Suddath," SOUTH
    CAROLINA HISTORICAL MAGAZINE 63
    (April 1962), 93-104. (7th South Carolina)
Young, John D. "A Campaign with Sharpshooters,"
    ANNALS OF WAR, 267-287.
Youngblood, William. "Personal Observations at Gettysburg,"
    CONFEDERATE VETERAN 19 (1911), 286-287.

2.   Books

Alexander, E. P. FIGHTING FOR THE CONFEDERACY:
    PERSONAL RECOLLECTIONS OF GENERAL E.
    PORTER ALEXANDER. ed. Gary Gallagher. Chapel
    Hill: University of North Carolina Press, 1989.
Andrews, Eliza Frances. WARTIME JOURNAL OF A
    GEORGIA GIRL. ed. Spencer King, Jr. Macon:
    Ardivan, 1960.
Andrews, Sidney. THE SOUTH SINCE THE WAR.
    Boston: Houghton Mifflin, 1971.
Andrews, W. H. FOOTPRINTS OF A REGIMENT:
    A RECOLLECTION OF THE FIRST GEORGIA REGULARS.
    Atlanta: Longstreet, 1992.
Austin, Aurelia. GEORGIA BOYS WITH STONEWALL.
    Athens: University of Georgia Press, 1967.
Avery, I. W. THE HISTORY OF THE STATE OF GEORGIA
    FROM 1850 TO 1881 EMBRACING THE THREE
    IMPORTANT   EPOCHS: THE DECADE BEFORE THE
    WAR 1861-1865; THE WAR; THE PERIOD OF
    RECONSTRUCTION WITH PORTRAITS OF THE
    LEADING PUBLIC MEN OF THIS ERA. New York:
    Derby, 1881.
Von Borcke, Heros. MEMOIRS OF THE CONFEDERATE WAR
    FOR INDEPENDENCE. New York: Smith, 1938.
Bigelow, John. THE PEACH ORCHARD, GETTYSBURG, JULY
    2, 1863. Minneapolis: Kimball-Stoner, 1910.
Bond, Nathan J. and O. J. Coward eds. THE SOUTH
    CAROLINIANS: COLONEL ASBURY COWAN'S
    MEMOIRS. New York: Vantage, 1968.
    (2nd South Carolina)
Caldwell, J. F. J. A HISTORY OF A BRIGADE OF SOUTH
    CAROLINIANS. Philadelphia: King and Baird, 1866.
Carter, Robert. FOUR BROTHERS IN BLUE: A TRUE STORY
    OF THE GREAT CIVIL WAR FROM BULL RUN TO
    APPOMATTOX. Washington, D. C.: Gibson, 1913.

Cockrell, Monroe, ed. GUNNER WITH STONEWALL:
    REMINISCENCES OF WILLIAM T. POAGUE. Jackson,
    Tennessee: McCowat-Mercer Press, 1957.
Cowtan, Charles. SERVICE OF THE TENTH NEW YORK
    VOLUNTEERS (NATIONAL ZOUAVES) IN THE WAR
    OF THE REBELLION. New York: Ludwig, 1882.
Dawes, Rufus. SERVICE WITH THE SIXTH WISCONSIN
    VOLUNTEERS. Dayton, Ohio: Morningside, 1984.
Dawson, F. H. REMINISCENCES OF CONFEDERATE
    SERVICE 1861-1865. ed. Bell Wiley. Baton Rouge:
    LSU Press, 1980.
Dickert, Augustus. HISTORY OF KERSHAW'S BRIGADE.
    Newberry, South Carolina: Aull, 1899.
Doubleday, Abner. CHANCELLORSVILLE AND
    GETTYSBURG CAMPAIGNS OF THE CIVIL WAR.
    New York: Blue and Gray, 1955.
Evans, Clement. CONFEDERATE MILITARY HISTORY 6.
    Atlanta: Confederate Publishing, 1889.
Everett, Donald. CHAPLAIN NICHOLAS DAVIS AND
    HOOD'S TEXAS BRIGADE. San Antonio:
    Principia, 1962.
Everson, Guy and E. W. Simpson, Jr. "FAR, FAR FROM
    HOME": THE WARTIME LETTERS OF DICK AND
    TALLY SIMPSON THIRD SOUTH CAROLINA
    VOLUNTEERS. New York: Oxford, 1994.
Felton, Rebecca L. MY MEMOIRS OF GEORGIA POLITICS.
    Atlanta: Index, 1911.
Figg, R. W. "WHERE MEN ONLY DARE TO GO!" OR THE
    STORY OF A BOY COMPANY BY AN EX-BOY.
    Richmond: Whittet and Shepperson, 1885.
Fletcher, William. REBEL PRIVATE FRONT AND REAR. ed.
    Bell Wiley. Washington D.C.: Zenger, 1985.
    (5th Texas)
Folsom, J. M. HEROES AND MARTYRS OF GEORGIA:
    GEORGIA'S RECORD IN THE REVOLUTION OF 1861.
    Macon: Burke and Boykin, 1864.

Fremantle, A. J. THREE MONTHS IN THE SOUTHERN
    STATES. Edinburgh and London, 1863.
Giles, Valmor. RAGS AND HOPE: RECOLLECTIONS OF
    VAL C. GILES. New York: Cowart-McCann, 1961.
    (4th Texas)
Harwell, Richard, ed. "DEAR MOTHER DO NOT GRIEVE
    ABOUT ME. IF I AM KILLED, I'LL ONLY BE DEAD":
    LETTERS FROM GEORGIA SOLDIERS IN THE CIVIL WAR.
    Savannah: Beehive Press, 1977.
Heller, J. R., III and Carolyn Heller. THE CONFEDERACY IS
    ON HER WAY UP THE SPOUT: LETTERS TO SOUTH
    CAROLINA 1861-1864. Athens: University of Georgia
    Press, 1992. (18th Georgia)
Holley, Thomas. RAMSEY VOLUNTEERS THE SIXTEENTH
    GEORGIA INFANTRY REGIMENT ARMY OF NORTHERN
    VIRGINIA C.S.A. Fernandino Beach, Florida: Wolfe, 1995.
Hood, John Bell. ADVANCE AND RETREAT.
    New Orleans: Hood Orphan Relief Fund, 1880.
Longstreet, James. FROM MANASSAS TO APPOMATTOX.
    Philadelphia: Lippencott, 1896.
MaGill, Robert. PERSONAL REMINISCENCES OF A
    CONFEDERATE SOLDIER BOY.
    Milledgeville: Boyd, 1993.
McGehee, J. B. AUTOBIOGRAPHY. Buena Vista, Georgia:
    Weaver, 1915.
Morgan, Dorothy Jones. A VERY PERSONAL GLIMPSE OF THE
    CIVIL WAR ERA FROM 1849-1863. Self-published, 1993.
Pollard, E. A. A HISTORY OF THE LOST CAUSE. New York:
    Treat, 1866.
Polley, J. B. HOOD'S TEXAS BRIGADE: ITS MARCHES, ITS
    BATTLES, ITS ACHIEVEMENTS.
    Dayton: Morningside, 1988.
_____ A SOLDIER'S LETTERS TO CHARMING NELLIE.
    New York: Meade, 1908. (4th Texas)
Priest, J. M. ed. STEPHEN ELLIOTT WELCH OF THE
    HAMPTON LEGION.
    Shippensburg, Maryland: Burd Street, 1994.

Reid, Whitlaw. AFTER THE WAR: A TOUR OF THE
    SOUTHERN STATES, 1865-1866.
    New York: Harper, 1963.
Roberson, Elizabeth. WEEP NOT FOR ME DEAR MOTHER.
    Washington, North Carolina: Venture, 1991.
    (18th Georgia).
Ross, Fitzgerald. CITIES AND CAMPFIRES OF THE
    CONFEDERATE STATES.
    ed. Richard Harwell. Urbana, Illinois:
    University of Illinois Press, 1958.
Schiller, H. M., ed. A CAPTAIN'S WAR: THE LETTERS AND
    DIARIES OF WILLIAM H. S. BURGWYN 1861-1865.
    Shippensburg: White Mane, 1994. (31st North Carolina)
Shaw, Robert Gould. BLUE-EYED CHILD OF FORTUNE:
    LETTERS OF ROBERT GOULD SHAW. ed. Russell
    Duncan. Athens: University of Georgia Press, 1992.
Sherwood, Adiel. GAZATEER OF GEORGIA.
    Atlanta: Richards, 1860.
Small, Samuel. BRIEF BIOGRAPHIES OF THE MEMBERS OF
    THE CONSTITUTIONAL CONVENTION 1877. Atlanta:
    Constitution Publishing, 1877.
Smith, Gerald J. "I'M GOING WHETHER YOU SWEAR ME IN
    OR NOT!" DIARIES, LETTERS, AND   REMINISCENCES OF
    THE UNION AND THE CONFEDERACY.
    Murfreesboro, Tennessee: Ambassador, 1995.
Sorrell, Moxley. RECOLLECTIONS OF A CONFEDERATE
    STAFF OFFICER.
    Jackson, Tennessee: McCowat-Mercer, 1958.
Stegeman, John. THESE MEN SHE GAVE: CIVIL WAR DIARY
    OF ATHENS,   GEORGIA. Athens: University of
    Georgia Press, 1964.
Stevens, J. W. REMINISCENCES OF THE CIVIL WAR.
    Hillsboro, Texas: Hillsboro Mirror Print, 1902.
    (5th Texas)
Stewart, Robert I. HISTORY OF THE ONE HUNDRED AND
    FORTIETH REGIMENT PENNSYLVANIA
    VOLUNTEERS. Philadelphia: Franklin, 1912.

Stiles, Robert. FOUR YEARS WITH MARSE ROBERT.
New York: Neale, 1908.
Survivors' Association. HISTORY OF THE CORN EXCHANGE
REGIMENT 118TH PENNSYLVANIA VOLUNTEERS.
Philadelphia: Smith, 1885.
Sutton, Elijah H. GRANDPA'S WAR STORIES.
Demorest, Georgia: n.p.n.d. (24th Georgia)
VOICES OF THE CIVIL WAR: SECOND MANASSAS.
Alexandria, Virginia: Time Life, 1996.
Wells, Charles. ARMY LIFE OF AN ILLINOIS SOLDIER.
Washington, D.C.: Neale, 1906.
Wiley, Bell I. ed. CONFEDERATE LETTERS OF JOHN W.
HAGAN. Athens: University of Georgia Press, 1958.
_____ LETTERS OF WARREN AKIN CONFEDERATE
CONGRESSMAN.
Athens: University of Georgia Press, 1959.

II.   Secondary Sources

1.   Articles

Ambrose, Stephen. "Yeoman Discontent in the Confederacy,"
    CIVIL WAR HISTORY 8 (September 1962), 259-268.
Ashe, S. V. "Poor Whites in the Occupied South," JOURNAL
    OF SOUTHERN HISTORY 58 (February 1991), 39-62.
Brandon, W. P. "Calling the Georgia Constitutional Convention
    of 1877," GEORGIA HISTORICAL QUARTERLY 17
    (September 1933), 189-203.
Brooks, R. P. "Howell Cobb and the Crisis of 1850,"
    MISSISSIPPI VALLEY HISTORICAL REVIEW 4
    (December 1917), 279-298.
Coffman, Richard. "A Vital Unit (Phillips' Legion)," CIVIL
    WAR TIMES ILLUSTRATED 20 (January 1982), 40-45.
Crawford, G. B. "Cotton, Land and Sustenance: Toward The
    Limits of Abundance in Late Antebellum Georgia,"
    GEORGIA HISTORICAL QUARTERLY 72
    (Summer 1988), 215-247.
Edwards, J. C. "Georgia's Political Schism in 1872: Two
    Letters," GEORGIA HISTORICAL QUARTERLY 56
    (Fall 1972), 432-434.
Escott, Paul. "Southern Yeomen and the Confederacy," MAJOR
    PROBLEMS IN THE CIVIL WAR AND RECONSTRUCTION.
    ed. Michael Perman. Lexington, Massachusetts: Heath,
    1991.
Flowers, Earl, Jr. "The Wofford Settlement on the Georgia
    Frontier," GEORGIA   HISTORICAL QUARTERLY 41 (Fall
    1977), 258-267.
Greene, Helene. "Politics in Georgia, 1853-54: The Ordeal of
    Howell Cobb," GEORGIA HISTORICAL QUARTERLY 30
    (September 1946), 185-211.
Harper, Roland. "The Development of Agriculture in Upper
    Georgia from 1850 to 1890," GEORGIA HISTORICAL
    QUARTERLY 6 (1922), 3-27.

Holland, L. M. "P. M. B. Young and the Restoration of
    Sovereignty to Georgia," EMORY UNIVERSITY
    QUARTERLY 7 (June 1951), 143-150.
Hudson, Travis. "A History of the 59th Georgia Volunteer
    Infantry Regiment, III," ATLANTA HISTORICAL
    JOURNAL 26 (Winter 1982-83), 19-30.
Huff, Lawrence. "Joseph Addison Turner's Role in Georgia
    Politics," GEORGIA HISTORICAL QUARTERLY 50
    (March 1966), 3-15.
"William Darrah Kelley," DICTIONARY OF AMERICAN
    BIOGRAPHY 5. ed. Dumas Malone. New York:
    Scribners, 1933, 299-300.
Klingberg, Frank. "The Southern Claims Commission: A
    Postwar Agency in Operation," MISSISSIPPI VALLEY
    HISTORICAL REVIEW 32 (Fall 1945), 234-256.
Mitchell Eugene. "H. I. Kimball: His Career and Its Defense,"
    ATLANTA HISTORICAL BULLETIN 3 (October 1938),
    250-261.
"National Party Conventions, 1831-1972," CONGRESSIONAL
    QUARTERLY May 1976.
Perman, Michael. "The Forked Road to Redemption, 1873-1876,"
    THE ROAD TO REDEMPTION: SOUTHERN POLITICS
    1869-1879. Chapel Hill: University of North Carolina
    Press, 1984, 149-177.
Roberts, L. E. "Educational Reform in Antebellum Georgia,"
    GEORGIA REVIEW 16 (Spring 1962), 74-80.
Sarris, Jonathan. "Anatomy of an Atrocity: The Madden Branch
    Massacre and Guerilla Warfare in North Georgia, 1861-
    1865," GEORGIA HISTORICAL QUARTERLY 77
    (Winter 1993), 679-710.
Smith, Gerald J. "Kershaw's Salient: A Time To Die,"
    MILITARY HISTORY, TBA
    _____ "Manassas, Georgia," CONFEDERATE PHILATELIST 39
    (November-December 1994), 223-224.
Stanton, E. F. "Manual Labor Schools," SOUTHERN LITERARY
    MESSENGER (March 1835), 15-16.

Talmadge, John E. "Peace Movement Activities in Civil War Georgia," GEORGIA REVIEW 7 (Summer 1953), 190-203.

Taylor, Elizabeth. "The Convict Lease System," GEORGIA HISTORICAL QUARTERLY 26 (March 1962), 113-128.

Tickell, Ian. "An Uncommon Soldier's Due Cover from Virginia", CONFEDERATE PHILATELIST 40 (May-June 1995), 104-105.

Ward, Judson C., Jr. "The New Departure Democrats of Georgia: An Interpretation," GEORGIA HISTORICAL QUARTERLY 41 (September 1957), 227-236.

Weller, James and Cornelia. "Georgia Boys at Gettysburg," ATLANTA HISTORY 33 (1989), 5-25.

Wender, Herbert. "The Southern Commercial Convention at Savannah," GEORGIA HISTORICAL QUARTERLY 15 (June 1931), 173-191.

2.   Books:

Austin, J. H. ABSTRACTS OF GEORGIA WILLS II. n.p., n.d.
Barkley, Norman Y. THE CREATION OF MODERN GEORGIA.
      Athens: University of Georgia Press, 1990.
Battey, George M. HISTORY OF ROME AND FLOYD COUNTY.
      Atlanta: Webb and Young, 1922.
Beringer, Richard E., Herman Hattaway, Archer Jones, and W.
      N. Still, Jr. WHY THE SOUTH LOST THE CIVIL WAR.
      Athens: University of Georgia Press, 1986.
Bonner, James C. A HISTORY OF GEORGIA AGRICULTURE.
      Athens: University of Georgia Press, 1964.
_____ and L. E. Roberts, eds. STUDIES IN GEORGIA HISTORY.
      Athens: University of Georgia Press, 1940.
Bragg, W. A. JOE BROWN'S ARMY: THE GEORGIA STATE LINE.
      Macon: Mercer University Press, 1987.
Bryan, T. Conn. CONFEDERATE GEORGIA.
      Athens: University of Georgia Press, 1953.
Carter, J. C. MAGNOLIA JOURNEY. Tuscaloosa, Alabama:
      University of Alabama Press, 1974.
Catton, Bruce. BRUCE CATTON'S CIVIL WAR: THREE
      VOLUMES IN ONE. New York: Fairfax, 1984.
Cooper, William J., Jr. THE SOUTH AND THE POLITICS OF
      SLAVERY 1828-1856.   Baton Rouge: LSU Press, 1978.
Coulter, E. Merton. COLLEGE LIFE IN THE OLD SOUTH.
      Athens: University of Georgia Press, 1951.
_____CONFEDERATE STATES OF AMERICA 1861-1865.
      Baton Rouge: LSU Press, 1950.
_____ GEORGIA A SHORT HISTORY. Chapel Hill:
      University of North Carolina Press, 1947.
Cunyus, Lucy. HISTORY OF BARTOW COUNTY, GEORGIA,
      FORMERLY CASS, Easley, South Carolina: Southern
      Historical Press, 1976.
Downey, Fairfax. THE GUNS AT GETTYSBURG.
      New York: Collier, 1958.

Dwight, B. W. HISTORY OF THE DESCENDANTS OF JOHN
    DWIGHT, II. New York: Trow, 1874.
Elliott, Joseph C. LIEUTENANT GENERAL RICHARD HERON
    ANDERSON: LEE'S   NOBLE SOLDIER.
    Dayton: Morningside, 1985.
Evans, Lawton. A HISTORY OF GEORGIA.
    New York: American Book Company, 1898.
Flanigan, James C. HISTORY OF GWINNETT COUNTY.
    Hapeville, Georgia: Tyler, 1943.
Freeman, Douglas Southall. LEE'S LIEUTENANTS 3 Volumes.
    New York: Scribners, 1944.
Furgurson, Ernest B. CHANCELLORSVILLE 1863: THE SOULS
    OF THE BRAVE. New York: Knopf, 1992.
Hahn, Steven. THE ROOTS OF SOUTHERN POPULISM:
    YEOMAN FARMERS AND THE TRANSFORMATION OF
    THE GEORGIA UP-COUNTRY. New York: Oxford, 1983.
Hait, Jane W. HISTORY OF THE WOFFORD FAMILY.
    Spartanburg,, South Carolina: Reprint Company, 1993.
Hennessey, John. SECOND MANASSAS BATTLEFIELD MAP
    STUDY. Lynchburg, Virginia: Howard, 1985.
Hesseltine, William B. CIVIL WAR PRISONS: A STUDY IN WAR
    PSYCHOLOGY. New York: Unger, 1964.
Holland, L. M. PIERCE M. B. YOUNG: THE WARWICK OF   THE
    SOUTH. Athens: University of Georgia Press, 1964.
Howe, David. A POLITICAL HISTORY OF SECESSION.
    New York: Putnam, 1914.
Jeffrey, William. RICHMOND PRISONS.
    New York: Republican, 1893.
Johnson, Amanda. GEORGIA AS A COLONY AND STATE.
    Atlanta: Cherokee, 1970.
Johnson, Michael. TOWARD A PATRIARCHAL REPUBLIC.
    Baton Rouge: LSU Press, 1977.
Johnson, Vicki C. THE MEN AND VISION OF THE   SOUTHERN
    COMMERCIAL CONVENTIONS 1845-1871.
    Columbia, Missouri: University of Missouri Press, 1992.
Johnston, John W. WESTERN AND ATLANTIC RAILROAD OF
    THE STATE OF GEORGIA. Atlanta: Stein, 1932.

Kimzey, H. E. EARLY GENEALOGICAL AND HISTORICAL
RECORDS, HABERSHAM COUNTY. n.p., 1988.
McElreath, Walter. CONSTITUTIONAL HISTORY OF
GEORGIA. Atlanta: Harrison, 1912.
McMurray, Richard. JOHN BELL HOOD AND THE WAR FOR
SOUTHERN INDEPENDENCE. Lincoln, Nebraska:
University of Nebraska Press, 1982.
Mancini, Matthew. ONE DIES GET ANOTHER: CONVICT
LEASING IN THE AMERICAN SOUTH 1866-1928.
Columbia, South Carolina: University of South Carolina
Press, 1996.
THE MEXICAN WAR AND ITS HEROES.
Philadelphia: Claxton, 1882.
Miers, Earl Schenck and R. A. Brown. GETTYSBURG.
New Brunswick, Connecticut: Rutgers, 1948.
Mims, Edwin. SIDNEY LANIER.
Boston: Houghton Mifflin, 1905.
Mitchell, Reid. CIVIL WAR SOLDIERS.
NewYork: Touchstone, 1988.
Montgomery, Horace. CRACKER PARTIES.
Baton Rouge: LSU Press, 1950.
Murfin, James. THE GLEAM OF BAYONETS: THE BATTLE OF
ANTIETAM SEPTEMBER 17, 1862.
Atlanta: Mockingbird, 1965.
Murray County Historical Commission. MURRAY COUNTY
HERITAGE. Roswell, Georgia: Wolfe, 1987.
Orr, Dorothy. A HISTORY OF EDUCATION IN GEORGIA.
Chapel Hill: University of North Carolina Press, 1950.
Parks, J. H. JOSEPH EMERSON BROWN OF GEORGIA.
Baton Rouge: LSU Press, 1977.
Pfanz, Harry W. GETTYSBURG THE SECOND DAY.
Chapel Hill: University of North Carolina Press, 1987.
Phillips, U. B. GEORGIA AND STATE RIGHTS.
Macon: Mercer University Press, 1984.
Randall, J. G. THE CIVIL WAR AND RECONSTRUCTION.
New York: Heath, 1937.

Range, Willard. A CENTURY OF GEORGIA AGRICULTURE
    1850-1950. Athens: University of Georgia Press, 1954.
Rhea, Gordon C. THE BATTLE OF THE WILDERNESS.
    Baton Rouge: LSU Press, 1994.
Ridpath, J. C. HISTORY OF THE UNITED STATES FROM
    ABORIGINAL TIMES TO THE PRESENT II.
    New York: Allen, 1876.
Roberts, Derrell. JOSEPH E. BROWN AND THE POLITICS OF
    RECONSTRUCTION.
    Tuscaloosa: University of Alabama Press, 1993.
Schiaf, Morris. THE BATTLE OF THE WILDERNESS.
    Boston: Houghton Mifflin, 1910.
Sears, Stephen. LANDSCAPE TURNED RED: THE BATTLE OF
    ANTIETAM. New York: Ticknor and Fields, 1983.
Shyrock, R. H. GEORGIA AND THE UNION IN 1850.
    New York: AMS, 1968.
Simpkins, Francis B. A HISTORY OF THE SOUTH.
    New York: Knopf, 1963.
Simpson, Harold. HOOD'S TEXAS BRIGADE: LEE'S GRENADIER
    GUARD.
    Waco, Texas: Texian Press, 1970.
Smith, Gerald J. "SMITE THEM HIP AND   THIGH!" GEORGIA
    METHODIST   MINISTERS IN THE CONFEDERATE
    MILITARY. Murfreesboro, Tennessee:
    Ambassador, 1993.
Swanberg, W. A. SICKLES THE INCREDIBLE.
    New York: Ace, 1956
Talmadge, John E. REBECCA LATIMER FELTON: NINE
    STORMY DECADES.
    Athens: University of Georgia Press, 1960.
Temple, Sarah. THE FIRST ONE HUNDRED YEARS: A
    SHORT HISTORY OF COBB COUNTY.
    Atlanta: Brown, 1935.
Thompson, Mildred. RECONSTRUCTION IN GEORGIA.
    Savannah: Beehive, 1972.
Trudeau, N. A. BLOODY ROADS SOUTH.
    Boston: Little, Brown, 1989.

Wallace, D. D. HISTORY OF WOFFORD COLLEGE.
        Nashville: Vanderbilt
        University Press, 1951.
Wiley, Bell I. PLAIN PEOPLE OF THE CONFEDERACY.
        Baton Rouge: LSU Press, 1943.
_____ THE ROAD TO APPOMATTOX.
        New York: Atheneum Press, 1968.
Wise, Jennings. THE LONG ARM OF LEE
        CHANCELLORSVILLE TO APPOMATTOX.
        Lincoln, Nebraska: University of Nebraska Press, 1991.

3.   Published Biographical Sketches of W. T. Wofford:

ACWORTH NEWS, August 15, 1887.
ATLANTA CONSTITUTION, May 24, 1884.
Boatner, Mark M., III. CIVIL WAR DICTIONARY (New York:
     McKay, 1959), 945.
Bohannon, Keith. "W. T. Wofford," THE CONFEDERATE
     GENERAL 6 ed. W. C. Davis (New York: National
     Historical Society, 1991), 156-57.
_____ "More Georgians in Gray," MILITARY IMAGES 8
     (1986), 6-13.
Coleman, ,Kenneth and C. S. Garr. DICTIONARY OF
     GEORGIA BIOGRAPHY 2 (Athens: University of
     Georgia Press, 1983), 1077-78.
Faust, Patricia, ed. HISTORICAL TIMES ILLUSTRATED
     ENCYCLOPEDIA OF THE CIVIL WAR (New York:
     Harper and Row, 1986), 839-840.
Hesseltine, W. B. and Larry Gamble. "Georgia's Confederate
     Leaders after Appomattox," GEORGIA HISTORICAL
     QUARTERLY 35 (1951), 1-15.
Isbell, Mrs. Luther. COLONEL WILLIAM WOFFORD, R. S.   1812;
     NATHANIEL WOFFORD 1812; GENERAL WILLIAM
     TATUM WOFFORD C.S.A. n.p., n.d.
     (Stephens County Library).
Kerlin, R. H. CONFEDERATE GENERALS OF GEORGIA.
     Fayetteville, Georgia: Historical Books, 1995.
Knight, L. L. A STANDARD HISTORY OF   GEORGIA AND
     GEORGIANS 6. (Chicago: Lewis, 1917), 2817.
Malone, Dumas, ed. DICTIONARY OF AMERICAN   BIOGRAPHY
     20 (New York: Scribners, 1936), 440-441.
Northern, William J. MEN OF MARK IN GEORGIA 3 (Atlanta:
     Caldwell, 1908), 293-94.
Spencer, Thomas. "Gen. William Wofford - A Confederate
     Great," CARTERSVILLE TRIBUNE, March 23, 1950.

3.   Theses and Dissertations:

Bryan, Lucy Dillard. "James Fielding Dillard, Confederate
        Soldier." M.A. Thesis, University of Georgia, 1940.
Mahan, J. B., Jr. "A History of Old Cassville 1833-1864."
        M. A. Thesis, University of Georgia, 1950.
Rock, Virginia. "The Making and Meaning of I'LL TAKE MY
        STAND: A Study in Utopian Conservatism, 1925-1939."
        Ph.D. Dissertation, University of Minnesota, 1961.
Smith, Gerald Judson, Jr., " 'Satisfaction Wherever He Served':
        The Career of Alexander Robert Lawton, 1818-1863."
        M.A. Thesis, Georgia Southern University, 1994.
Steeliman, Lala. "The Georgia Constitutional Convention of
        1877." M.A. Thesis, University of North Carolina, 1946.
Wallenstein, Peter B. "From Slave South to New South: Taxes
        and Spending from 1850 Through Reconstruction."
        Ph.D. Dissertation, Johns Hopkins University, 1973.

4.   Unpublished Papers

Stevenson, John. "The Georgia Convention of 1877."
        Western Carolina University, 1994. Used by permission
        of author.

INDEX

—1—

16th Georgia, 65, 69, 70, 72, 76, 79, 80, 86, 90, 103, 104, 117, 121, 130, 137
18th Georgia, 27, 29, 30, 32, 35, 39, 42, 43, 46, 47, 48, 51, 52, 56, 57, 59, 60, 65, 66, 69, 81, 98, 104, 122, 137

—2—

24th Georgia, 65, 73, 74, 82, 85, 92, 101, 113, 118, 129, 137

—A—

Akin, Warren, 11, 132
Anderson, R. H. 67
Appomattox, 109
Athens Southern Banner, 5, 9
Athens Southern Watchman, 94
Atlanta and Blue Ridge Railroad Company, 156
Atlanta Daily Intelligencer, 10
Atlanta Southern Confederacy, 42, 73, 97, 109
Atlanta Sun, 156
Augusta Daily Chronicle and Sentinel, 25

—B—

Bartow, Francis, 32
Bell, John, 18, 32
Breckinridge, John C., 18
Brown, Joseph E., 14, 18, 20, 23, 24, 25, 26, 27, 50, 99, 100, 101, 133, 141, 142, 143, 150, 154, 157, 158, 159, 169
Burke, John W., 5, 11

—C—

Camp McDonald, 24, 27, 36
Cartersville and Van Wert Railroad, 154
Cartersville Express, 156
Cass County, 1, 5, 12, 13, 19, 32
Cass Station, 6, 155, 158
Cassville, 1, 3, 5, 6, 10, 11, 12, 15, 18, 20, 31, 32, 36, 61, 63, 127, 131, 132, 133, 143, 155, 159, 169
Cassville Female Institute, 12
Cassville Standard, 5, 10, 12, 18
Chancellorsville, 63, 67, 68, 71, 72, 75, 99, 107, 112
Cherokee Baptist College, 15
Chester's Gap, 95
Chickamauga Creek, 98
Chinn Ridge, 48, 49
Cobb's Legion, 65, 81, 119, 122, 123, 129
Cobb, Howell, 17, 135, 136
Cobb, T. R. R., 60, 65
Cold Harbor, 119, 121, 126, 127
Compromise of 1850, 8
Conscription Act, 36, 60
Constitutional Unionists, 9, 18

—D—

Davis, Jefferson, 23, 143
DeBow's Review, 14
DeBow, James, 13
Douglas, Stephen, 18
Dunkard Church, 52, 53, 58

—E—

Eltham's Landing, 35
Eugenius Nesbit, 19

—F—

Felton, Rebecca, 160,169
Fort Sanders, 103
Franklin College, 2
Fredericksburg, 28, 29, 32, 34, 65, 66, 67, 68, 72, 74, 76, 77

—G—

Gaines Mill, 39, 40, 49
Gatewood, John P., 100
Georgia Hospital and Relief Association, 98
Georgia Military Institute, 12, 24
Georgia Platform, 8, 9
Gettysburg, 63, 75, 76, 80, 84, 87, 99
Grant, U. S., 107, 145
Guard Hill, 107, 129
Gwinnett Manual Labor Institute, 2

—H—

Hampton's Legion, 39, 42, 47, 49, 51, 52, 53, 56, 57, 60
Hill, D. H., 51
Hood, John Bell, 32
Hooker, Joseph, 52, 55, 66
Howard, Charles Wallace, 12
Howard, Oliver O., 153

—J—

Jackson, Stonewall, 41, 42, 43, 45, 46, 51, 55, 56, 60, 67, 68, 69, 75, 76, 146
Jenkins, Charles, 8, 151
Johnson, H. V., 18, 133
Johnston, Joseph, 32, 39
Judah, H. M., 142

—K—

Kelley, William Darrah, 152
Kelly's Ford, 41, 67, 68, 77
Kershaw, Joseph, 74
Kingston, 6, 131, 145, 146, 156

—L—

Langdon, Margaret, 168
Law, Evander M., 29
Lawton, A. R., 53
Lee, Robert E., 39, 41, 43, 51, 65, 66, 67, 68, 72, 75, 76, 80, 93, 94, 95, 98, 99, 100, 105, 107, 108, 113, 114, 115, 119, 127, 128, 129, 130, 135, 139, 140, 143, 145, 146
Little Round Top, 81, 82, 88, 92
Longstreet, 41, 42, 43, 49, 51, 58, 60, 65, 76, 80, 81, 83, 85, 90, 91, 93, 95, 102, 103, 105, 107, 108, 111, 113, 114, 115, 127, 129, 135, 139
Lumpkin Independent, 160

—M—

McClellan, 35, 39, 41, 51, 60
McLaws, Lafayette, 37, 59, 65, 67, 68, 69, 72, 74, 75, 77, 80, 81, 82, 83, 85, 91, 94, 108
Mexican War, 4, 5, 37
Miller's Farm, 53, 55
Missouri Compromise, 8

—N—

New Departure Democrats, 158

—O—

Omnibus Bill, 7

—P—

Peach Orchard, 81, 82, 86
Phillips' Legion, 65, 67, 72, 73, 77, 80, 81, 84, 89, 94, 97, 103, 123, 138
Pope, John, 41
Populist Movement, 168

—R—

Richmond Dispatch, 30
Richmond Sentinel, 69, 85
Richmond Whig, 39

—S—

Sellars, W. H., 45
Seven Days' Campaign, 39
Seven Pines, 39
Sharpsburg, 50, 52, 54, 60, 109
Sherman, W. T., 107
Shiloh, 36
Smith, Charles Henry, 2
Smith, G. W., 29
Southern Commercial Convention, 13
Southern Countryman, 12
Southern Cultivator, 12
Southern Rights Party, 9, 10
Spottsylvania, 108, 115, 116, 117, 118
Steedman, James, 146

ABOUT THE AUTHOR

The author was born in Marshallville, Georgia in 1941. He holds degrees from Andrew College, LaGrange College, Emory University, West Georgia College, and the University of Georgia. Presently, he is Professor of English and Chair of the Division of Humanities at Paine College, Augusta, Georgia. He lectures widely in American Civil War history and publishes regularly in such diverse fields as Methodist history, Civil War history, philately, literature, and folklore. He is a member of the Society of Civil War Historians.

Join The Civil War Society Today

The magazine.

Civil War magazine is the cornerstone of the Society. Published bi-monthly, *Civil War* features original scholarly articles covering all facets of the war. Our writers are opinionated, often conflicting in their interpretations, but that is the essence of scholarship. We work to ensure that each issue is balanced in its representation of the subject matter, and covers as large a geographical area as possible. *Civil War* does not shrink from controversial or unconventional subjects, and we present the traditional topics in a fresh light to broaden understanding.

Our seminars. We believe

in action. Our Society seminars, held year-round, are hosted by the leading academic experts and regularly attract participants from as far as the west coast, Canada and Europe. Come to one and you'll see why. Some of our recent seminars have included an intense focus on the Seven Days Battles in Richmond, and a novel perspective of Antietam by canoe. Our seminars are excellent for deepening your appreciation of the mastery of a successful strategy, the strengths and limitations of field command, and the personalities of the commanders themselves. They are also relaxing social events that allow members to become acquainted. Anyone can visit a battlefield — we bring it alive!

The **Civil War Society** is a unique organization: personal, yet far-reaching, impartial yet provocative, informed, yet entertaining. Our publications have won awards, our seminars have drawn praise, and our funds have helped save battlefields. We have a vibrant, active, and growing membership — we invite you to become a part of it!

Membership Includes:

- *Civil War* bi-monthly magazine

- Our historical **calendar,** thoroughly researched and really stunning

- The **Society newsletter,** where members keep abreast of preservation activities and society events.

- A personalized parchment **membership certificate**

- Our **guide** to tracing your Civil War ancestors

- The opportunity to obtain a **Civil War Society MasterCard,** with a portion of every purchase going towards preservation.

Call 1-800-247-6253

or use the order form below

☐ For a Gift ☐ For Myself/ ☐ 1 yr. $39.00 ☐ 2 yrs. $68.00 (save $10) ☐ 3 yrs. $89.00 (save $28)

Name _____

Address _____

City _____ State _____

Zip _____

gift card to read _____

☐ Check ☐ 💳 ☐ 💳 ☐ 💳 ☐ 💳

Card Number _____

Exp. Date _____

Signature _____

The Civil War Society • P.O. Box 770-CW • Berryville, Virginia 22611
Please allow 4 to 6 weeks for delivery For foreign shipping please add $10, $8 for Canada